Advance Praise

Green Careers

Green Careers fills a long-standing gap in what we know about green careers. Cassio and Rush have created a detailed, accessible, and easy-to-read compendium of green careers that covers a wide spectrum of jobs — from highly technical positions to trade jobs to business-related opportunities. The engaging interviews with green job holders give readers a rich, hands-on introduction to a wide variety of interesting green positions. I already know this book will have a prominent place on my bookshelf.

> — CAROL MCCLELLAND, PhD, Founder and Executive
> Director of Green Career Central and author
> of *Your Dream Career For Dummies*

This is a valuable resource for people looking to find a career in sustainability. It pulls together information that would be otherwise hard to find: salaries, employment prospects and advice from those in the field.

> — DARCY HITCHCOCK is co-author of the award-winning book,
> *The Business Guide to Sustainability*, and co-founder of the
> International Society of Sustainability Professionals.

Green Careers is a marvelous career guide for the 21st century. It outlines the career possibilities, defines the roles of various occupations, provides examples of each, and outlines for the reader the ways and means of entering or even transferring into these new pathways. It should be in all career collections.

> — MARGARET RILEY DIKEL,
> author, Rileyguide.com

Cassio and Rush inspire readers to consider sustainability issues and perspectives when choosing a career. They provide helpful advice and resources for career decision-makers at all levels a must-read for current career service professionals, students in high school through graduate school, and mid-career job seekers. This book encourages all of us to find ways to "go green" on the job!

> — MELISSA VENABLE, PhD, Member, National Career
> Development Association, College of Education,
> University of Hawaii at Manoa

Green Careers

Green Careers

*Choosing Work for
a Sustainable Future*

JIM CASSIO & ALICE RUSH

NEW SOCIETY PUBLISHERS

Cataloging in Publication Data:
A catalog record for this publication is available
from the National Library of Canada.

Copyright © 2009 by Jim Cassio & Alice Rush.
All rights reserved.

Cover design by Diane McIntosh.
Cover photo: © iStock/Robert Churchill.

Printed in Canada. First printing March 2009.

Paperback ISBN: 978-0-86571-643-8

Inquiries regarding requests to reprint all or part of *Green Careers*
should be addressed to New Society Publishers at the address below.

To order directly from the publishers,
please call toll-free (North America) 1-800-567-6772,
or order online at newsociety.com

Any other inquiries can be directed by mail to:

New Society Publishers
P.O. Box 189, Gabriola Island, BC V0R 1X0, Canada
(250) 247-9737

New Society Publishers' mission is to publish books that contribute in fundamental ways to building an ecologically sustainable and just society, and to do so with the least possible impact on the environment, in a manner that models this vision. We are committed to doing this not just through education, but through action. This book is one step toward ending global deforestation and climate change. It is printed on Forest Stewardship Council-certified acid-free paper that is **100% post-consumer recycled** (100% old growth forest-free), processed chlorine free, and printed with vegetable-based, low-VOC inks, with covers produced using FSC-certified stock. Additionally, New Society purchases carbon offsets based on an annual audit, operating with a carbon-neutral footprint. For further information, or to browse our full list of books and purchase securely, visit our website at: newsociety.com

NEW SOCIETY PUBLISHERS
newsociety.com

Recycled
Supporting responsible use
of forest resources

FSC   www.fsc.org Cert no. SW-COC-1271
© 1996 Forest Stewardship Council

Contents

Part II: Additional Information and Resources

This book is dedicated to Al Gore
for helping to wake people up about global warming
and about personal and collective responsibility.

Acknowledgments

Alice would like to thank her husband Dave and kids Rebecca and Robert, for their support while writing this book, and her mother, Nonette Hanko, as her first "green role model" and environmentalist. Others she wishes to thank are California Lieutenant Governor John Garamendi, Bobette Parsons, Val Hanko, DeAnne Musolf and all those we interviewed for this book in generously donating their time and expert advice.

Alice would also like to thank Al Gore for personally inspiring her to help write this book. If through our book we can provide knowledge and empower our youth and adults of all ages with direction on how to work and prosper in green careers — while helping to save the planet with their gifts, strengths and aptitudes — then we've done our job right. The economy and our Mother Earth can both thrive!

Jim would like to thank his family, friends and colleagues for their support and assistance in the development of this book, specifically, his daughters, Marina and Isabelle Cassio, and his wife, Deborah Moreno Cassio. Also a warm thanks to all those generous individuals who allowed us to interview them and to learn from them.

Introduction

Congratulations on choosing this book and embarking on a journey toward pursuing your life's work! We wrote this book because we know many people of all ages and backgrounds want to work in career fields that help save the planet in some way. And yet few people seem to know "what" and "where" these careers are. What green careers are available? What kind of salary can I expect? What demand is there for these kinds of jobs? What degree or certificate do I need? How do I get my first job? How do I change to a green career? What resources can help me?

This book grew out of a free resource guide on green careers that Jim developed for career development professionals. During his research, it became apparent that there were no current books specifically focused on green careers. So Alice and Jim teamed up to develop this book, which includes comprehensive career profiles that cover approximately 90 different occupations, plus over 65 profiles of real people who work in those career fields, including green entrepreneurs. We selected the occupations profiled in this book — not because that's how many green occupations exist, but because those selected reflect a variety of career and job opportunities that represent almost every area of career interest and aptitude. Note, however, that most of these career fields can also lead to jobs that are not green. In fact, there are probably only a handful of occupations that are exclusively green in terms of real jobs. But every day, more green jobs are created and more non-green jobs are becoming greener. This is happening because, increasingly, employers are going green. Some are transitioning slowly, while others are reinventing themselves almost overnight. Some are doing it out of responsibility for the environment, while others are doing it because it makes financial sense.

In brief, our goal in writing this book is to help people of all ages and backgrounds learn about their green career choices and become inspired. We know that aptitudes, values, interests, personality and skills vary from individual to individual; so we did not want to focus solely on green careers that require aptitudes in math and science — as some environmental career books have done. Rather, we wanted a new book that would meet the needs of a wide variety of individuals interested in preserving and protecting the environment through their careers. We wanted to help people with an interest in construction work learn how they can specialize in green building as a niche career area. We wanted to help people who have an interest or aptitude for business or sales learn about alternative energy and entrepreneurial careers. We wanted to help people who are strong with communication skills learn about green public relations, marketing and journalism. We wanted to help people who love to travel and explore other cultures learn about careers in ecotourism. We wanted to help teens and young adults explore tomorrow's green career choices.

We hope as you read this book that you will be inspired to pursue your green career dreams with confidence and direction. We want you to find a career you feel passionate about and to prosper doing what you love. Enjoy this next chapter of your life. You will make a difference!

What is a *Green Career* and Where are the *Green Jobs*?

Going Green

Before we get into a discussion of green industries, jobs and careers, it might be good to discuss the principal values that help to define a person who has "gone green." However, it's not a checklist. There is no absolute list of green values or agreement on how to define them. But together these and other green values reflect an approach to life — including home, family, community and work — that centers on an awareness of our impact on the planet and its people:

- Environmental protection/preservation
- Eco-friendly design
- Sustainable development
- Renewable energy
- Organic/natural products
- Fair trade
- Holistic health
- Clean technology
- Peace and justice
- Social conscience

What is a green career?

Green careers involve working in green jobs that are focused on sustainability and/or environmental protection and preservation. These jobs can be defined either by the nature and purpose of the job or by the nature and purpose of the employer.

Merriam-Webster defines "sustainability" as a method of harvesting or using a resource so that the resource is not depleted or permanently damaged.

Sustainable agriculture refers to the ability of a farm to produce food indefinitely without causing irreversible damage to ecosystem health.

A sustainable business or organization generally means that they are committed to:

- Conserving energy
- Using renewable energy sources

1

- Preventing pollution
- Reducing waste
- Conserving water

An "occupation" is a way of categorizing similar jobs. For example, the occupation of journalist encompasses a variety of journalist jobs, including those that specialize in politics, technology or entertainment. Some journalists specialize in environmental issues. Occupations are not defined on the basis of the *greenness* of their jobs or the employers they work for. There are two important consequences of this reality:

1. You can't judge an individual job for greenness on the basis of its title or on the basis of the parent occupation to which it is related. There are scarce few occupations in which *all* of its jobs are green. Therefore you must look at the nature and purpose of the individual job, or the nature and purpose of the employer, in order to determine if it's a green job.
2. You can't know how many green jobs currently exist or how many will exist in the future — based on our government's current employment statistics research programs. These employment statistics depend on the Standard Occupational Classification (SOC) system which is never up-to-date on current workforce trends. Therefore valid statistics on individual green jobs are impossible without doing an extensive survey of the employment in specific green industries or in a specific geographic area.

Just to be clear, the above definition of "green careers" includes "green collar jobs," which can be defined in any number of ways, depending on your perspective and/or agenda. The definition of "green collar jobs" can range from manual labor jobs that are green to any green job, without regard to education level.

Our definition of "green careers" includes jobs at every level of skill and experience, including manual labor jobs as well as the environmental science and engineering professions that form the traditional foundation for green/environmental work. But the definition also includes a wide variety of other career fields, including those of management, support and administrative staff that can be found in virtually all industries — if and when those jobs meet our green jobs criteria.

Where Are the Green Jobs?

In response to climate change and other concerns, our society is going green, and that includes the workplace. Many employers are creating new green jobs and changing their existing jobs in terms of how the work is done. Others are starting up new businesses built on a foundation of green values. Although we don't know the exact number of green jobs, recent studies are now suggesting that five to seven percent of the jobs in the US are green jobs, and that percentage is expected to increase significantly through 2030 to where green jobs may account for one of every four or five jobs. So it is clear that both the number and the percentage of green jobs is growing. It is also clear that green jobs now represent a wide variety of occupational choices that didn't exist just two to three years ago. They can now be found in every corner of the workplace and economy.

The following list shows the industries and their sectors where most green jobs can be found.

Advertising and Public Relations Services Industry (Green)
- All sectors

Agriculture and Food Industry
Green sectors include:
- Green/Natural/Organic Food Restaurants
- Makers of Natural/Organic Food Products
- Sellers of Prepared Natural/Organic Food
- Sustainable/Organic Farms
- Sustainable/Organic Nurseries/Greenhouses
- Sustainable Aquaculture Farms/Fish Hatcheries

Alternative Fuel Vehicles Industry
Green sectors include:
- Advanced Technology Vehicle Manufacturers (electric, hybrids, fuel cell, hydrogen)
- Alternative Fuel Vehicle Manufacturers
- Alternative Fuel Producers/Distributors
- Alternative Fuel Vehicle Repairers (technicians, first-responders)
- Alternative Fuel Vehicle Sales/Service
- Battery Manufacturers

Bicycle Industry
Green sectors include:
- Bicycle Courier and Cargo Services
- Bicycle Manufacturing
- Bicycle Sales and Service

Biotech/Life Sciences Industry

Green sectors include:

- Blue Biotechnology (marine and aquatic applications)
- Green Biotechnology (agricultural applications)
- Red Biotechnology (medical applications)
- White Biotechnology (industrial applications)
- Bioeconomy (investments and economic output)

Building Industry (Green/Sustainable)

Green sectors include:

- Architectural Services
- Building Materials
- Building/Construction/Specialty Trade Contractors
- Furniture/Cabinet Makers (using environmentally certified/recycled wood)
- Salvage and Deconstruction Services

Cleaning and Janitorial Services Industry (Green Cleaning)

- All sectors

Clothing and Accessories Industry (Organic/Natural/Recycled Material)

Green sectors include:

- Design
- Manufacturing
- Wholesale
- Retail

Ecotourism Industry

- All sectors

Engineering Services Industry (Green)

Green sectors include:

- Chemical
- Civil
- Construction Management Services
- Environmental
- Land Planning
- Manufacturing/Production
- Surveying
- Transportation

Environmental Health and Safety Services Industry (Consulting)
- All sectors

Environmental and Hazardous Materials (HazMat) Services Industry
Green sectors include:
- Environmental Consulting Services
- Hazardous Materials (HazMat) Services
- Environmental Engineering Services — see Engineering Services Industry

Geography and GIS Services Industry
- All sectors

Government
Green sectors include:
- Federal: e.g., Army Corps of Engineers; Bureau of Land Management (BLM); Centers for Disease Control and Prevention (CDC); Department of Energy; Environmental Protection Agency; Fish and Wildlife Service; Forest Service; Geological Survey (USGS); National Oceanic and Atmospheric Administration (NOAA); National Park Service; Natural Resources Conservation Service (NRCS)
- State: e.g., Agriculture and Food Safety; Coastal Zone Management; Community and Economic Development; Emergency Services; Energy; Fisheries and Wildlife Protection; Parks and Recreation; Planning; Pollution Control and Prevention; Public Health; Water Resources
- Local (cities, towns, counties, special districts): e.g., Air Quality Management; Conservation/Park Land Management; Electricity; Green Building; Green Business; Public Transportation; Recycling; Regional Planning; Waste Management; Water and Wastewater Treatment

Investment Services Industry (Sustainable/Socially Responsible Investing/SRI)
- All sectors

Journalism and Publishing Industry (Green/Sustainable)
- All sectors

Landscaping and Habitat Restoration Services Industry (Green)
Green sectors include:
- Arborist/Tree Services
- Gardening/Landscape Maintenance Services
- Habitat Restoration Services

- Landscape Architectural Services
- Landscape Contractors

Legal Services Industry (Environmental and Land Use Law)

- All sectors

Natural Sciences Consulting Services

Specialties include:

- Atmospheric and Space Scientists
- Biochemists, Biophysicists and Toxicologists
- Chemists and Forensic Toxicologists
- Environmental Scientists
- Epidemiologists
- Foresters and Forest Pathologists
- Geoscientists, Environmental Geologists, Hydrogeologists and Marine Geologists
- Hydrologists and Water Resources Managers
- Microbiologists and Environmental Health Microbiologists
- Physicists and Health Physicists
- Soil and Plant Scientists
- Soil and Water Conservationists
- Zoologists, Wildlife Biologists and Marine Biologists

Non-profit Organizations (Green/Environmental)

- All environmental sectors

Printing Industry (Green/Sustainable)

- All sectors

Recycling Industry (Green)

Green sectors include:

- Electronics (cell phones, computers)
- Glass
- Metal
- Paper
- Plastics
- Textiles
- Wood

Renewable Energy Industry

Green sectors include:

- Biomass

- Solar Systems Manufacturing
- Solar Systems Sales, Installation and Service
- Wind Turbines Manufacturing
- Wind Turbines Sales, Installation and Service

Utilities Industry

Green sectors include:

- Electric Power Generation, Transmission and Distribution
- Natural Gas Distribution
- Water, Sewage and Other Systems

Other: Misc. Retail (Green/Sustainable/Organic Products)

Green sectors include:

- Crafts/Artwork made by Third World Artisans
- Gardening Supplies
- Recycled, Reclaimed and Earth-friendly Products
- Outdoor Apparel/Equipment
- Scooters

What Occupations?

Remember that an occupation is a way of categorizing similar jobs. Therefore a given occupation typically describes both green jobs and non-green jobs. The reason for this is simply that occupations are not defined on the basis of the *greenness* of their jobs. The same principle is true for industries; they are not generally defined on the basis of the *greenness* of their employers. Take recycling, for example. The recycling industry is largely green, but not always. That may come as a shock to some of us who have been conditioned to think that all recycling is good for the environment. But even with the best intentions, some recycling is inefficient and some is even harmful to the environment. So whether you are looking at occupations or industries, you still have to assess each individual job and each individual employer to know to what extent a job is green.

The career fields (occupations) that we chose to profile in this book do not constitute a comprehensive list of green careers. And there is good reason for this: The more occupations you add to any list of green careers, the more you get into the gray area between green and non-green jobs. Is veterinarian a green career? Not by our definition, but you could certainly be a green veterinarian. What about forest firefighters — is this not a green career? While it's true that they protect our natural resources by fighting forest fires, the reality is that their priority is to protect personal property — even at the expense of our natural resources. So, by our definition, this career field doesn't quite meet our green criteria. But that doesn't mean you can't be green *and* work as a forest firefighter. In fact, it should be said that it is equally noble to be a green individual working for a non-green employer, where you can use your skills and values to help your employer become meaningfully green. If not you, then who will do it?

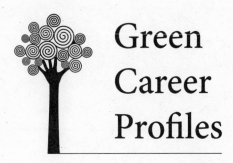

Green
Career
Profiles

Engineering Group

- Chemical Engineers, including Green Chemical Engineers
- Civil Engineering Technicians
- Civil Engineers, including Green Building, Irrigation/Reservoir and Waste Management Engineers
- Conservation, Biological and Agricultural Engineers
- Electrical Engineering Technicians, including Photovoltaic, Wind and Biomass Energy Technicians
- Electrical Engineers, including Recycling, Solar/Photovoltaic, Wind and Biomass Engineers
- Environmental Engineering and Pollution Control Technicians
- Environmental Engineering Professors
- Environmental Engineers, including Ecological and Air Quality Engineers
- Mechanical Engineers

Chemical Engineers, including Green Chemical Engineers

Chemical engineers design chemical plant equipment and devise processes for manufacturing chemicals and products, such as gasoline, synthetic rubber, plastics, detergents, cement, paper and pulp, by applying principles and technology of chemistry, physics and engineering.

Qualifications and Advancement
A bachelor's degree in chemical engineering is the typical education requirement. However, a graduate degree is usually necessary for college and university teaching positions and for many jobs in research and development.

Entry-level engineers usually begin their careers as junior engineers, working under the supervision of experienced engineers. As they gain experience and knowledge, they generally advance to positions of greater responsibility. For engineers, advancement can lead to senior engineer, project manager, research and development manager and vice president for engineering. Some

become consultants or start their own engineering firms. Those with a graduate degree can also become college and university professors.

Salary Survey

Median salary: $78,860 (very high)
Typical range: $62,410 to $98,100

Job Outlook and Employment

Average growth is projected for this occupation in the US, from 30,444 jobs in
2006 to 32,842 in 2016. Although overall employment in the chemical manufacturing industry is expected to decline, chemical companies will continue to
research and develop new chemicals and more efficient processes to increase
output of existing chemicals. However, most employment growth for chemical engineers will be in service-providing industries such as professional,
scientific and technical services, particularly for research in energy and the
developing fields of biotechnology and nanotechnology.

Where the Jobs Are

Research and development in the physical, engineering and life sciences
(12.54%); Basic chemical manufacturing (11.09%); Resin, synthetic rubber
and artificial synthetic fibers and filaments manufacturing (6.16%); Petroleum and coal products manufacturing (5.77%); Pharmaceutical and medicine manufacturing (4.86%); Federal government, excluding postal service
(3.79%); Self-employed: 1.9%

Resources

American Chemical Society (ACS): portal.acs.org
American Institute of Chemical Engineers (AIChE): aiche.org
Engineering Central: engcen.com
Green Chemistry Institute: chemistry.org
National Society of Professional Engineers: nspe.org
O*NET OnLine: online.onetcenter.org (see chemical engineers)
US Dept. of Labor, Bureau of Labor Statistics: bls.gov/oco/ocos027.htm

Q&A   **TONY KINGSBURY**
Executive, Dow Chemical; Executive in
Residence, Haas School of Business, University of
California, Berkeley, from an interview with Jim in 2008.

*How did you get into this career field? What was your edu-
cation and experience, including any green–related training or certification?*

My educational background is chemical engineering. My first job at Dow Chemical was actually in production — making plastics. As I worked in that environment, I kept asking more and more questions, like "What are the customers doing with the plastic we're making?" And that led to a technical troubleshooting/product development job where I worked with plastics customers. So in that job I would work with customers to figure out if there was something wrong with the way they were working with the plastic or if was there something wrong in terms of what Dow had supplied. In some cases, this meant there was a need for a new product to be developed to meet their needs. And that was a great job. I worked with folks in packaging, consumer electronics, toys, medical — a whole broad range of industry segments. And then, as environmentalism grew in late 80s, I asked if I could move into that area. More and more of our customers were asking: "How do we recycle this stuff?" "What do we need to be doing?" "What's Dow doing?" "How will this law being proposed affect me?" And I had a passion for that. I also had an interest in politics. You look how things have emerged in sustainability and in environmentalism, and there's a clear link between what's going on in the political realm and what's going on in business development. You can't separate the two. So, at the same time that my career was advancing through production and product development, I was also very much aware of what was going on from a political standpoint. I was working in Southern California at the time, so I asked to get involved in lobbying up in Sacramento and with various industry groups that were working on things which gave me a greater insight into how the twists and turns of all this were going. And then, one thing led to another.

What is your current job title and how would you describe the work you do in a typical day? What are your most common tasks, including those that make yours a green job?

There's what I'm doing now, and then there's what I was just doing. Right now, I am on loan from Dow Chemical to the University of California, Berkeley to start up a new sustainability program. That also includes teaching a graduate class on measuring sustainability. But to get here, I spent 25 years at Dow Chemical. My last role at Dow was as their global plastics sustainability leader — looking at sustainability in plastics on a global basis for Dow, which is the largest plastic manufacturer in the world. Right now my official title is executive in residence at the Haas School of Business at UC Berkeley. I'm starting up what we're calling the sustainable products and solutions program, which is a multidisciplinary program with start-up funding provided by the Dow Chemical Company Foundation. Not from the company, but from the foundation. They asked me to come here and get it up and rolling for the first couple of years.

If you could give advice to a young person who wants to work in this career field someday, what would you tell them? How can they best groom themselves for this field?

Build a broad base of work experience wherever you can. If you look at the dynamics of what's going on in the world and what's going on in society, then being able to deal with multiple industries and with multiple people within a company is helpful. To be able to talk to the business folks, the technical folks, the marketing folks and the public policy folks — any chance you have to interact with all those folks is valuable experience. And that's beneficial, because to truly come up with sustainable solutions you have to think about all of those various aspects. You can't just think about one area, anymore, which kind of goes back to what I'm trying to do here at UC Berkeley with this program. We're trying to break down some of the walls that exist here on campus. For example: where chemistry just does chemistry and doesn't look at the business aspects of what they're doing. They need to think about the business aspect, and we need to get the business people talking with the chemistry people, talking with the engineers and so forth, so that we can come up with a viable sustainable solution at the end of the day. The world is the marketplace. You never know where your competition is going to come from. You never know where your products are going to come from. So you have to think globally. Read the *Economist*, the *New York Times*, the *San Francisco Chronicle*. Also, travel to expand your view of the world.

What kind of career advancement opportunities can one expect in this field? What kind of salary range would reflect that career path (from entry-level to the more advanced position)?

I would suggest starting with a technical degree. With that, you can always go into business or into public affairs or public policy. But if you get a degree in public policy or public affairs, it is extremely difficult to go into a technical area. Chemical engineering is one example of a technical degree. Mechanical engineering is another. Chemistry is yet another. Even things like toxicology and public health. Dow Chemical's current vice president of sustainability has a PhD in public health and toxicology from Harvard. So from a career-path standpoint, you can go anywhere you want, or you can stay on the technical side and work on a specific area that may become your specialty. But by the same token, if you've got talents in some of these other areas, you can move up the ladder. You can start as a basic engineer or chemist and you've got a good starting salary. Then you can look at senior management positions at $150,000 or more per year. A chief sustainability officer can be well over $200,000 per year.

In your opinion, what are some of the best schools, degrees and certificates for jobs in this career field, including green–specific training?
Obviously UC Berkeley is an excellent school. But there are a lot of great schools out there. It is important to pick a quality school for the subject you are majoring in. Beyond that, make sure you are comfortable with the professors and staff you will be working with. Look for schools that offer you the ability to take classes and explore your interests in areas like business or politics — in addition to your science degree. I have a chemical engineering degree from Oregon State, and I had the opportunity to do a lot of things outside of chemistry and chemical engineering, and that expanded my horizons. So I think that's what you want to look for in a school. Obviously the popular schools for engineering are a bonus in terms of recruiting opportunities, but look for schools that also give you the opportunity to think outside the box. I think schools like Arizona State, that are trying to integrate sustainability into a broad spectrum of class offerings, will be helpful for students that want to get into this area in their careers. Also, look for opportunities to volunteer outside of the school experience. Internships are great, but if you can't do something on the social side of sustainability, and if you enjoy the political side, volunteer and get involved in these things. I think that's the kind of stuff that not only looks good on a resumé, but also gives you a sense of what you want to be engaged in and what kind of company you want to work for in the future. One of the things I always tell people is that I had great summer jobs in college. And one of the things I found out from my summer jobs was not so much what I wanted to do when I graduated, but what I didn't want to do. As far as what degree, I think that you can go far with a bachelor's degree. My advice would be to get your bachelor's degree and get into the working world before you pursue a master's degree. I wouldn't recommend jumping right into a master's program unless you really know what it is you want. With some work experience, you may decide that you need to pursue something on the business side, like an MBA.

How does someone without previous experience in this career field land a job? What are the best strategies for job-hunting in this field?
These days you need to search for jobs both online and offline. Online job searching is a key tool in looking for positions. But I also think networking is a key thing. Pursuing internships and summer jobs in areas that you are

interested in is an awfully good way to get an "in" with a company. And if not with that company, maybe they don't end up hiring the summer that you graduate, for example, but if you've made good contacts there, those folks can get you in touch with other folks who might be hiring. So the networking side of things is critical.

Are there any professional associations that you would recommend joining?
There are all sorts of associations for technical folks. So pick your favorite: chemical engineering, or AIChE; chemistry, or ACS; mechanical engineering; industrial engineering or whatever. And getting really involved in these organizations also shows that you're a leader. And it presents the opportunity to network with folks who are engaged in what they're doing.

What emerging careers do you see developing now and into the future for this career field? What new technologies will have the greatest impact on this field?
The whole energy area is a huge area of opportunity and will include many opportunities for chemical engineers, chemists and mechanical engineers. The jobs could be related to power, or to transport, or to design, or to energy storage. Or, on the other side of it, if you think about climate change as it relates to energy, how do you siphon off the CO_2 and store it so that it's not released into the atmosphere? That's a huge opportunity for chemists, chemical engineers and the whole engineering field in general. And all of those fields need great thinkers. And bio-derived fuels — what makes sense from a sustainability standpoint? There has been a lot of criticism lately of ethanol from corn. For example, can we afford to divert half of our corn crop to making fuel while the world starves? I'm guessing the answer is no, we can't. So what are the other things we can do without using food crops and food acreage to supply bio-derived fuels? Energy conservation is going to need a lot of engineering and chemistry behind it. Even things like toxicology, with chemists getting into the whole toxicology area. If you look at what's happening in Europe, there's a law that basically says chemistry tests have to be done and approved before you can put a product on the market. So that's going to lead to huge opportunities in terms of being able to evaluate those things and to predict what's going to be successful or not. And we're going to have to change how we use materials, how we recycle materials and how we reuse materials. That kind of thing is going to lead to great opportunities. At the same time, you're going to need chemists and chemical engineers and engineers to think about the business side of all this. At the end of the day, how do you make money doing these things? And think about the global aspects of where the stuff is manufactured and used. What are the end-of-life implications of making this? What are the

social implications of this stuff being made by 11-year-olds in a third-world country? We live in a world where you have to look at all three legs of that sustainability stool.

Resources from Q&A

American Chemical Society (ACS): portal.acs.org
American Institute of Chemical Engineers (AIChE): aiche.org
Arizona State University: asu.edu
Dow Chemical Company: dow.com
Economist: economist.com
Harvard University: harvard.edu
New York Times: nytimes.com
Oregon State University: oregonstate.edu
San Francisco Chronicle: sfgate.com/chronicle/
University of California, Berkeley | Haas School of Business: haas.berkeley.edu

Civil Engineering Technicians

Civil engineering technicians apply theory and principles of civil engineering in planning, designing and overseeing construction and maintenance of structures and facilities under the direction of engineering staff or physical scientists.

Qualifications and Advancement

An associate's degree in civil engineering technology or a related field is the typical education/training requirement. Although employers don't usually require engineering technicians to be certified, such certification can provide job-seekers with a competitive advantage. The National Institute for Certification in Engineering Technologies has established a voluntary certification program for civil engineering technicians.

Entry-level engineering technicians usually begin by performing routine duties under the close supervision of an experienced technician, technologist or engineer. As experience is gained, they are given more difficult assignments with decreasing supervision. Some civil engineering technicians may become supervisors. Some others will go on to complete a bachelor's degree and become professional engineers.

Salary Survey

Median salary: $40,560 (high)
Typical range: $31,310 to $51,230

Job Outlook and Employment

Average growth is projected for this occupation in the US, from 90,650 jobs in 2006 to 99,888 in 2016. Spurred by population growth and the related need to improve the nation's infrastructure, more civil engineering technicians will be needed to expand transportation, water supply and pollution control systems, as well as large buildings and building complexes. They also will be needed to repair or replace existing roads, bridges and other public structures.

Where the jobs are

State government (25.45%); Local government (17.54%); Testing laboratories (3.33%).

Resources

National Institute for Certification in Engineering Technologies (NICET): nicet.org
Natural Resources Conservation Service (NRCS): nrcs.usda.gov
American Society of Certified Engineering Technicians (ASCET): ascet.org
O*NET OnLine: online.onetcenter.org (see civil engineering technicians)
US Dept. of Labor, Bureau of Labor Statistics: bls.gov/oco/ocos112.htm
See also resources for civil engineer

Q&A   GEORGE A. RILEY, JR.
Civil Engineering Technician, Natural Resources Conservation Service, from an interview with Alice in 2008

How did you get into this career field? What was your education and experience, including any green-related training or certification?
Well I always had a great love of the outdoors and was always in the creek or woods with my best friend while growing up. I caught and released my first fish at age six, and the beauty and spectacular power of the moment has inspired me ever since. Growing up on a farm allowed me to gain an appreciation of the environment, the connection and relationship of all life. When in school, I thrived with the Earth Science classes. I started going to a community college and was able to get into a special program that helped by providing jobs for students with state and federal agencies. I worked with the USDA Soil Conservation Service, now the Natural Resources Conservation Service (NRCS).

The great thing about these agencies was that they provided a very good training program, and they encouraged your participation. They also had programs to advance your education, but this would require a career change into the management field. I never took advantage of this because I wanted to work one on one with the local landowners, get my hands dirty and see the positive benefits of our working together. I enjoyed that down-to-earth communal, plus it kept me close to the outdoors — which I love so much. I only had 1.5 years of community college in forestry and geology. But I had a fair knowledge and experience working on farms prior to going to college, and that aided in understanding the issues faced by the farm community.

What is your current job title and how would you describe the work you do in a typical day? What are your most common tasks, including those that make yours a green job?

I'm currently a civil engineering technician; prior to that, I did a lot of farm planning, developing management systems and operation plans, along with some engineering practice designs. Now all I do is engineering designs and practice installations and assist resource planners with best-fit engineering methods to solve resource concerns. Generally, I'm either in the field collecting design data, in the office running through design computations and developing project designs or in the field reviewing planned designs with the landowners or assisting with the installation of the designed projects. Most of our projects will have significant positive impacts on the environment, which is great, but most of the time when working with farmers — these are side benefits for them. It's great when you can design a project that will collect waste that may be going into a stream or ditch and, at the same time, create an opportunity for farmers to benefit their crop production. At the same time, you helped clean up the streams and improved the habitat for so many critters.

If you could give advice to a young person who wants to work in this career field someday, what would you tell them? How can they best groom themselves for this field?

You definitely need to get a degree to get hired with most agencies. But going to school also provides job opportunities, as there are some programs out there where one can do summer work with the agencies and go to school during the winter. This gives both parties a chance to check each other out to see if this would be a desirable career opportunity or not. Take soil classes, geology, math and engineering classes. We do a lot of survey work, and that field has changed so much with GPS and all the other electronic gadgets out there.

What kind of career advancement opportunities can one expect in this field? What kind of salary range would reflect that career path (from entry-level to the more advanced position)?

As a civil engineering technician or soil conservation technician with USDA NRCS, there are some limitations in the career advancement, as you may start out at a GS-4 or 5, depending on your experience and background, and will top out your grade at a GS-9 or 10. There are some agencies that do go a little bit higher, but not much.

The pay will vary around the country, but in the local Puget Sound area, it will range from +/− $28,000 to $68,000.

In your opinion, what are some of the best schools, degrees and certificates for jobs in this career field, including green-specific training?

Washington State University has a good engineering program, as well as Gonzaga in Spokane, Washington, and St Martin's in Lacey, Washington. I think either civil engineering or ag engineering degrees would set you up well, and any training you can get in computer-aided drawing (CAD) would also be a big boost for your career.

How does someone without previous experience in this career field land a job? What are the best strategies for job-hunting in this field?

I would try and find an agency that has the summer work program in your field of interest. Check with the human resources department of the different agencies.

What emerging careers do you see developing now and into the future for this career field? What new technologies will have the greatest impact on this field?

Survey and CAD areas seem to be going strong and would seem an area to focus on currently and in the next ten years.

Resources from Q&A

Gonzaga University: gonzaga.edu
Natural Resources Conservation Service (NRCS): nrcs.usda.gov
Saint Martin's University: stmartin.edu
Washington State University: wsu.edu

Civil Engineers, including Green Building, Irrigation/ Reservoir and Waste Management Engineers

Civil engineers perform engineering duties in planning, designing and overseeing construction and maintenance of building structures and facilities, such as roads, railroads, airports, bridges, harbors, channels, dams, irrigation projects, pipelines, power plants, water and sewage systems and waste disposal units. Includes architectural, structural, traffic, ocean and geo-technical engineers.

Qualifications and Advancement
A bachelor's degree in civil engineering is the typical education requirement. However, a graduate degree is usually necessary for college and university teaching positions and for many jobs in research and development.

Entry-level engineers usually begin their careers as junior engineers, working under the supervision of experienced engineers. As they gain experience and knowledge, they generally advance to positions of greater responsibility and/or develop specialties. For engineers, advancement can lead to senior engineer, project manager, research and development manager and vice president for engineering. Some become consultants or start their own engineering firms. Those with a graduate degree can also become college and university professors.

Salary Survey
Median salary: $68,600 (very high)
Typical range: $54,520 to $86,260

Job Outlook and Employment
Faster than average growth is projected for this occupation in the US, from 256,330 jobs in 2006 to 302,409 in 2016. This will be spurred by general population growth and the related need to improve the nation's infrastructure, including the design, construction and expansion of transportation, water supply and pollution control systems and buildings and building complexes.

Where the Jobs Are
State government (11.57%); Local government (11.55%); Non-residential building construction (5.47%); Federal government, excluding postal service (3.84%); Self-employed: 4.41%

Resources
American Society of Civil Engineers (ASCE): asce.org
Engineering Central: engcen.com
National Society of Professional Engineers: nspe.org
O*NET OnLine: online.onetcenter.org (see civil engineers)
US Dept. of Labor, Bureau of Labor Statistics: bls.gov/oco/ocos027.htm
US Green Building Council/LEED AP Certification: usgbc.org

Erica Fifer, Area Engineer, US Department of Agriculture, from an interview with Alice in 2008

How did you get into this career field? What was your education and experience, including any green-related training or certification?

I was interested in working in an environmental career. After talking to a family friend working in a conservation career, I felt that getting a degree in environmental engineering would be the best fit for me. I received a civil engineering degree with an emphasis in environmental engineering from UW (University of Washington). I also worked for NRCS (Natural Resources Conservation Service) in the summers as a student trainee. While attending school, I pursued and received my engineer-in-training certificate.

What is your current job title and how would you describe the work you do in a typical day? What are your most common tasks, including those that make yours a green job?

As area engineer, I perform a wide variety of tasks. I assist in site visits on new projects and help develop alternatives; I complete field data collection and design. I also review designs and plans prepared by others, assist in coordinating projects and project designs and provide training and engineering leadership for Western Washington. On an "office day," I field questions on projects, work on designs and review work completed by others. On a "field day," I go to project sites and assist in developing and discussing alternatives for landowners. Projects vary from assisting agricultural producers, to improving waste management on their farms, to assisting with habitat restoration projects.

If you could give advice to a young person who wants to work in this career field someday, what would you tell them? How can they best groom themselves for this field?

Getting on-the-job experience is key. I would recommend trying to get into a summer intern program. This gives a person some hands-on experience with their selected field and can help you decide if this is right for you.

What kind of career advancement opportunities can one expect in this field? What kind of salary range would reflect that career path (from entry-level to the more advanced position)?

There are many career advancement opportunities within the agency I work for and in the field in general. I can't speak to the salary range in "private practice," but for the federal government, the range is from $34,000 to $77,000.

How does someone without previous experience in this career field land a job? What are the best strategies for job-hunting in this field?
A good strategy would be to get on with an agency as an intern. This would allow you to gain experience while working towards your career. Even volunteering in the field is a good way to get your foot in the door.

Are there any professional associations that you would recommend joining?
American Society of Civil Engineers.

Resources from Q&A
American Society of Civil Engineers (ASCE): asce.org
Natural Resources Conservation Service (NRCS): nrcs.usda.gov
University of Washington: washington.edu

 JAMES M. LITTLE, Vice President of Engineering,
Waste Connections, Inc., from an interview with Alice in 2008

How did you get into this career field? What was your education and experience, including any green-related training or certification?
I have bachelor of science and master of science degrees in geology. I joined an environmental consulting company out of grad school and was exposed to a wide array of industrial/mining environmental issues. I got a professional geologist license. There really was no "green" training at that time. Learned a lot about regulations and corporate risk management — which is the foundation for what I do today.

What is your current job title and how would you describe the work you do in a typical day?
As Vice President of Engineering, I direct corporate initiatives while developing and acquiring new facilities around the United States. I resolve and monitor environmental compliance issues and direct our field operations in a manner that protects the environment and lowers our corporate risk profile.

If you could give advice to a young person who wants to work in this career field someday, what would you tell them?
Do a consulting stint to get exposure to a lot of viewpoints and figure out where you want to be in the big picture. Get as much business exposure as you can because ultimately — to influence people or business to do the right thing — you have to understand how it impacts them and be able to convince them it is in their best interest. Internships are an excellent way to gain experience for college students.

What kind of career advancement opportunities can one expect in this field? What kind of salary range would reflect that career path (from entry-level to the more advanced position)?

Depends on the track. If they remain technical, the advancement is somewhat limited to supervisory status. If they develop management and business skills, they can end up in a boardroom. Entry level: $50,000. For purely technical folks, the upper range is $120,000 to $150,000. Management can go as high as $500,000.

In your opinion, what are some of the best schools, degrees and certificates for jobs in this career field, including green-specific training?

Almost all major universities are providing environmental education these days. I would recommend a hard discipline bachelor of science degree in chemistry/physics, geology or engineering, with some business training. Here in California, several University of California schools offer excellent curricula. Stanford and Cal Poly also produce a lot of good young talent.

How does someone without previous experience in this career field land a job? What are the best strategies for job-hunting in this field?

Most likely working for a consulting company. The work is tedious and typically requires field work. Be willing to start at the bottom. Good jobs in this field rely heavily on networking. I don't hire anyone without solid references.

How much experience is necessary before a person should venture into self-employment in your field? What positions should that experience be in?

I think 5 to 10 years, and even then you need networked clients. There are far too many people in consulting companies with 20 years of experience to expect someone like me to hire you with minimal experience.

Are there any professional associations that you would recommend joining?

The associations are typically highly specialized, such as the American Society of Civil Engineers.

What emerging careers do you see developing now and into the future for this career field?

Carbon management and alternative energy solutions. Water and air purification technology is advancing as well.

Resources from Q&A:

American Society of Civil Engineers (ASCE): asce.org
Cal Poly, San Luis Obispo: calpoly.edu

Stanford University: stanford.edu

University of Washington: washington.edu

Waste Connections, Inc.: wasteconnections.com

Conservation, Biological and Agricultural Engineers

Agricultural engineers apply knowledge of engineering technology and biological science to agricultural problems concerned with power and machinery, electrification, structures, soil and water conservation and processing of agricultural products.

Qualifications and Advancement

A bachelor's degree in agricultural engineering or a related field is the typical education requirement. However, a graduate degree is usually necessary for college and university teaching positions and for many jobs in research and development.

Entry-level engineers usually begin their careers as junior engineers, working under the supervision of experienced engineers. As they gain experience and knowledge, they generally advance to positions of greater responsibility. For engineers, advancement can lead to senior engineer, project manager, research and development manager and vice president for engineering. Some become consultants or start their own engineering firms. Those with a graduate degree can also become college and university professors.

Salary Survey

Median salary: $66,030 (very high)

Typical range: $53,040 to $80,370

Job Outlook and Employment

Average growth is projected for this occupation in the US, from 3,133 jobs in 2006 to 3,401 in 2016. More engineers will be needed to meet the increasing demand for using biosensors to determine the optimal treatment of crops. Employment growth should also result from the need to increase crop yields to feed an expanding population and produce crops used as renewable energy sources.

Where the Jobs Are

Federal government, excluding postal service (14.5%); Management of companies and enterprises (11.14%); Colleges, universities and professional schools (6.88%); Local government (5.11%); Grain and oilseed milling (4.97%); Animal slaughtering and processing (4.73%); Sugar and confectionery product manufacturing (3.45%); Other food manufacturing (3.41%); Fruit and vegetable preserving and specialty food manufacturing (3.39%)

Resources

American Society of Agricultural and Biological Engineers: asabe.org
Association of Conservation Engineers (ACE): conservationengineers.org
Engineering Central: engcen.com
National Society of Professional Engineers: nspe.org
O*NET OnLine: online.onetcenter.org (see agricultural engineers)
US Dept. of Labor, Bureau of Labor Statistics: bls.gov/oco/ocos027.htm

Electrical Engineering Technicians, including Photovoltaic, Wind and Biomass Energy Technicians

Electrical engineering technicians apply electrical theory and related knowledge to test and modify developmental or operational electrical machinery and electrical control equipment and circuitry in industrial or commercial plants and laboratories. Usually work under direction of engineering staff.

Qualifications and Advancement

An associate's degree in electrical engineering or a related field is the typical education/training requirement. Although employers don't usually require engineering technicians to be certified, such certification can provide jobseekers with a competitive advantage. The National Institute for Certification in Engineering Technologies has established a voluntary certification program.

Entry-level engineering technicians usually begin by performing routine duties under the close supervision of an experienced technician, technologist or engineer. As experience is gained, they are given more difficult assignments with decreasing supervision. Some electrical engineering technicians may become supervisors. Some others will go on to complete a bachelor's degree and become professional engineers.

Salary Survey

Median salary: $50,660 (high)
Typical range: $39,270 to $60,470

Job Outlook and Employment

Slower than average growth is projected for this occupation in the US, from 170,433 jobs in 2006 to 176,530 in 2016. The rising demand for electrical products will be somewhat offset by foreign competition in design and manufacturing.

Where the Jobs Are

Semiconductor and other electronic component manufacturing (11.11%); Navigational, measuring, electromedical and control instruments manufacturing (7%); Employment services (6.59%); Wired telecommunications carriers (5.49%); Federal government, excluding postal service (5.23%); Postal service (4.31%); Electric power generation, transmission and distribution (4.15%); Communications equipment manufacturing (3.23%); Research and development in the physical, engineering and life sciences (3.07%)

Resources

National Institute for Certification in Engineering Technologies (NICET): nicet.org

Solar Energy Industries Association (SEIA): seia.org

See also resources for electrical engineers

O*NET OnLine: online.onetcenter.org (see electrical engineering technicians)

US Dept. of Labor, Bureau of Labor Statistics: bls.gov/oco/ocos112.htm

Electrical Engineers, including Recycling, Solar/ Photovoltaic, Wind and Biomass Engineers

Electrical engineers design, develop, test or supervise the manufacturing and installation of electrical equipment, components or systems for commercial, industrial, military or scientific use.

Qualifications and Advancement

A bachelor's degree in electrical engineering is the typical education requirement. However, a master's degree is often necessary for advancement. Since this field is so broad, electrical engineers often earn a master's degree in their area of specialty.

Entry-level engineers usually begin their careers as junior engineers, working under the supervision of experienced engineers. As they gain experience and knowledge, they generally advance to positions of greater responsibility. For engineers, advancement can lead to senior engineer, project manager, research and development manager and vice president of engineering. Some become consultants or start their own engineering firms. Those with a graduate degree can also become college and university professors.

Salary Survey
Median salary: $75,930 (very high)
Typical range: $60,640 to $94,050

Job Outlook and Employment
Slower than average growth is projected for this occupation in the US, from 153,375 jobs in 2006 to 162,965 in 2016. Although job growth will be spurred by the strong demand for electrical devices, including electric power generators, wireless phone transmitters, high-density batteries and navigation systems, international competition and manufacturing will limit employment growth.

Where the Jobs Are
Navigational, measuring, electromedical and control instruments manufacturing (9.29%); Electric power generation, transmission and distribution (7.98%); Semiconductor and other electronic component manufacturing (7.92%); Research and development in the physical, engineering and life sciences (4.68%)

Resources
Engineering Central: engcen.com
Green Energy Jobs: greenenergyjobs.com
Institute of Electrical and Electronics Engineers: ieeeusa.org
National Society of Professional Engineers: nspe.org
O*NET OnLine: online.onetcenter.org (see electrical engineers)
Solar Energy Industries Association (SEIA): seia.org
US Dept. of Labor, Bureau of Labor Statistics: bls.gov/oco/ocos027.htm

Environmental Engineering and Pollution Control Technicians

Environmental engineering technicians apply theory and principles of environmental engineering to modify, test and operate equipment and devices used in the prevention, control and remediation of environmental pollution, including waste treatment and site remediation. May assist in the development of environmental pollution remediation devices under the direction of an engineer.

Qualifications and Advancement
An associate's degree is the typical education/training requirement. However, it is sometimes possible to qualify for environmental engineering technician jobs without formal training. Although employers usually do not require

environmental engineering technicians to be certified, such certification may provide jobseekers a competitive advantage.

Environmental engineering technicians usually start as an assistant to an environmental engineer. As they gain experience and knowledge, technicians are given more difficult assignments and have less supervision. Some environmental engineering technicians may advance to supervisory positions. With a bachelor's degree, technicians can become environmental engineers.

Salary Survey
Median salary: $40,560 (high)
Typical range: $30,920 to $53,250

Job Outlook and Employment
Much faster than average growth is projected for this occupation in the US, from 21,126 jobs in 2006 to 26,362 in 2016. More environmental engineering technicians will be needed to comply with environmental regulations and to develop methods of cleaning up existing hazards. A shift in emphasis toward preventing problems rather than controlling those that already exist, as well as increasing public health concerns resulting from population growth, also will spur demand.

Where the Jobs Are
Local government (11.68%); Management, scientific and technical consulting services (11.43%); Testing laboratories (10.53%); Remediation and other waste management services (5.42%); State government (5.26%)

Resources
American Society of Certified Engineering Technicians (ASCET): ascet.org
Association of Environmental Professionals (AEP): califaep.org
Green Engineering Jobs: greenengineeringjobs.com
O*NET OnLine: online.onetcenter.org (see environmental engineering
    technicians)
US Dept. of Labor, Bureau of Labor Statistics: bls.gov/oco/ocos112.htm
See also resources for environmental engineers

Environmental Engineering Professors

Engineering teachers, postsecondary, teach courses pertaining to the application of physical laws and principles of engineering for the development of machines, materials, instruments, processes and services. Includes both teachers primarily engaged in teaching and those who combine teaching and research.

Qualifications and Advancement

A doctorate degree in engineering is the typical education requirement, although a master's degree is often adequate for positions with community colleges and some four-year colleges.

Engineering instructors generally have several years of experience in their field before going into teaching, usually as lecturers or adjunct (part-time) professors or instructors. Eventually they find a full-time position. The next step for college and university professors is to become tenured — meaning that the professor has received a permanent job contract, granted after a probationary period of several years (depending on the institution). Advancement for tenured professors involves moving into administrative positions, such as department chairperson, dean, vice president and president.

Salary Survey

Median salary: $64,780 (very high)
Typical range: $46,500 to $89,680

Job Outlook and Employment

Much faster than average growth is projected for this occupation in the US, from 4,310 jobs in 2006 to 5,301 in 2016. Many job openings in this occupation will be created by growth in enrollments and the need to replace the many postsecondary teachers who are likely to retire over the next decade.

Where the Jobs Are

Colleges, universities and professional schools (70.8%); Community colleges (21.54%); Technical and trade schools (3.04%)

Resources

American Association for Aerosol Research (AAAR): aaar.org
American Chemical Society (ACS): portal.acs.org
American Geophysical Union (AGU): agu.org
Association of Environmental Engineering and Science Professors (AEESP):
    aeesp.org
Green Engineering Jobs: greenengineeringjobs.com
Preparing Future Faculty (PFF) program: preparing–faculty.org
O*NET OnLine: online.onetcenter.org (see engineering teachers, postsecondary)
US Dept. of Labor, Bureau of Labor Statistics: bls.gov/oco/ocos066.htm
See also resources for environmental engineers

MICHAEL J. KLEEMAN, Professor of Civil and Environmental Engineering, University of California, Davis, from an interview with Jim in 2008

How did you get into this career field? What was your education and experience, including any green-related training or certification?

I earned a bachelor of applied science degree in mechanical engineering from the University of Waterloo in Ontario, Canada, and an MS/PhD in Environmental Engineering Science from Caltech in Pasadena, California. The undergraduate degree gave me a lot of quantitative tools that were very flexible. So I was ready to take advantage of the opportunities in environmental engineering when they came my way. I couldn't have predicted that ahead of time, but chance favors the prepared mind.

How would you describe the work you do in a typical day? What are your most common tasks, including those that make yours a green job?

I am a professor in the Civil and Environmental Engineering Department at the University of California, Davis. I teach classes and perform research related to urban and regional air quality problems, including climate effects on air quality and mechanistic links between air quality and human health effects. My research program is diverse. On any given day, I may be collecting samples in the field, building parallel computer systems, writing computer programs, performing data analysis, writing reports, papers, etc. In the classroom, I may be teaching, grading assignments or preparing exams. UC faculty are also expected to perform significant service for the university and the general community, so I have served on numerous committees and aided the State of California as an expert witness in court cases.

If you could give advice to a young person who wants to work in this career field someday, what would you tell them?

Get a degree in a quantitative field related to chemistry, engineering or computer programming. Build quantitative skills early in your career.

What kind of career advancement opportunities can one expect in this field? What kind of salary range could be expected?

Researchers in this field work in academia, government labs, regulatory agencies and private consulting firms. It is a competitive field, with many bright minds working on the tough problems that we face. Until we completely understand climate impacts on air quality and the mechanistic links between air quality and human health, opportunities in the field should be plentiful.

Salary ranges that I have seen for freshly minted PhDs in this area range from $70,000 to $150,000 per year. More advanced positions range from $100,000 to $200,000 per year.

What are some of the best schools, degrees and certificates for jobs in this career field, including green-specific training?
An undergraduate degree in chemical or mechanical engineering should lay the foundation for any of the following advanced degrees:

- Caltech: Environmental Science and Engineering, MS/PhD
- Carnegie Mellon University (CMU): Chemical Engineering, MS/PhD
- Georgia Tech: Civil and Environmental Engineering, MS/PhD
- Stanford University: Civil and Environmental Engineering, MS/PhD
- UC Davis: Civil and Environmental Engineering, MS/PhD

Are there any professional associations that you would recommend joining?
- American Association for Aerosol Research
- American Geophysical Union
- American Chemical Society

What emerging careers do you see developing now and into the future for this career field? What new technologies will have the greatest impact on this field?
Climate impacts on air pollution and health. Computer modeling and enhanced sensor networks will have a major impact on this field in the future.

Resources from Q&A
American Association for Aerosol Research (AAAR): aaar.org
American Chemical Society (ACS): portal.acs.org
American Geophysical Union (AGU): agu.org
California Institute of Technology (Caltech): caltech.edu
Carnegie Mellon University: cmu.edu
Georgia Institute of Technology (Georgia Tech): gatech.edu
Stanford University: stanford.edu
University of California, Davis: ucdavis.edu
University of Waterloo: uwaterloo.ca

Environmental Engineers, including Ecological and Air Quality Engineers

Environmental engineers design, plan or perform engineering duties in the prevention, control and remediation of environmental health hazards utilizing various engineering disciplines.

Environmental engineering disciplines include: air quality control; water supply; wastewater disposal; stormwater management; solid waste management; and hazardous waste management.

Qualifications and Advancement

A bachelor's degree in environmental engineering is the typical education requirement. However, a graduate degree is usually necessary for college and university teaching positions and for many jobs in research and development.

Environmental engineers usually begin as junior engineers. Once they pass the professional exam and get licensed, they have many options for advancement. They may be given more complex projects and be assigned as a lead or senior engineer. They may move into management positions. They may become consulting engineers. The American Academy of Environmental Engineering recommends that engineers obtain a master's degree, since employers increasingly prefer job candidates with advanced degrees. Most research and teaching positions also require a master's degree or higher.

Salary Survey

Median salary: $69,940 (very high)
Typical range: $54,150 to $88,480

Job Outlook and Employment

Much faster than average growth is projected for this occupation in the US, from 54,341 jobs in 2006 to 68,161 in 2016. More environmental engineers will be needed to comply with environmental regulations and to develop methods of cleaning up existing hazards. A shift in emphasis toward preventing problems rather than controlling those that already exist, as well as increasing public health concerns resulting from population growth, also are expected to spur demand.

Where the Jobs Are

Management, scientific and technical consulting services (14.42%); State government (12.46%); Local government (8.86%); Federal government, excluding postal service (7.84%); Self–employed: 2.66%

Resources

Air & Waste Management Association (A&WMA): awma.org
American Academy of Environmental Engineers (AAEE): aaee.net
American Chemical Society (ACS): portal.acs.org
American Geophysical Union (AGU): agu.org
Association of Environmental Professionals (AEP): califaep.org

Engineering Central: engcen.com
Green Engineering Jobs: greenengineeringjobs.com
National Society of Professional Engineers: nspe.org
O*NET OnLine: online.onetcenter.org (see environmental engineers)
US Dept. of Labor, Bureau of Labor Statistics: bls.gov/oco/ocos027.htm

 CAROLYN CRAIG, Air Quality Engineer,
El Dorado County Air Quality Management District,
from an interview with Alice in 2008

How did you get into this career field? What was your education and experience, including any green-related training or certification?
I started in the environmental engineering field in 1981, just as the federal hazardous waste regulations (RCRA) were promulgated. After spending 15 years working in water quality, hazardous waste and hazardous materials, I switched to air quality as the Federal Clean Air Act was amended and expanded. I worked in the industry for 25 years and have been working at the El Dorado County Air Quality Management District for 3 years. I have a bachelor of science degree in chemical engineering and a certificate in hazardous materials management. I'm also an avid bike rider, I use public transit whenever possible, and I try to minimize my impact on the environment in both my personal and professional life.

What is your current job title and how would you describe the work you do in a typical day? What are your most common tasks, including those that make yours a green job?
My current title is air quality engineer. I administer grants for projects that reduce air emissions, I promulgate and provide assistance for the implementation of regulations that reduce air emissions, and I prepare plans and work with other organizations on how the region can meet air quality standards. In addition, I oversee the requirements for testing to determine whether equipment is meeting the required limits for air emissions. I spend about ⅔ of my time in the office and ⅓ in the field, with the opportunity to interface with and educate both the public and business community.

If you could give advice to a young person who wants to work in this career field someday, what would you tell them? How can they best groom themselves for this field?
I would tell them to get a technical background with a bachelor's degree in science so they can understand why the reduction of air emissions is critical.

They should become informed about current technologies that reduce air emissions. They should also strive to minimize their own generation of air emissions so they can understand how to encourage others to do so.

What kind of career advancement opportunities can one expect in this field? What kind of salary range would reflect that career path (from entry-level to the more advanced position)?
With the current state of air quality, there are many opportunities with government, industry and equipment and service suppliers. Salary ranges are commensurate with technical requirements and with experience. From this path, advancement is usually into management, but opportunities are also available in larger organizations for technical experts in specific types of air pollutants, equipment or regulations.

In your opinion, what are some of the best schools, degrees and certificates for jobs in this career field, including green-specific training?
After a technical four-year degree, many colleges have certificate programs that blend experience with traditional course work.

How does someone without previous experience in this career field land a job? What are the best strategies for job-hunting in this field?
A candidate without prior experience would need to have a good technical education and be informed about current trends in air quality. That could be gained by attending technical workshops, being involved with environmental groups or reading educational information provided by air quality and health organizations.

Are there any professional associations that you would recommend joining?
The Air & Waste Management Association.

What emerging careers do you see developing now and into the future for this career field? What new technologies will have the greatest impact on this field?
Emerging careers will be in developing new products that operate with less air emissions; helping industry comply with the myriad of new regulations; and working in regulatory organizations to implement regulations which provide environmental benefit with a minimum impact to businesses.

Resources from Q&A
Air & Waste Management Association (A&WMA): awma.org
El Dorado County Air Quality Management District (AQMD):
  co.el-dorado.ca.us/EMD/apcd/

Mechanical Engineers, including Green Mechanical Engineers

Mechanical engineers perform engineering duties in planning and designing tools, engines, machines and other mechanically functioning equipment. Oversee installation, operation, maintenance and repair of such equipment as centralized heat, gas, water and steam systems.

Qualifications and Advancement

A bachelor's degree is the typical education requirement. However, a graduate degree is usually necessary for advancement and for college/university faculty positions.

Entry-level engineers usually begin their careers as junior engineers, working under the supervision of experienced engineers. As they gain experience and knowledge, they generally advance to positions of greater responsibility. For engineers, advancement can lead to senior engineer, project manager, research and development manager and vice president of engineering. Some become consultants or start their own engineering firms. Those with a graduate degree can become college and university professors.

Salary Survey

Median salary: $69,850 (very high)
Typical range: $55,420 to $87,550

Job Outlook and Employment

Slower than average growth is projected for this occupation in the US, from 225,797 jobs in 2006 to 235,169 in 2016. The slow overall growth for this occupation is expected because total employment in manufacturing industries — in which employment of mechanical engineers is concentrated — is expected to decline.

Where the Jobs Are

Navigational, measuring, electromedical and control instruments manufacturing (5.42%); Aerospace product and parts manufacturing (4.79%); Federal government (4.56%); Motor vehicle parts manufacturing (4.14%); Research and development in the physical, engineering and life sciences (3.83%); Other general purpose machinery manufacturing (3.4%); Self-employed: 2.24%

Resources

American Society of Mechanical Engineers (ASME): asme.org
American Solar Energy Society (ASES): ases.org

Engineering Central: engcen.com
Green Energy Jobs: greenenergyjobs.com
Green Mechanical Council (GreenMech): greenmech.org
National Society of Professional Engineers: nspe.org
O*NET OnLine: online.onetcenter.org (see mechanical engineers)
US Dept. of Labor, Bureau of Labor Statistics: bls.gov/oco/ocos027.htm
US Green Building Council/LEED AP Certification: usgbc.org

Environmental Health and Safety Group

○ Environmental Health and Safety Engineers

○ Environmental Health and Safety Technicians

○ Hazardous Materials (HazMat) and Asbestos Abatement Workers

○ Industrial Hygienists and Environmental Health and Safety Analysts/ Managers

Environmental Health and Safety Engineers

Industrial health and safety engineers plan, implement and coordinate safety programs, requiring application of engineering principles and technology, to prevent or correct unsafe environmental working conditions.

Qualifications and Advancement

A bachelor's degree in health and safety engineering or a related field is the typical education requirement. However, a graduate degree is usually necessary for advancement and for college and university teaching positions.

Entry-level engineers usually begin their careers as junior engineers, working under the supervision of experienced engineers. As they gain experience and knowledge, they generally advance to positions of greater responsibility. For engineers, advancement can lead to senior engineer, project manager, research and development manager and vice president of engineering. Some become consultants or start their own engineering firms. Those with a graduate degree can also become college and university professors.

Salary Survey

Median salary: $66,290 (very high)

Typical range: $51,630 to $83,240

Job Outlook and Employment

Average growth is projected for this occupation in the US, from 25,380 jobs in 2006 to 27,823 in 2016. Because health and safety engineers make production processes and products as safe as possible, their services should be in demand as concern increases for environmental health and safety.

Where the jobs are (for all health and safety engineers)

Non-residential building construction (8.08%); State government (5.23%); Management, scientific and technical consulting services (5.05%); Local government (4.6%); Basic chemical manufacturing (3.61%); Management of companies and enterprises (3.22%)

Resources

American Society of Safety Engineers: asse.org

Board of Certified Safety Professionals (BCSP): bcsp.org

EHSCareers.com: ehscareers.com

Engineering Central: engcen.com

National Association for EHS Management (NAEM): naem.org

National Safety Council (NSC): nsc.org

National Society of Professional Engineers: nspe.org

O*NET OnLine: online.onetcenter.org (see industrial health and safety engineers)

US Dept. of Labor, Bureau of Labor Statistics: bls.gov/oco/ocos027.htm

Environmental Health and Safety Technicians

Occupational health and safety technicians collect data on work environments for analysis by occupational health and safety specialists. Implement and conduct evaluation of programs designed to limit chemical, physical, biological and ergonomic risks to workers.

Qualifications and Advancement

A bachelor's degree in occupational health, safety or a related field, such as engineering, biology or chemistry, is the typical education requirement. There are also two-year associate's degree and one-year certificate programs available, but a bachelor's degree is often the minimum requirement for career advancement. There are also a number of voluntary certifications available through several organizations (see Resources).

Environmental health and safety technicians who work for federal agencies advance to a specified full-performance level if their work is satisfactory. Advancement beyond this level usually leads to supervisory positions, such as environmental health and safety specialist. Advancement opportunities in state and local government and the private sector are often similar to those in the federal government. With a graduate degree in industrial hygiene or a related field, specialists can become professors or researchers.

Salary Survey
Median salary: $42,160 (high)
Typical range: $32,550 to $53,840

Job Outlook and Employment
Faster than average growth is projected for this occupation in the US, from 10,468 jobs in 2006 to 11,992 in 2016. This growth reflects the continuing demand for a safe and healthy work environment. Emergency preparedness will also continue to increase in importance, creating additional demand for these workers. In private industry, employment growth will reflect overall business growth and continuing self-enforcement of government and company regulations and policies.

Where the Jobs Are
Local government (14.93%); Federal government (12.23%); State government (11.93%); General medical and surgical hospitals (6.25%); Management, scientific and technical consulting services (5.53%); Colleges, universities and professional schools (5%)

Resources
American Board of Industrial Hygiene (ABIH): abih.org
American Industrial Hygiene Association (AIHA): aiha.org
Board of Certified Safety Professionals (BCSP): bcsp.org
Council on Certification of Health, Environmental and Safety Technologists (CCHEST): cchest.org
EHSCareers.com: ehscareers.com
O*NET OnLine: online.onetcenter.org (see occupational health and safety technicians)
US Dept. of Labor, Bureau of Labor Statistics: bls.gov/oco/ocos017.htm

Hazardous Materials (HazMat) and Asbestos Abatement Workers

Hazardous materials removal workers identify, remove, pack, transport or dispose of hazardous materials, including asbestos, lead-based paint, waste oil, fuel, transmission fluid, radioactive materials and contaminated soil. Specialized training and certification in hazardous materials handling or a confined entry permit are generally required. May operate earth-moving equipment or trucks.

Qualifications and Advancement

No formal education beyond a high-school diploma is required to become a hazardous materials removal worker. However, federal, state and local governments set training and certification requirements for this occupation, so the training can range from a few days to several months. Regulations vary by specialty and sometimes by state or locality. Employers are responsible for employee training, although some training can be done at Occupational Safety and Health Administration (OSHA) training centers.

Advancement usually takes the form of greater responsibility and higher pay, although some hazardous materials removal workers can become lead workers or supervisors. Beyond that, however, advancement generally requires a bachelor's degree or higher.

Salary Survey

Median salary: $35,450 (low/moderate)
Typical range: $27,680 to $47,320

Job Outlook and Employment

Average growth is projected for this occupation in the US, from 39,497 jobs in 2006 to 43,929 in 2016. Numerous Superfund projects will require cleanup of hazardous materials waste sites, spurring demand for hazardous materials removal workers. However, employment growth will largely be determined by federal funding, which has been declining in recent years. The often dangerous aspects of these jobs lead to high turnover because many workers do not stay in the occupation long. Therefore, opportunities for decontamination technicians, radiation safety technicians and decontamination workers should be particularly good.

Where the jobs are

Remediation and other waste management services (67.41%); Waste treatment and disposal (8.62%); Waste collection (3.46%)

Resources

Academy of Certified Hazardous Materials Managers (ACHMM):
   achmm.org
Continuing Challenge Hazmat Workshop: hazmat.org
International Association of Hazardous Materials Technicians (IAHMT):
   iahmt.com
Occupational Safety and Health Administration (OSHA): osha.gov
Restoration Industry Association (RIA): ascr.org

O*NET OnLine: online.onetcenter.org (see hazardous materials removal
    workers)
US Dept. of Labor, Bureau of Labor Statistics: bls.gov/oco/ocos256.htm

Laura Greer with her hazmat crew on a
river retrieval mission.

 LAURA GREER
HazMat Division Manager,
PARC Specialty Contractors,
from an interview with Jim in 2008

*How did you get into this career field?
What was your education and experience, including any green-related training or certification?*
I started out with a cannery. The first
thing I did was quality control where
I went out and found problems that they had with what they shipped. Then
I went into coordinating how the material came off the line and was labeled
and shipped. Then I interviewed for a job in a hazardous waste facility where
transportation played a big part. But I clicked really well with the person who
was running that hazmat site, and he taught me everything so that I learned
the whole operation.

*What is your current job title and how would you describe the work you do in a
typical day? What are your most common tasks?*
I'm the HazMat Division Manager. That means I do everything. I do compliance for all of our permitting. I run our hazmat crew. I do the business development end. I do the customer service — keeping the clients. I do all the
contract writing. I work with my field crews at times. Our clients include law
enforcement agencies — cities, counties and state. But we also work with the
private sector. We have a very close relationship with a lot of the counties and
law enforcement agencies, and we do a lot of emergency response type work.
We also do illegal drug cleanup and remediation. I used to work for another
hazmat company that went through 10 acquisitions in almost 11 years. But the
company I work for now is my ideal because I like staying local and not traveling all over the United States.

*If you could give advice to a young person who wants to work in this career field
someday, what would you tell them? How can they best groom themselves for
this field?*

You have to have a clean DMV record and the ability to pass a background check, because a lot of our customers need that to get on their site. Even to get your hazmat license is much stricter than it was ten years ago. A lot of our people who work up through the ranks don't necessarily have a college degree, but they have a good knowledge of construction, good problem-resolution skills and good interpersonal skills. And then you also need to have really good safety ethics. Sometimes we have to ask: How can we get this done safely and do a good thing for the environment, but also not put our employees at risk? At a minimum, take a basic chemistry class at college. That's important for you to know what you're working with. For me, I can't hire people with less than six months experience, and I can't hire a field supervisor with less than four years experience. So a certificate or associate's degree in an environmental science program would give you an excellent background for hazmat work. Also, there's the Continuing Challenge Hazmat Workshop that travels from town to town. Most of it is really fire-related, but I've gone to it for 15 years, and we teach at it, too. It's a good place to pick up some classes if you're in the industry or even just starting out. Getting your initial 40 hours of training is key, so that can be your step in the door.

What kind of career advancement opportunities can one expect in this field?
The career ladder usually goes from a field technician to a foreman and from a foreman to a project manager. If they wanted to get into administrative work, they could get into estimating. All of our field technicians and foremen are our drivers, too. But some companies have specific jobs for drivers — which would be an entry-level position. But here, we're a little more diversified because of the nature of what we do. Our people have to be able to do a little bit of everything, so we wear more hats.

How does someone without previous experience in this career field land a job? What are the best strategies for job-hunting in this field?
I use a local job board, and I use Craigslist, and I get better responses than I get from a newspaper ad. Some of the other companies I work with use Monster, too.

Are there any professional associations that you would recommend joining?
I used to belong to a whole bunch, but that's kind of dwindled back. Our asbestos people belong to some associations, but I'm not as familiar with those. This industry has changed a lot in the last ten years, and now there's less networking.

What emerging careers do you see developing now and into the future for this career field? What new technologies will have the greatest impact on this field?
Laws are changing all the time. Some of the environmental laws are changing regarding how you do things. Even the OSHA (Occupational Safety and Health Administration), with more regulations changes. And technology changes all the time when it comes to the use of equipment or how you do the job. So that's something we just have to keep up with. I can't say that there's any one big thing, but there's always something changing. For example, the Lumex mercury detector machine that we bought a couple years ago to replace an older machine — the new one fine-tunes our mercury clean up a lot better.

Resources from Q&A
Continuing Challenge Hazmat Workshop: hazmat.org
Craigslist: craigslist.org
Monster: monster.com
Occupational Safety and Health Administration (OSHA): osha.gov
OhioLumex Co: ohiolumex.com

Industrial Hygienists and Environmental Health and Safety Analysts/Managers

Occupational health and safety specialists review, evaluate and analyze work environments and design programs and procedures to control, eliminate and prevent disease or injury caused by chemical, physical and biological agents or ergonomic factors. May conduct inspections and enforce adherence to laws and regulations governing the health and safety of individuals.

Qualifications and Advancement
A bachelor's degree in occupational health, safety or a related field, such as engineering, biology or chemistry, is the typical education requirement. Some have a master's degree in industrial hygiene. All occupational health and safety specialists are trained in the applicable laws and inspection procedures through a combination of classroom and on-the-job training.

Occupational health and safety specialists begin as trainees or are promoted from technician positions. As they gain experience and knowledge, they advance to positions of greater responsibility. Eventually, advancement leads to supervisory or management positions, although this often requires a graduate degree.

Salary Survey

Median salary: $58,030 (very high)

Typical range: $45,050 to $72,660

Job Outlook and Employment

Average growth is projected for this occupation in the US, from 45,206 jobs in 2006 to 48,882 in 2016. The average growth reflects a balance of continuing public demand for a safe and healthy work environment against the desire for smaller government and fewer regulations. Emergency preparedness will continue to increase in importance, creating demand for these workers. More specialists will be needed to cope with technological advances in safety equipment and threats, changing regulations and increasing public expectations. In private industry, employment growth will reflect overall business growth and continuing self-enforcement of government and company regulations and policies.

Where the jobs are

Local government (14.93%); Federal government (12.23%); State government (11.93%); General medical and surgical hospitals (6.25%); Management, scientific and technical consulting services (5.53%); Colleges, universities and professional schools (5%)

Resources

American Board of Industrial Hygiene (ABIH): abih.org

American Industrial Hygiene Association (AIHA): aiha.org

Board of Certified Safety Professionals (BCSP): bcsp.org

Council on Cert. of Health, Env. and Safety Technologists (CCHEST):
     cchest.org

EHSCareers.com: ehscareers.com

Indoor Air Quality Association (IAQA): iaqa.org

Indoor Environmental Institute (IEI): ieinstitute.org

Institute of Inspection, Cleaning and Restoration Certification (IICRC):
     iicrc.org

National Environmental Health Association (NEHA): neha.org

O*NET OnLine: online.onetcenter.org (see occupational health and safety
     specialists)

US Dept. of Labor, Bureau of Labor Statistics: bls.gov/oco/ocos017.htm

Q&A **JOHN BANTA**
Certified Associate Industrial Hygienist, RestCon Environmental, from an interview with Jim in 2008

How did you get into this career field? What was your education and experience, including any green-related training or certification?

My initial experience was while I was an animal health technician working in medical research at the University of California, Davis. During that time, my hobby was to purchase homes that were in distress and fix them up. My wife and I would live in the homes as we were working on them. In 1980 I purchased an old Victorian home and proceeded to sand and burn old paint off and scrape and get the place painted. In the process, I managed to poison the whole family. My wife and myself and our two-year-old daughter ended up with some pretty significant blood lead levels. But we were fortunate, as my daughter's pediatrician was a very bright woman who recognized the problem. It was like being hit with a ton of bricks. It had never occurred to me that any of the remodeling things that I was doing might be adversely affecting me or my family. And so that probably was the major event that I could point to that led to an awakening. For the next few years, I started reading everything I could about indoor air quality and various concerns with regards to building health and safety. I started talking with people. My name got out there. People started calling and asking me questions. One day my wife looked at our phone bill and asked me who all these people were that I was talking to, and I told her that they were people that were having indoor air quality problems in their buildings and were calling and asking questions. She said the long-distance phone bill is over $200 a month; you've got to start charging them! And so I kind of phased into it, and within a few more years, I was providing full-time indoor environmental quality investigations and services. But I did not have a degree in that field. At that time, there were no degrees, really. In fact, there still are no specific degrees with regard to indoor air and environmental quality, or at least none that are routinely offered. I became recognized by the Environmental Protection Agency (EPA) as being proficient in radon gas measurements. In fact, I was one of the first people in California to take part in the EPA's radon gas proficiency program. Then I got certified in asbestos inspection and management planning. By 1990 it became apparent to me

I needed to have an educational background to back up the experience I had already gained. So our family moved to Arizona so I could attend Prescott College and get a degree in Environmental Health Sciences. That and five additional years of experience also prepared me for the Industrial Hygienist board exam.

What is your current job title and how would you describe the work you do in a typical day? What are your most common tasks, including those that make yours a green job?

I'm a certified associate industrial hygienist, but I consider myself a general purpose indoor environmental consultant. My job breaks down into three different categories: One, I'm an investigator. I go out and do field investigations. Two, I'm a teacher. Our company teaches people how to perform mold remediation, sewage damage cleanup and water damage restoration activities, and we provide various health and safety classes. And then third, which is probably the smallest portion of my job, is doing expert witness work. Sometimes these cases end up going to court, and so you've got to have thick enough skin and recognize that the attorneys' line of questioning isn't personal. It's just their job, and you just have to be cognizant of the facts of the case and tell the truth. A more typical industrial hygienist provides health and safety services for the working environment. And so you have some industrial hygienists that are available for hire on multiple types of projects. One day they might be working at an auto mechanics facility, another day they might be at a construction site, and another day they might be in a hospital. Then you have other industrial hygienists who work on workplace safety issues within a specific industry, such as mining or manufacturing. Another type of industrial hygienist are those associated with a university where they are often quite specialized.

If you could give advice to a young person who wants to work in this career field someday, what would you tell them? How can they best groom themselves for this field?

The minimum is a bachelor's degree that gives them a background in the sciences. But a degree in industrial hygiene and then the necessary experience for becoming certified as an industrial hygienist is basically like preparing for a master's degree. Either way, having a good background in chemistry, physiology and biology is very important from the standpoint of having a foundation to strike out from. The thing that I find kind of sad about my field is that it has been approached more as a technical type of career as opposed to a professional type of career. So what ends up happening with a lot of the state and federal certifications that are offered is people are taught a cookbook approach in terms of what they're supposed to do. For example, how many samples do you collect from which type of material in order to make an asbestos determination? There is so much that happens in this field that is outside of the box. So I think it's important for people to have a broad-based understanding of what goes on in order to be able to think through the problems and figure out what's going on. In addition to a basis in the sciences, they need a firm understanding of construction; how buildings are put together and how they function when they are operating properly. Today, whenever some homeowner doesn't know what type of environmental quality issue they are having in their building, they seem to believe they have a mold problem. And the problem with indoor environmental quality professionals not having the broad-based background is that it may not be a mold problem. There may be something else going on in the building that needs to be recognized. For example, I had an elderly woman call our company a while back, and she was absolutely certain that she had a mold problem. She'd had two other companies that specialize in mold come in to find the mold, and they couldn't. And she called and wanted me to come in because she had heard that I was the best. So I got to her place, and as I was looking around, I discovered that the vent stack was disconnected from her furnace system. Her furnace system was basically pumping carbon monoxide into her house every time it came on, and so she was literally being poisoned with carbon monoxide. But she didn't want to believe me. She'd been feeling bad for some time and was absolutely convinced that it was mold and that none of us mold specialists were competent. I asked her if she had any relatives nearby, and it happened that her son only lived about five minutes away. So I reached him by phone and explained what I had discovered. It just so happened that he had recently gone to work for a heating, ventilation and air-conditioning company a couple of months earlier. So he immediately knew what I was talking about and came rushing over and took his mom to the hospital where it was confirmed that she had carbon monoxide poisoning. A couple of weeks later, I got a call from her apologizing for calling me a quack and saying that it had been a long time since she'd been able to think straight. Although I'm a specialist, I believe it's important that when we go into these investigations we don't go in with blinders on and forget about all the other types of indoor environmental quality problems that exist. In fact, the majority of time, indoor air quality problems probably have something going on other than mold. In physics every reaction has an equal and opposite reaction. Likewise, every change that we make to the living environment is going to have reactions. Sometimes they're the positive reaction that we want, but there may be unintended consequences. I would say that most of what goes on in terms of indoor air quality issues in buildings these days is a consequence of the energy crisis that occurred back in the 1970s. We took our buildings and tightened them up and reduced the amount of air infiltration and air exchange that was occurring with the outdoors. From an energy conservation standpoint, that was a very good thing. But the unintended consequences were that we ended up having various types of chemicals that were used as part of the manufacturing processes that would accumulate in the indoor environment. We had moisture that began to accumulate. And there was less margin for error with regard to buildings and how they operate. Case in point is carpeting: Certain carpet manufacturers take part in programs like the Carpet and Rug Institute's Green Label program and make a safer carpet product that doesn't emit the same levels of chemicals from their carpet that can cause problems for infants and others. If you're a carpet end-user or distributor, you have these substitute options that can lessen the risk. And that was one of the reasons that my co-authors and I wrote the book *Prescriptions for a Healthy House: A Practical Guide for Architects, Builders and Homeowners*. It deals with specifying the types of substitute materials and processes that exist so you can construct a healthier building. For example, instead of gluing everything together with glue that contains formaldehyde, what kinds of mechanical fasteners can you use?

What kind of career advancement opportunities can one expect in this field? What kind of salary range would reflect that career path (from entry-level to the more advanced position)?

I think at this point the sky is the limit. An entry-level position would probably start out with the individual doing technical types of investigation work and then, as they become more proficient, move into different and more challenging aspects of the field. It's a good idea for an individual who's going to be doing this type of work to get a broad base of experience in the various types of problems that are out there and to get the various certifications. Also, there are now a number of colleges offering certificate programs that are a part of a continuing education program, and those are the types of things people should be looking at, too. An organization I am associated with is called the Indoor Environmental Institute, and we're in the process of developing a certification that would be aimed and focused primarily on indoor environmental quality — to try to fill the gap that's out there. At some point I wouldn't be surprised if this becomes a formal degree type of program, and I look forward to that day. But this is something we've been working on, and I'm hoping it's available within the next year. I think that a starting salary in this field would probably be somewhere around $45,000 to $50,000 a year. Perhaps a range of $60,000 to $80,000 a year is fairly typical for those with experience.

How does someone without previous experience in this career field land a job? What are the best strategies for job-hunting in this field?
Going to companies and talking with people that are doing this type of work. Maybe start out doing some of the actual installations. For example, here at our company we specialize in investigating mold problems, but we want all of our people to have gone through the process of what you do when a building gets water damaged? How do you go about drying a building out rapidly? How do you go about doing mold remediation? Some people come to us with indoor air quality experience, but they don't have those basics. So I would put them back out in the field working with some of the companies that perform remediation or abatement to get the kind of experience they need to understand the business, not only from a scientific standpoint, but from a practical aspect as well. And that's not a bad place to start.

Are there any professional associations that you would recommend joining?
A good one for remediation is the Institute of Inspection Cleaning and Restoration Certification. The certification organization that is under development would be the Indoor Environmental Institute, while a trade organization would be the Indoor Air Quality Association. For mainstream industrial hygienists, the American Board of Industrial Hygiene is the certifying organization, and the American Industrial Hygiene Association is the trade organization.

Resources from Q&A
American Board of Industrial Hygiene (ABIH): abih.org
American Industrial Hygiene Association (AIHA): aiha.org
Environmental Protection Agency (EPA): epa.gov
Indoor Air Quality Association (IAQA): iaqa.org
Indoor Environmental Institute (IEI): ieinstitute.org
Institute of Inspection, Cleaning and Restoration Certification (IICRC): iicrc.org
John Banta's EcoTip Blog: 1510365blog.wordpress.com
Prescott College: prescott.edu
RestCon Environmental: restcon.com
University of California, Davis: ucdavis.edu

 Tom Rivard
Senior Environmental Health Specialist,
City/County of San Francisco,
from an interview with Jim in 2008

How did you get into this career field? What was your education and experience, including any green-related training or certification?

I have a bachelor's degree in zoology and a master's degree in environmental health. When I had graduated with a degree in zoology, I couldn't find a job. So I applied for a job with the county as an environmental health trainee, which is a really good starting point for people that have science degrees, but don't go to medical or dental school. So I started in environmental health before it became green — when it was basic health and safety work, like inspections and water quality. Then I went back and got my graduate degree in industrial hygiene at UC Berkeley. After that, I worked as the noise control officer for the county. Then I worked as an industrial hygienist at a hospital and a medical center. And then I worked as a noise control officer for the city/county of San Francisco.

What is your current job title and how would you describe the work you do in a typical day? What are your most common tasks?

I'm the senior environmental health specialist for the city. In recent years, I've been doing air pollution and noise modeling, health impact assessments and looking at the impact of traffic on the population. I've developed assessment tools to look at smart growth and to see where smart growth doesn't work. And to look at this concept of putting people in areas of high traffic volume, next to freeways and near transportation corridors, in order to expedite transit, but at the same time putting people in areas where the environmental pollutants are the highest and where the air quality and noise are the worst. And so my job is to look at how we can do that successfully. But environmental health is a broad field. There are a lot of places for a person to find a little niche. But if you don't have drive and you don't have a creative interest, you get channeled. You'll find yourself inspecting dirty restaurants and answering dog-dropping complaints.

If you could give advice to a young person who wants to work in this career field someday, what would you tell them? How can they best groom themselves for this field?

The conservative way would be to get a bachelor's degree in environmental health and then you could be an environmental health specialist, registered with the state. That's the simplest way to start. To do what I'm doing, you'll need at least a master's degree and lots of classes in chemistry and particle analysis. If you want to do noise, you'll also need to take classes in acoustics. And you'll need to work where people are really interested in understanding health issues, whereas most cities and counties are not. I think San Francisco is really a leader in that respect at the moment.

What kind of career advancement opportunities can one expect in this field? What kind of salary range would reflect that career path (from entry-level to the more advanced position)?

With San Francisco, we're probably the highest paid in the nation. A public environmental health specialist here makes somewhere between $80,000 and $110,000 per year. But a similar position with a small or rural county might only pay $40,000 to $80,000 per year. Generally the larger and more urbanized counties pay better. But I've looked at what they pay in New York, and it's not great.

In your opinion, what are some of the best schools, degrees and certificates for jobs in this career field, including green-specific training?

For the undergraduate degree, Cal State Northridge has a terrific program. For graduate school, there's UC Berkeley, UCLA, Washington State, the University of Washington, the University of Michigan and Harvard University, among others.

How does someone without previous experience in this career field land a job? What are the best strategies for job-hunting in this field?

It should be easy to get a job anywhere in the United States if you're a registered environmental health professional or a certified industrial hygienist. Generally speaking, in today's society where everybody wants to get into the technology areas because they pay really well, you're not finding a lot of people with good technical skills go into environmental health. But if someone has a passion, the job opportunities are good. And if you don't mind the relatively low pay, you can get a job working in a nice rural area like Yosemite or Lake Tahoe. The beauty of environmental health is that every county has jobs. In California, there are two websites to find out about job openings: one is CCDEH .com — the California Conference of Directors of Environmental Health; the other is CEHA.org — the California Environmental Health Association.

Outside of California, I would use the National Environmental Health Association (NEHA) website to look for jobs.

Are there any professional associations that you would recommend joining?
The California Environmental Health Association was worthwhile — especially when I was younger and just getting started. Also, the National Environmental Health Association. And the American Industrial Hygiene Association is very good. The Acoustical Society of America is quite good for a person interested in that. The California Air Pollution Control Officer Association would be another good one to look at for that kind of work.

What emerging careers do you see developing now and into the future for this career field? What new technologies will have the greatest impact on this field?
In environmental health, if you want to get out of the box and do cool stuff, you'd better take classes in geographical information systems (GIS). We use GIS to model all 15,000 streets of our city to look at noise and air quality levels and to understand traffic volume. GIS is where the action is.

Resources from Q&A
Acoustical Society of America (ASA): asa.aip.org
American Industrial Hygiene Association (AIHA): aiha.org
California Air Pollution Control Officer Association (CAPCOA): capcoa.org
California Conference of Directors of Environmental Health (CCDEH):
    ccdeh.com/jobs/
California Environmental Health Association (CEHA): ceha.org
California State University, Northridge (Cal State Northridge): csun.edu
Harvard University: harvard.edu
National Environmental Health Association (NEHA): neha.org
San Francisco (City and County of): sfgov.org
University of California, Berkeley: berkeley.edu
University of California, Los Angeles: ucla.edu
University of Michigan: umich.edu
University of Washington (UW): washington.edu
Washington State University (WSU): wsu.edu

Government Regulations and Planning Group

○ Construction and Building Inspectors, including Green Building Inspectors

○ Environmental and Regulatory Compliance Inspectors and Specialists

○ Urban and Regional Planners, including City/County, Environmental/Land Use and Transportation Planners

○ Urban and Regional Planning Aides, Assistants and Technicians

Construction and Building Inspectors, including Green Building Inspectors

Construction and building inspectors inspect structures using engineering skills to determine structural soundness and compliance with specifications, building codes and other regulations. Inspections may be general in nature or may be limited to a specific area, such as electrical systems or plumbing.

Qualifications and Advancement

Most employers require at least a high-school diploma or equivalent, plus several years of experience in one or more of the skilled trade professions. However, a college degree can sometimes substitute for some of the previous experience requirements. Employers often look for persons who have studied engineering or architecture or who have a certificate or associate's degree in building inspection technology. More than half of all new entrants to this occupation have completed one to four years of college. The amount of on-the-job training required varies by type of inspector and state. Construction and building inspectors generally receive much of their training on the job and must learn building codes and standards on their own.

Working with an experienced inspector, they learn about inspection techniques; codes, ordinances and regulations; contract specifications; and recordkeeping and reporting duties. A bachelor's degree in engineering or architecture is often required for advancement to supervisory positions.

Salary Survey

Median salary: $46,570 (high)

Typical range: $36,610 to $58,780

Job Outlook and Employment

Faster than average growth is projected for this occupation in the US, from 109,730 jobs in 2006 to 129,739 in 2016. Concern for public safety and a desire for improvement in the quality of construction should continue to stimulate demand for construction and building inspectors in government as well as in firms specializing in architectural, engineering and related services. In addition, the growing focus on natural and man-made disasters is increasing the level of interest in and need for qualified inspectors. Issues such as green and sustainable design are new areas of focus that will also drive the demand for construction and building inspectors.

Where the Jobs Are

Local government (41.38%); State government (8.03%); Self-employed: 8.13%

Resources

American Construction Inspectors Association (ACIA): acia.com

American Society of Home Inspectors (ASHI): ashi.org

International Code Council (ICC): iccsafe.org

National Association of Home Inspectors (NAHI): nahi.org

O*NET OnLine: online.onetcenter.org (see construction and building inspectors)

US Dept. of Labor, Bureau of Labor Statistics: bls.gov/oco/ocos004.htm

US Green Building Council/LEED AP Certification: usgbc.org

Q&A   LAURENCE KORNFIELD
Chief Building Inspector,
City/County of San Francisco,
from an interview with Jim in 2008

How did you get into this career field? What was your education and experience, including any green-related training or certification?

For almost 20 years, I've been the chief building inspector for the city. I went to graduate school in environmental design and taught in graduate school for a number of years. And then I did subdivision layout in design and construction, until the company I worked for moved.

And so I needed a job, and there it was: Take the exam for building inspector! It was mostly to see if you can read and write, as it turns out that most building inspector jobs were retirement jobs for carpenters with bad backs. But those times have changed, as the standards have gone tremendously up. Building inspectors have prerequisites for experience in construction or architecture, and there are some equivalency and offsets if you have degrees in various fields. It takes a few years to have the necessary qualifications, but not a lot of time. But it's become a very competitive field because it pays relatively well and it's a very secure job with good retirement benefits. So it's become a very desirable field to work in.

What is your current job title and how would you describe the work you do in a typical day? What are your most common tasks, including those that make yours a green job?

What I do at this point in my career is not typical at all. I sit in an office and think about codes and help people write legislation and problem solve. But, typically, inspectors have two major activities: One is plan review, and the other is field inspections. In San Francisco, we generally rotate our inspectors through both of those activities. The plan review function requires inspectors at a very high level of working knowledge of the codes to be able to find stuff and communicate their concerns. That function is overlapped by structural engineers who often do the structural review, although inspectors are also trained to do that at a basic level. And then there's also overlap by mechanical plan checkers because many of the green provisions of our building codes actually reside in the State's energy code which can be very complex. And then we have other specialties as well, such as geo-technical. The plan review process includes going through the planning department, the fire department, the health department and so on, as all the conditions of approval from the various agencies are recorded on a set of approved documents. And so the building inspector is the person who has to make sure the construction conforms to those conditions for all departments. So there's a very broad base of knowledge required for building inspectors who work in plan review.

If you could give advice to a young person who wants to work in this career field someday, what would you tell them? How can they best groom themselves for this field?

One approach is to have a general knowledge of the world of construction. So working for a developer or an architect or whatever — it doesn't matter. Just so you understand how things work. Because people who may be able to pass the inspector exam based on technical knowledge often find that they're not really prepared for this work unless they have actual knowledge. A second approach is to participate in some formal training. And there are a whole bunch of colleges that offer training for building inspectors. For example, Butte College in Oroville, California, has a very intense, two- year program for building inspectors. This is such a difficult and technical field these days that you really need to have formal technical training. A third approach I might suggest is to do volunteer work for agencies. For example, we hire interns and volunteers over the summer. That allows you to get to know people and to learn your way around the bureaucracy.

What kind of career advancement opportunities can one expect in this field? What kind of salary range would reflect that career path (from entry level to the more advanced position)?
We have some positions that may allow someone to start out and then gradually work their way up into inspector positions. But most people enter as building inspectors. Career advancement in this field is a challenge because they typically start and end their careers as inspectors. Certainly some can become chief inspectors or move into administrative jobs. But typically building inspection work does not train people for those other administrative jobs, whereas engineering classes may train people to be managers or administrators. So a building inspector who wants to advance beyond the normal ladder that leads to chief inspector may need to go to school in public administration or somehow get on a different track. Another option that some of my friends have done is they go and become directors of building departments for smaller jurisdictions. I don't know what the official salary range is here in San Francisco, but I think the building inspectors start at over $70,000 per year. Of course, in San Francisco we have a very high cost of living.

In your opinion, what are some of the best schools, degrees and certificates for jobs in this career field, including green–specific training?
Butte College is just one example, as there are lots of colleges that have building inspection programs. You can also check out the colleges that are offering the new ICC (International Code Council) Building Inspectors Certificate. Plus there are many courses out there that are designed to help you pass the standard exam. And someone might take such a course that's less than a year in length and then take the exam and pass it. But, for many, they will be surprised at the extent of the required knowledge, and they will have to delay taking the exam so they can take more classes or get more experience first. It's not easy these days.

How does someone without previous experience in this career field land a job? What are the best strategies for job-hunting in this field?
Building inspection is a conservative field, although the green building stuff is challenging many of them to look forward. But we're essentially a bunch of conservative people who are trying to protect people who basically aren't even around yet. We're not just here to protect the current user; we're trying to assure the safety of people 20, 30 or 40 years from now. We get all sorts of newfangled stuff, and we are slow to adopt it, and for good reason! And so, while many people these days are searching for jobs online, someone looking for a job as a building inspector shouldn't overlook traditional job search methods.

Also, I think that we will find in the next five years that being LEED AP certified is going to be very desirable as agencies will be increasingly looking to hire someone who can help them deal with all the green building initiatives coming along. I think there's going to be a niche for people who specialize in green building.

Are there any professional associations that you would recommend joining?
The big one for building inspectors is ICC, the International Code Council. They have the monthly magazine that everyone in the profession reads. That is pretty much the standard.

What emerging careers do you see developing now and into the future for this career field? What new technologies will have the greatest impact on this field?
There are new technologies in construction, including the green building initiatives, so there's constant learning required of the inspectors. The future for building inspectors will include going out to a job site and pulling up a screen with all the stuff you need to look at right there and then. Not having to go back to the office and write up the paper work. Building inspectors have been using computers since the early 90s, but computer skills are going to become increasingly important.

Resources from Q&A
Butte College: butte.edu
International Code Council (ICC): iccsafe.org/training/contract/insp–c.html
San Francisco (City and County of): sfgov.org
US Green Building Council/LEED AP Certification: usgbc.org

Environmental and Regulatory Compliance Inspectors and Specialists

Environmental compliance inspectors inspect and investigate sources of pollution to protect the public and environment and ensure conformance with federal, state and local regulations and ordinances.

Qualifications and Advancement

An associate's degree in chemistry, biology or a related field is the typical education/training requirement for some jobs, while others require a bachelor's degree. About three out of five new entrants to this occupation have completed a bachelor's degree.

Employers often have several levels within this occupation (i.e., I, II and III), as well as different specialties requiring various certifications. Advancement can lead to supervisory or management positions, but extensive experience, as well as a bachelor's degree or higher, are the typical requirements.

Salary Survey

Median salary: $47,050 (high)
Typical range: $33,920 to $62,760

Job Outlook and Employment

Slower than average growth is projected for all compliance officer occupations in the US, including environmental compliance inspectors, from 237,035 jobs in 2006 to 248,709 in 2016. However, most of the job growth for environmental compliance inspectors is likely to be with local government (cities and counties) where job growth is projected to reflect increasing population growth and an increasing emphasis on environmental protection and preservation.

Where the Jobs Are

Federal, state and local government, including cities and counties (specific numbers for environmental compliance inspectors are not available)

Resources

Environmental Protection Agency (EPA): epa.gov
International Network for Environmental Compliance and Enforcement
    (INECE): inece.org
National Registry of Environmental Professionals (NREP): nrep.org
O*NET OnLine: online.onetcenter.org (see environmental compliance
    inspectors)

US Dept. of Labor, Bureau of Labor Statistics: bls.gov/oco/oco20051.htm (see
    compliance officers)
USAJOBS: usajobs.gov

Q&A **ANDY HESS**
Environmental Scientist,
US Environmental Protection Agency,
from an interview with Jim in 2008

*How did you get into this career field? What was
your education and experience, including any
green-related training or certification?*

After receiving a bachelor of science degree in oceanography from Humboldt
State University, California, I went to work for the Naval Oceanographic Office in Bay St. Lewis, Mississippi, for about one and a half years. I then transferred to the Puget Sound Naval Shipyard in Bremerton, Washington, to work
as a radiological control technician. It was another one and a half years before I started my career with the Environmental Protection Agency (EPA) in
Seattle. My initial responsibilities with EPA were to manage the field equipment and supplies for Region 10, which includes the states of Washington,
Oregon, Idaho and Alaska. These duties included servicing, calibrating, re-
pairing, ordering and shipping field gear for environmental studies and inspections. With time, my duties evolved to assisting, and then leading, field
studies and compliance inspections.

*What is your current job title and how would you describe the work you do in a
typical day? What are your most common tasks, including those that make yours
a green job?*

My title is environmental scientist. With this job, there is no such thing as a
typical day. In general, there are three main components to my current position: one is performing compliance inspections and field studies; two is training, writing standard operating procedures and providing other assistance for
our environmental projects; and three is managing our field equipment and
supply center for the region. An example of a project I'm currently working on
is a Columbia River study where we're using an electro-shocking boat to collect fish for toxicology analysis. We're also collecting water samples and taking
field measurements to characterize the water. My support includes preparing
water quality monitors, sampling gear, going over sampling procedures and
preparing all the tools that are needed to go out and do the study. Another

project I'm involved in is an oceanographic research project on the northwest coast where we're doing sediment and water sampling analysis. If you asked me about a typical day on a week when I'm doing compliance inspections, the story would be quite different. I would be going through files, reading permits on various types of facilities — be it a water treatment plant, an oil and gas facility or a seafood processor. A fair amount of travel is often required to perform our duties. Inspectors also need to receive a certain amount of training and can become instructors themselves. I have prepared training materials and provided training to regional, national and international inspectors. In some regions, the EPA uses what we call multimedia inspectors. These are inspectors who theoretically can go into a facility and evaluate their wastewater, their air discharge and their hazardous waste generation. Those are the three main programs, but there are several other programs, such as underground injection, underground storage tanks, leaking underground storage tanks, asbestos and the Toxic Substances Control Act for PCBs and for Lead. Depending on the EPA region, some inspectors will perform inspections in more than one media, referred to as multimedia inspectors, while others will just specialize in one program. Also, depending on the region and/or program, an inspector might also perform compliance determinations and be involved in the enforcement process.

If you could give advice to a young person who wants to work in this career field someday, what would you tell them? How can they best groom themselves for this field?
Depending on the particular field of interest, I would recommend an education which includes a good basic science background. With advancing technology, computer skills are also an asset. For understanding the more technical aspects of a facility, an engineering background would be helpful.

What kind of career advancement opportunities can one expect in this field? What kind of salary range would reflect that career path (from entry-level to the more advanced position)?
From my experience, and within my region, I would say there's excellent job potential. They encourage people to pursue career advancement, and the personnel office here is always providing courses or seminars for people to develop their skills and to think about what they need to do to advance. One thing about career advancement within the EPA — there's a lot of different roads or avenues you can take. It's common for employees to move to a different program or type of job from the one they were initially hired for. I think

this field offers great career potential and pays quite well for a government agency. You could look up the federal salaries online. Going up to a GS12 is usually the top end for an inspector, but in some instances you could go up to a GS13.

In your opinion, what are some of the best schools, degrees and certificates for jobs in this career field, including green-specific training?
I don't know that your choice of a college is that critical. What I feel is important is that a prospective employee has an ability to apply what they've learned and have an aptitude and desire to learn specific job applications. Most likely a new employee will need to learn specific skills and gain the related knowledge on the job. Good interpersonal skills are also essential. You probably heard of Libby, Montana? Well, in Libby they mine vermiculite. And it turns out that vermiculite was laced with asbestos, and there were a lot of people dying from that — even though it's naturally occurring. A co-worker of mine got involved in doing a study on that with another person, and it just evolved. He bought an electron microscope, and now he does all kinds of field studies and analysis for asbestos. He wasn't trained in college for that, but he has an aptitude to learn, and he was able to work with people, learn, pick up books, read and get training. The EPA is very good at providing training for people who want to advance their skills, and that's what he did. And it's taken him probably seven to eight years to advance his skills to where he's now considered a national expert on some of the things he does. I would say he does very little, if any, compliance inspection work now, but that is where he started. That's why I say that this agency offers a great opportunity to let people develop their skills, and their work will evolve to fit the skills that they're strong in.

How does someone without previous experience in this career field land a job? What are the best strategies for job-hunting in this field?
Some people have started out working for private contractors or other government agencies such as the state, county or local agencies where you can get started in this field. Keep your eyes open and try to tailor your experience to fit a future position that you're shooting for. I believe all the EPA job openings are listed on the Internet at USAJOBS.gov.

Are there any professional associations that you would recommend joining?
Not for compliance inspectors. For other types of positions that are more science related, yes, but in terms of a resumé, anything you can do to show that you are serious beyond just the normal education packet would be good.

What emerging careers do you see developing now and into the future for this career field? What new technologies will have the greatest impact on this field?
As I mentioned earlier, computer skills are an asset, as most new field instrumentation is designed to interface with computers to some degree. An understanding of chemistry will also allow a field sampler to better communicate with the chemists who will be analyzing his or her samples.

Resources from Q&A
Environmental Protection Agency (EPA): epa.gov
Humboldt State University: humboldt.edu
Naval Oceanographic Office: navo.navy.mil
USAJOBS: usajobs.gov

Urban and Regional Planners, including City/County, Environmental/Land Use and Transportation Planners

Urban and regional planners develop comprehensive plans and programs for use of land and physical facilities of local jurisdictions, such as towns, cities, counties and metropolitan areas.

Qualifications and Advancement
A bachelor's degree in urban planning or a related field is the typical education requirement for some jobs, while others require a master's degree. However, a bachelor's degree from an accredited planning program, coupled with a master's degree in architecture, landscape architecture or civil engineering, is excellent preparation as well.

Some planners begin their careers as city/county planning aides or technicians, working under the supervision of experienced planners. As they gain experience and knowledge, they can advance into city or county planner positions. Planners may advance to assignments requiring a high degree of independent judgment, such as designing the physical layout of a large development or recommending policy and budget options. Public sector planners are sometimes promoted to community planning or community development director where they spend much of their time meeting with officials, speaking to civic groups and supervising staff. Further advancement usually takes the form of a new job with a larger jurisdiction with generally more complex problems.

Salary Survey

Median salary: $56,630 (very high)
Typical range: $44,480 to $71,390

Job Outlook and Employment

Faster than average growth is projected for this occupation in the US, from 33,809 jobs in 2006 to 38,716 in 2016. Most new jobs will be in affluent, rapidly expanding communities. Growth will be driven by the need for local governments in particular to provide public services such as regulation of commercial development, the environment, transportation, housing and land use and development for an expanding population. Non-governmental initiatives dealing with historic preservation and redevelopment will also create employment growth.

Where the Jobs Are

Local government (67.79%); State government (8.91%)

Resources

American Planning Association (APA): planning.org
Association of Collegiate Schools of Planning (ACSP): acsp.org
Planetizen: The Planning & Development Network: planetizen.com
O*NET OnLine: online.onetcenter.org (see urban and regional planners)
US Dept. of Labor, Bureau of Labor Statistics: bls.gov/oco/ocos057.htm

Q&A   LILIA SCOTT
Senior Transportation Planner, Santa Clara Valley Transportation Authority/URS Corporation, from an interview with Jim in 2008

How did you get into this career field? What was your education and experience, including any green-related training or certification?
I studied literature and art in college. I thought I would go into publishing or journalism, but I had no idea how to go about that. Then I met a man, and we fell in love. He was finishing his degree in landscape architecture, and when he finished, he won a fellowship to travel around the world and study design approaches to water in an attempt to address the urban runoff issue. I tagged along. I'd traveled before, but not to this extent. We went all over Southeast Asia, the Indian subcontinent, the Middle East and Europe. We rode planes,

trains, donkey carts, rickshaws, auto-rickshaws and bicycles, and we walked. When we came back from the trip, I got a job at an insurance company doing administration and writing. It was a part-time job, so I took calculus and business classes at night. My boyfriend's former roommate was also a landscape architect, and he dated a woman who was a planner. I met her and her friends, and I was impressed with how smart they were. My first thought was, I wish I was that smart. My second thought was, maybe I am. So I quit my insurance job to find an admin job in planning to see if the work interested me. I let a temp agency assign me to work as an administrative assistant for the regional rideshare program. I revamped their systems, built a new database for their marketing department and improved the tracking system. I guess they were impressed because, within a few months, the director of planning agreed to hire me as his staff planner. It was a tremendous break, since normally you have to have a relevant degree for a job like that. I completely loved that job. And then I started getting bored with the limits of our perspective. For example, I wanted to take land use into consideration when looking at the region's transportation problems. But that was outside our realm. So I applied to graduate school at UC Berkeley, and they admitted me. I wanted to do land use planning, but I kept getting pushed one way or another back to transportation. The reality remains that there is more interesting work in transportation, so that's where I've stayed.

What is your current job title and how would you describe the work you do in a typical day? What are your most common tasks, including those that make yours a green job?

My current job title is senior transportation planner. Since grad school, I have worked in transportation, but not always in planning. I've done a lot of transportation demand management work as well. Common tasks would include: research, such as reading and synthesizing reports; talking to people; surfing the net for relevant information; writing memos, reports and e-mails; public speaking; meeting facilitation; determining how to frame an idea for the right response; and project management — paying attention to schedules and budgets, checking in with people about their schedule and budget, organizing people, paper, ideas, motivations.

If you could give advice to a young person who wants to work in this career field someday, what would you tell them? How can they best groom themselves for this field?

Get trained and volunteer because all the planners I know volunteer all the time. You will need the master's degree. Be well-rounded. Pay attention.

What kind of career advancement opportunities can one expect in this field? What kind of salary range would reflect that career path (from entry-level to the more advanced position)?

Opportunities for advancement are endless. I guess the best you can do is run a planning department for a big city, region, state or country. But you could also get out of the field a little and climb even more. You could run a successful planning non-profit organization or consulting firm. Salaries vary substantially based on your location, focus and sector — non-profit organization, consulting firm or public agency. You can definitely be comfortable, but probably not get rich. My best guess on salary ranges is $30,000–$60,000 per year at the entry level, $50,000–$100,000 per year at the mid level and $80,000–$150,000 per year at the upper level.

In your opinion, what are some of the best schools, degrees and certificates for jobs in this career field?

Planetizen has a ranking. I think UC Berkeley is best. MIT is also supposed to be good, but it doesn't have a transportation concentration. As with all things, see which professors/researchers/professionals you admire and ask them.

How does someone without previous experience in this career field land a job? What are the best strategies for job-hunting in this field?

You get a master's degree in planning. With administrative or marketing skills and only a bachelor's degree, you may be able to get a job working with planners. I would shoot for non-profits or private consulting firms for the best exposure. You can get a planning job without the master's degree, but you'll probably have to get the master's eventually. I've had the most luck networking as opposed to responding to job listings.

Are there any professional associations that you would recommend joining?

Join advocacy groups relevant to your interests. Attend the public meetings to watch the proceedings and speak your mind. There are a lot of professional associations — I'm not a member of any of them, though.

What emerging or high-growth careers do you see developing now and into the future for this career field? What new technologies will have the greatest impact on this field?

I wouldn't use the words "high growth." I would use words like "steady" or "solid" or "recession–proof" — at least regarding transportation. Urban design is probably more volatile, and the salaries are lower, but you get to design things. Most people become planners because they are practical and they care about people and the planet, not because they want to "emerge" or "grow." We leave that to the politicians. People who succeed in planning generally do so because they are convincing and have natural social skills, but you can wonk out and be a techie too, if that compels you.

Resources from Q&A
Massachusetts Institute of Technology (MIT): web.mit.edu
Planetizen: planetizen.com
Santa Clara Valley Transportation Authority: vta.org
University of California, Berkeley: berkeley.edu

Urban and Regional Planning Aides, Assistants and Technicians

City and regional planning aides compile data from various sources, such as maps, reports and field and file investigations, for use by planners in making planning studies.

Qualifications and Advancement
An associate's degree is the typical education/training requirement. However, almost half of all new entrants to this occupation have a bachelor's degree.

This is generally an entry-level position without much chance of advancement unless one attains a bachelor's degree in urban planning or a related field. As planners, one may advance to assignments requiring a high degree of independent judgment, such as designing the physical layout of a large development or recommending policy and budget options. Public sector planners may be promoted to community planning or community development director where much time is spent meeting with officials, speaking to civic groups and supervising staff. Further advancement usually takes the form of a new job with a larger jurisdiction with generally more complex problems.

Salary Survey
Median salary: $33,860 (low/moderate)
Typical range: $26,270 to $43,310

Job Outlook and Employment
Average growth is projected for this occupation in the US, from 17,777 jobs in 2006 to 19,977 in 2016. As with city and county planners, most new jobs will be in affluent, rapidly expanding communities. Growth will be driven by the need for local governments, in particular, to provide public services such as regulation of commercial development, the environment, transportation,

housing and land use and development for an expanding population. Non-governmental initiatives dealing with historic preservation and redevelopment will also create employment growth.

Where the Jobs Are

Colleges, universities and professional schools (35.77%); Research and development in the physical, engineering and life sciences (20.85%); Research and development in the social sciences and humanities (16.71%); Local government (4.94%); Management, scientific and technical consulting services (3.29%)

Resources

American Planning Association (APA): planning.org
Association of Collegiate Schools of Planning (ACSP): acsp.org
Planetizen: The Planning & Development Network: planetizen.com
O*NET OnLine: online.onetcenter.org (see city and regional planning aides)
US Dept. of Labor, Bureau of Labor Statistics: bls.gov/oco/oco20052.htm
    (see city and regional planning aides)

Green Building
and Landscaping Group

○ Architects, including Green and Natural Building Architects

○ Green Building/Construction Trades Workers and Supervisors

○ Landscape Architects, including Habitat Restoration Specialists

○ Landscaping and Groundskeeping Workers (Eco-friendly)

Architects, including Green and Natural Building Architects

Architects plan and design structures, such as private residences, office buildings, theaters, factories and other structural property.

Qualifications and Advancement

A bachelor's degree in architecture is the typical education requirement. All states require individuals to be licensed (registered) before they can provide architectural services. Prior to becoming licensed, architecture school graduates generally work in the field under the supervision of a licensed architect.

Most architects start out as junior architects, gaining experience on the job, taking on increasing responsibilities and eventually managing entire projects. Some begin their careers as CAD operators/drafters before getting their bachelor's degree in architecture. In larger architectural firms, architects may advance to supervisory or management positions. Some architects become partners in established firms, while others start their own practices. Some architects go into real estate development, civil engineering or construction management. Some go into teaching.

Salary Survey

Median salary: $64,150 (very high)
Typical range: $49,780 to $83,450

Job Outlook and Employment

Faster than average growth is projected for this occupation in the US, from 131,873 jobs in 2006 to 155,258 in 2016. Employment of architects is strongly tied to the activity of the construction industry.

Where the Jobs Are

Architectural, engineering and related services (67.28%); Construction of buildings (3.76%); Government (3.1%); Self-employed: 20.33%

Resources

American Institute of Architects (AIA): aia.org
Architects/Designers/Planners for Social Responsibility (ADPSR): adpsr.org
BuildingGreen.com: buildinggreen.com
Intern Development Program (IDP): aia.org/ep_home_getlicensed
National Council of Architectural Registration Boards (NCARB): ncarb.org
Natural Building Network: naturalbuildingnetwork.org
O*NET OnLine: online.onetcenter.org (see architects)
US Dept. of Labor, Bureau of Labor Statistics: bls.gov/oco/ocos038.htm
US Green Building Council/LEED AP Certification: usgbc.org

 PAUL ALMOND
Architect, Sage Architecture, Inc., from an interview with Jim in 2008

How did you get into this career field? What was your education and experience?
I've always loved to draw and design things. I knew I wanted to be an architect early on, so I went to architecture school at the University of Minnesota, worked at various architectural firms during my schooling and then moved to California for the weather and apparent design interest.

What is your current job title and how would you describe the work you do in a typical day? What are your most common tasks?
I own my own architectural firm with my wife, who is also an architect. We provide a mixture of residential and commercial design work, but primarily modern residential design work for highly tailored homes that include green architecture. Hence, the name of our company: Sage Architecture. When we decided to open up a firm and do residential work, we felt morally obligated to take advantage of the technologies and techniques available to build better houses. Our work is limited to a very small percentage of the residential design market — it is very much a niche market dedicated to those who really value architecture and design. Every one of our projects is shaped to accommodate site conditions. The basic elements of green architectural work include technology, material and passive solar design. Technology includes things like

solar panels and geothermal heat source pumps. Materials include things like bamboo flooring and NO VOC paints. The third element, which we think is most important, is passive solar design. It's particularly important in places where we can take advantage of the environment to allow the building to heat and cool itself. Most commonly, our daily work consists of sketching raw design ideas, drafting details, coordinating with contractors on construction issues and meeting with clients to discuss their projects.

If you could give advice to a young person who wants to work in this career field someday, what would you tell them? How can they best groom themselves for this field?

Talk to architects before you even start college. During college you should work in the offices of architectural firms of varying sizes to experience the enormous variation in experiences. Your personal interest and proficiency can lead you to a technical (CAD) experience, a business experience or an artistic experience. Different firms focus on different areas, and within firms, employees are stratified into the many different tasks of architecture as the field continues to become more specialized — for better or for worse. But in our profession, the college education is really critical due to the licensing process required for architects.

What kind of career advancement opportunities can one expect in this field? What kind of salary range would reflect that career path (from entry level to the more advanced position)?

Again, enormous variation depending on your interest. Advancement can be very quick, depending on interest, talent and opportunity. A good talent for pure design, along with presentation and social skills, allows you to present design work to clients which can become extremely important. It's like being the lead singer in a band — it gets attention.

From there, starting your own architectural firm can be daunting, but depending on the type of firm, can actually be quite easy to run. You need to deal well with long days and surround yourself with the best people, including consultants. Salaries are low in the beginning, but advancement can be quick. Owning your own firm can mean the sky is the limit, depending on your skills, priorities and interests.

In your opinion, what are some of the best schools, degrees and certificates for jobs in this career field?

Architecture is an artistic profession. I have enormous respect for the big-name schools, but my experience is that you are more likely to be hired based on your personal design portfolio, experience and social skills. Of course, better schools are likely to help you develop a superior portfolio, but they can't do it for you. In the end, it comes down to you and you alone.

How does someone without previous experience in this career field land a job? What are the best strategies for job-hunting in this field?
A lot of internships. In fact, there's something called the Intern Development Program (IDP) that a lot of states have now adopted. You work at various firms, and you document the specific tasks that you're doing. And you have to fulfill a certain quota for different types of tasks, whether it's writing specifications, meeting with clients, doing design work, site work — all the various aspects of what an architect does.

Are there any professional associations that you would recommend joining? Is there an association specifically for green architects?
The AIA, or American Institute of Architects, is the professional organization for us. There are categories within the AIA, like COTE, as in Committee on the Environment, that support green architecture. You can join as an associate AIA member without being a licensed architect.

What emerging or high-growth careers do you see developing now and into the future for this career field? What new technologies will have the greatest impact on this field?
CAD certainly has had the biggest effect over the last 20 years within architecture. Integrating construction drawings, bidding and construction process documentation is becoming more and more popular for large projects. Pure design work remains, in my opinion, in the low-tech world of the pad and pencil. And that highlights the variability of our profession — spanning aspects from the purely technical to the purely artistic. As far as the field of green architecture, there's solar. But I wouldn't call that a new technology, although they're making improvements all the time. To me the new stuff is more the materials.

Resources from Q&A
American Institute of Architects (AIA): aia.org
Intern Development Program (IDP): aia.org/ep_home_getlicensed
Sage Architecture: sagearchitecture.com
University of Minnesota: umn.edu

Green Building/Construction Trades Workers and Supervisors

Green building and construction trades workers and supervisors represent a wide variety of occupations, including the 21 occupations described below, as well as helpers and laborers and the various types of licensed contractors who are responsible for their work.

In addition, there are solar contractors who tend to specialize in either photovoltaic or solar thermal energy. They or their workers design, install and service solar energy systems of all sizes. Depending on their size, solar contractors often employ helpers, installers, installer supervisors, installation managers, service technicians, service managers and sales representatives. Installers are generally jack-of-all-trades who have some carpentry, electrical and plumbing skills or abilities. Sometimes photovoltaic solar installations are performed or supervised by journey level electricians. With solar thermal, plumbing skills are generally more important than electrical skills, although both skill sets are required.

Brick masons and **block masons** lay and bind building materials, such as brick, structural tile, concrete block, cinder block, glass block and terra cotta block, with mortar and other substances to construct or repair walls, partitions, arches, sewers and other structures.

Carpet installers lay and install carpet from rolls or blocks on floors. Install padding and trim flooring materials.

Cement masons and **concrete finishers** smooth and finish surfaces of poured concrete, such as floors, walks, sidewalks, roads or curbs using a variety of hand and power tools. Align forms for sidewalks, curbs or gutters; patch voids; use saws to cut expansion joints.

Construction carpenters construct, erect, install and repair structures and fixtures of wood, plywood and wallboard, using carpenters' hand tools and power tools.

Drywall and ceiling tile installers apply plasterboard or other wallboard to ceilings or interior walls of buildings. Apply or mount acoustical tiles or blocks, strips or sheets of shock-absorbing materials to ceilings and walls of buildings to reduce or reflect sound. Materials may be of decorative quality. Includes lathers who fasten wooden, metal or rockboard lath to walls, ceilings or partitions of buildings to provide support base for plaster, fireproofing or acoustical material.

Electricians install, maintain and repair electrical wiring, equipment and fixtures. Ensure that work is in accordance with relevant codes. May install or service street lights, intercom systems or electrical control systems.

Floor layers (except carpet, wood and hard tiles) apply blocks, strips or sheets of shock-absorbing, sound-deadening or decorative coverings to floors.

Floor sanders and finishers scrape and sand wooden floors to smooth surfaces, using floor-scraper and floor-sanding machine, and apply coats of finish.

Glaziers install glass in windows, skylights, storefronts and display cases or on surfaces, such as building fronts, interior walls, ceilings and tabletops.

Insulation workers (floor, ceiling and wall) line and cover structures with insulating materials. May work with batt, roll or blown insulation materials.

Painters (construction and maintenance) paint walls, equipment, buildings, bridges and other structural surfaces, using brushes, rollers and spray guns. May remove old paint to prepare surface prior to painting. May mix colors or oils to obtain desired color or consistency.

Paperhangers cover interior walls and ceilings of rooms with decorative wallpaper or fabric or attach advertising posters on surfaces, such as walls and billboards. Duties include removing old materials from surface to be papered.

Plasterers and **stucco masons** apply interior or exterior plaster, cement, stucco or similar materials. May also set ornamental plaster.

Plumbers assemble, install and repair pipes, fittings and fixtures of heating, water and drainage systems, according to specifications and plumbing codes.

Roofers cover roofs of structures with shingles, slate, asphalt, aluminum, wood and related materials. May spray roofs, sidings and walls with material to bind, seal, insulate or soundproof sections of structures.

Rough carpenters build rough wooden structures, such as concrete forms, scaffolds, tunnel, bridge or sewer supports, billboard signs and temporary frame shelters, according to sketches, blueprints or oral instructions.

Stonemasons build stone structures, such as piers, walls and abutments. Lay walks, curbstones or special types of masonry for vats, tanks and floors.

Terrazzo workers and finishers apply a mixture of cement, sand, pigment or marble chips to floors, stairways and cabinet fixtures to fashion durable and decorative surfaces.

Tile and marble setters apply hard tile, marble and wood tile to walls, floors, ceilings and roof decks.

First-line supervisors/managers of construction trades and extraction workers directly supervise and coordinate activities of construction or extraction workers.

Construction managers plan, direct, coordinate or budget, usually through subordinate supervisory personnel, activities concerned with the construction and maintenance of structures, facilities and systems. Participate in the conceptual development of a construction project and oversee its scheduling and implementation.

Qualifications and Advancement

Construction workers generally learn their trade through formal and informal apprenticeships that typically take three to four years to complete (depending on the occupation) and to achieve journey-level status. Apprentices often begin as helpers until they find an employer who is willing to take them on as an apprentice. Union employers offer formal apprenticeship programs that include a combination of on-the-job training with some classroom instruction. Non-union employers generally provide less formal training. Hands-on vocational programs in construction technology are available through high schools, community colleges and private vocational schools, and while these programs can be valuable and often improve entry level job opportunities, they don't usually eliminate the need for apprenticeship or on-the-job training. To specialize in green building or sustainable construction usually requires additional on-the-job training and experience working on green or sustainable building projects.

Carpenters generally have more opportunities than other construction trades workers to become construction supervisors and managers because they are exposed to the entire construction process. Because Spanish-speaking workers make up a large part of the construction workforce in many areas, it is becoming increasingly important to be able to communicate in both English and Spanish in order to advance to supervisory positions. From supervisory positions, advancement usually leads to project manager. Some construction trades workers will become general or specialty contractors. A few will go into upper management of larger construction companies. A few others will change careers and become building inspectors for their local city or county.

For construction managers, a bachelor's degree is becoming increasingly important. Anyone interested in becoming a construction manager needs a

solid background in building science, business and management, as well as related work experience.

Salary Survey

Occupation	Median salary	Typical salary range
Brickmasons and Blockmasons	$42,980	$33,190 to $54,610
Carpet Installers	$34,560	$25,080 to $48,380
Cement Masons and Concrete Finishers	$32,650	$25,750 to $43,060
Construction Carpenters	$36,550	$28,190 to $49,600
Drywall and Ceiling Tile Installers	$36,140	$28,290 to $46,960
Electricians	$43,610	$33,420 to $57,650
Floor Layers	$34,190	$26,440 to $49,450
Floor Sanders and Finishers	$28,890	$22,540 to $38,420
Glaziers	$34,610	$26,730 to $46,140
Insulation Workers	$30,510	$23,420 to $41,600
Painters	$31,190	$25,340 to $40,580
Paperhangers	$33,710	$27,280 to $42,880
Plasterers and Stucco Masons	$34,700	$44,200 to $56,800
Plumbers	$42,770	$32,490 to $57,280
Roofers	$32,260	$25,210 to $43,250
Rough Carpenters	$36,550	$28,190 to $49,600
Stonemasons	$35,960	$27,290 to $45,850
Terrazzo Workers and Finishers	$31,630	$24,970 to $42,640
Tile and Marble Setters	$36,590	$27,360 to $48,890
Construction Supervisors (First Line)	$53,850	$41,990 to $69,310
Construction Managers	$73,700	$56,090 to $98,350

Job Outlook and Employment

Most of the construction trades worker occupations are projected to have average job growth through 2016. The exceptions include: roofers, tile/marble
setters and construction managers, which are projected to have faster than average job growth; carpet installers and floor sanders/finishers, which are projected to have little or no growth; and floor layers and paperhangers, which
are both projected to have an overall decline in jobs. In general, the need for
construction trades workers should grow as the level of construction activity continues to grow. Population and business growth will result in more
construction of residential homes, office buildings, shopping malls, hospitals, schools, restaurants and other structures that require construction trades
workers, supervisors and managers. There is insufficient data to project the
growth of green and sustainable-related construction jobs; however, there is

little doubt that this is a growing field (within construction) that will offer more and more job opportunities in the future. LEED AP certification from the US Green Building Council is becoming increasingly important for those who want to specialize in green building work.

Where the Jobs Are

General construction and specialty contractors

Resources

Americas Glass Association: americasglassassn.org

Associated Builders and Contractors (ABC): abc.org

Associated General Contractors of America (AGC): agc.org

Association of the Wall and Ceiling Industry (AWCI): awci.org

Certified Floorcovering Installers Association (CFI): cfiinstallers.com

Certified Sustainable Development Professional (CSDP) Program:
    aeecenter.org/certification/csdppage.htm

Flooring Contractors Association (FCICA): fcica.com

Home Builders Institute: hbi.org

Independent Electrical Contractors (IEC): ieci.org

International Brotherhood of Electrical Workers (IBEW): ibew.org

International Society of Sustainability Professionals (ISSP):
    sustainabilityprofessionals.org

International Union of Bricklayers and Allied Craftworkers (BAC):
    bacweb.org

International Union of Painters and Allied Trades (IUPAT): iupat.org

Insulation Contractors Association of America (ICAA): insulate.org

Mason Contractors Association of America (MCAA): masoncontractors.org

Masonry Institute of America (MIA): masonryinstitute.org

Master Painters and Decorators Association (MPDA):
    paintinfo.com/assoc/mpda/

National Association of Home Builders (NAHB): nahb.org

National Center for Construction Education and Research (NCCER):
    nccer.org

National Concrete Masonry Association (NCMA): ncma.org

National Electrical Contractors Association (NECA): necanet.org

National Insulation Association (NIA): insulation.org

National Joint Apprenticeship Training Committee (NJATC): njatc.org

National Roofing Contractors Association (NRCA): nrca.net

National Sustainable Building Advisor Program (NaSBAP): nasbap.org

National Terrazzo and Mosaic Association (NTMA): ntma.com

National Tile Contractors Association (NTCA): tile–assn.com

North American Board of Certified Energy Practitioners (NABCEP): nabcep.org

O*NET OnLine: online.onetcenter.org (see occupation titles described in this section)

Operative Plasterers' and Cement Masons' International Association (OPCMIA): opcmia.org

Painting & Decorating Contractors of America (PDCA): pdca.org

Plumbing–Heating–Cooling Contractors Association (PHCC): phccweb.org

Solar Energy International (SEI): solarenergy.org

Solar Living Institute: solarliving.org

US Dept. of Labor, Bureau of Labor Statistics: stats.bls.gov/oco/cg/cgs003.htm

US Green Building Council/LEED AP Certification: usgbc.org

United Association of Journeymen and Apprentices of the Plumbing and Pipefitting Industry: ua.org

United Brotherhood of Carpenters and Joiners of America (UBC): carpenters.org

United Union of Roofers, Waterproofers and Allied Workers: unionroofers.org

Q&A   **NEIL THOMSON**
Carpenter/Project Manager,
GreenBuilt Construction,
from an interview with Jim in 2008

How did you get into this career field? What was your education and experience, including any green-related training or certification?

I went to school at Humboldt State University, which is a pretty environmentally focused school. I lived at the Campus Center for Appropriate Technology. There's a pretty strong focus on green living there, and so that was a great start. I've always been interested in the building and construction fields, and I have worked in those fields for a number of years since college. And I would say the jobs were of varying levels of green — depending on the people I worked for. And then I met Scott Blunk of GreenBuilt Construction. The focus of his company is green building. When I started with them, maybe only 10% of our clients came to us because they were interested in green building. But over the past couple of years, there's been more and more interest. And now it's gone the whole other direction, where I would say that 90% to 95% of the people that come to us are interested in green building.

What is your current job title and how would you describe the work you do in a typical day? What are your most common tasks?
I'm the project manager, and my job is to go around and manage the different projects that our company is working on and focusing on quality control. If there are areas that we can address and make them more green, then that's the kind of thing that I focus on. And also just having the knowledge of the green products and building materials, and being able to help them make the right decisions in the field. Most decisions have been made beforehand. For instance, we might find that the job we're working on has inadequate insulation and a poorly functioning duct. And so we recommended fixing those little things, and now the client has a much more energy-efficient home and a much more comfortable kitchen. If we hadn't fixed those things, the kitchen would still look the same, but it wouldn't have changed the comfort level unless we had done the things behind the wall. So it's important to have someone in the field that knows those things and can address them as they come up. So I work with both the clients, as well as the subcontractors, in making sure they're doing their job as green as possible.

If you could give advice to a young person who wants to work in this career field someday, what would you tell them? How can they best groom themselves for this field?
Well, there's certainly a lot of training available, and that's valuable, but getting directly involved in the construction field is best. If you wanted to get into green construction and there wasn't a green construction company in your area, or one who would hire you, get a job with a regular construction company and then — eventually — you can talk people into going green. There's a lot of advantages to it, so in today's climate, it's not too hard to talk people into going green.

What kind of career advancement opportunities can one expect in this field? What kind of salary range would reflect that career path (from entry-level to the more advanced position)?
The salary range is probably $30,000 to $ 60,000 per year, depending on what level you get to and how long you've been in this field. A vice president of operations for a large company could be $100,000 to $150,000 per year. But like any construction field, you start off as a helper or apprentice. Once you're a

journey-level worker with several years of experience, you can become a lead worker or foreman. Then superintendent, project manager and other management positions — depending on the size of company. Or get a license and become the contractor.

In your opinion, what are some of the best schools, degrees and certificates for jobs in this career field, including green-specific training?
Here in Northern California, Sonoma State University has a green building program. But if you're more interested in the design side of things, the San Francisco Institute of Architecture has an environmental architecture program. Outside of Northern California, Boston Architectural College has a sustainability track that's supposed to be very good. As far as training in the green building industry, there are a lot of training opportunities. For example, public utilities like PG&E offer classes related to energy efficiency, such as appropriate insulation, home performance testing and those kinds of things. And there's also different green building associations that offer classes and trainings. There's also solar energy classes and training programs. And solar is definitely a part of green building, but green building is not just solar — despite what some people think. So we try and do everything we can for our clients before we even consider solar because you get a lot more bang for your buck.

How does someone without previous experience in this career field land a job? What are the best strategies for job-hunting in this field?
Any contractors who are at these trainings are going to be more interested in people who are already at those trainings. And a lot of contractors are going to these kinds of trainings. Also get involved with your local chapter of the US Green Building Council.

What emerging careers do you see developing now and into the future for this career field? What new technologies will have the greatest impact on this field?
Testing tools are going to have one of the biggest effects in the energy efficiency field. Infrared cameras, blower doors, duct blasters, CO_2 monitors — as those get used more and more, we're able to better find out how homes and buildings are performing. So I think those tools will create new jobs.

Resources from Q&A
Boston Architectural College (BAC): the–bac.edu
GreenBuilt Construction, Inc.: greenbuilt.com
Humboldt State University: humboldt.edu
Humboldt State University, Campus Center for Appropriate Technology
    (CCAT): humboldt.edu/~ccat/

San Francisco Institute of Architecture: sfia.net
Sonoma State University: sonoma.edu
US Green Building Council/LEED AP Certification: usgbc.org

 Tony Ortiz, Solar Installer Foreman, Aztec Solar, Inc.,
from an interview with Jim in 2008

How did you get into this career field? What was your education and experience, including any green-related training or certification?
I got out of high school with a GED, and I had one uncle who owned a solar company and another uncle who owned a roofing company. So those were my choices. I went for solar and learned everything on the job. I've also taken all kinds of different classes for solar.

What is your current job title and how would you describe the work you do in a typical day? What are your most common tasks?
I'm the installation manager for Aztec Solar. In a typical day, I meet the crew in the morning and go over the job. I make sure they have all the parts they need, that they understand that system and how it's going to be plumbed and answer any questions. From there, I go back to the office, answer phone calls, and then I go check on jobs. Sometimes I go out in the field and do service calls for customers. I also work directly with our customers when, after the salesman sells the job, I go out to the customer's site to be sure that what the salesman sold will fit and that it works for that customer.

If you could give advice to a young person who wants to work in this career field someday, what would you tell them? How can they best groom themselves for this field?
Take any vocational classes that have to do with hydraulics, plumbing and soldering with copper. Make sure you're not afraid of heights, because you have to be able to work on roofs. Learning county building codes would also help them get started. Like most construction jobs, you can come into the field right after high school. So college isn't really necessary unless you eventually want to go into management. But you'll get on-the-job training. And, if necessary, push management to get you into training classes — which they usually do in the fall and winter months. All our vendors have classes, so you can get all the training you need.

What kind of career advancement opportunities can one expect in this field? What kind of salary range would reflect that career path (from entry-level to the more advanced position)?

We always joke that we're the jack of all trades of all the trade occupations. You have to know carpentry, electrical and plumbing. But you start out as a helper, which might pay $13–$15 per hour. Then you can become a crew leader, which might pay $16–$20 per hour. Then you can become a service technician, which might pay $18–$20 per hour. From there you could become a service manager or move into sales.

In your opinion, what are some of the best schools, degrees and certificates for jobs in this career field, including green-specific training?
They've got various NABCEP certifications for people in this field. That was one of the things I did.

How does someone without previous experience in this career field land a job? What are the best strategies for job-hunting in this field?
Go out at the peak time when the solar companies are doing their hiring — which is in early spring. Go straight to the company, walk in, fill out an application and then pester them until they give you an interview. We and other companies use newspaper ads. Not many companies like ours do online job ads.

Are there any professional associations that you would recommend joining?
No.

What emerging careers do you see developing now and into the future for this career field? What new technologies will have the greatest impact on this field?
Not new technologies, but we're hoping for tax incentives and rebates that will help push the growth of this industry.

Resources from Q&A
Aztec Solar, Inc.: AztecSolar.com
North American Board of Certified Energy Practitioners (NABCEP):
    nabcep.org

Landscape Architects, including Habitat Restoration Specialists

Landscape architects plan and design land areas for such projects as parks and other recreational facilities, airports, highways, hospitals, schools, land subdivisions and commercial, industrial and residential sites.

Qualifications and Advancement

A bachelor's degree in landscape architecture is the typical education/training requirement. However, some employers require a master's degree. Some states require landscape architects to be licensed.

Landscape architects generally begin their careers as apprentices or interns. After gaining experience and becoming licensed, landscape architects can carry a design through all stages of development. After several years, they may advance to project manager, or they may become associates or partners of a landscape architecture firm. Many landscape architects choose to be self-employed. Some may pursue related jobs, such as construction supervisors, land/environmental planners or landscape consultants.

Salary Survey

Median salary: $55,140 (very high)
Typical range: $42,720 to $73,240

Job Outlook and Employment

Faster than average growth is projected for this general occupation in the US, estimated from 27,839 jobs in 2006 to 32,402 in 2016. Construction projects spur demand for landscape architects to help plan sites that meet with environmental regulations and zoning laws and integrate new structures with the natural environment in the least disruptive way. For example, landscape architects will be needed to manage stormwater runoff to avoid pollution of waterways and conserve water resources. Landscape architects also will be increasingly involved in preserving and restoring wetlands and other environmentally sensitive sites. In addition to the work related to new development and construction, landscape architects are expected to be involved in historic preservation, land reclamation and refurbishment of existing sites.

Where the Jobs Are

Architectural, engineering and related services (52.01%); Administrative and support services (13.01%); Services to buildings and dwellings (12.95%); State and local government (5.89%); Self-employed: 18.54%

Resources

American Society of Landscape Architects (ASLA): asla.org
Association of Professional Landscape Designers (APLD): apld.com
California Society for Ecological Restoration (SERCAL): sercal.org
Council of Landscape Architectural Registration Boards: clarb.org

Society for Ecological Restoration (SER): ser.org
O*NET OnLine: online.onetcenter.org (see landscape architects)
US Dept. of Labor, Bureau of Labor Statistics: bls.gov/oco/ocos039.htm

Q&A GREG MELTON
Landscape Architect, Land Image,
from an interview with Jim in 2008

*How did you get into this career field? What
was your education and experience, including
any green-related training or certification?*
It really started back when I was a kid. My
grandpa had an orchard, and I got into hor-
ticulture and farming. And then my dad had always doodled in architecture
and designed his own house. So he enlightened me on drawing and stuff. So
I kind of had a horticulture background and a drawing background in going
to college. I thought I wanted to be an engineer, but I didn't really enjoy physics and calculus. So I headed down the horticulture path and went to Chico
State. But about halfway through the program, I realized I was interested in
the plant material and design, but not really interested in the greenhouse stuff.
I took a class called recreation design, and I kind of found my home there.
My drawing skills kind of opened some doors. And with those doors opening
and having a horticulture background, the professor said, "You know you're a
perfect candidate for landscape architecture. You need to go to UC Davis and
complete your degree there." But I was real close to completing my horticulture degree at Chico State, so I completed that first. Then the next year I went
to UC Davis and enrolled in their landscape architecture school.

*What is your current job title and how would you describe the work you do in a
typical day? What are your most common tasks?*
I am a principle in a 14-person landscape architecture firm. I have a partner,
and I'm the senior planner in the office. I'm also the senior landscape architect. In a typical day, I would get to the office — having done my to-do list the
night before. So I get into the office and see what I finished working on the
day before. It may include designing one new design on a park project that we
have. I usually try to leave about an hour for that. Secondly I look at all the design projects. I review what my staff has created and let them have their own
design on that. The park projects, though, are my bread and butter, so I spend
a lot of time designing those. Then my third thing would be getting all my in-

voices out. Maybe halfway through the park job, I'd have a drop-in visitor who would either represent a new project or be a client from an old project that needs something. So we go down to the conference room for that. While I'm down there, I might have one or two employees or project managers catch me with questions. And that could extend to bringing a couple of other designers in on the conversation. Or bring in the specialty people if we're talking irrigation or whatever. The next thing you know, it's lunch time. Or, if not quite lunch time, I usually try to work out right before lunch. But that usually happens twice a week — if I'm lucky. By the way, the athletic club is a perk for us because we designed the place. So we got free memberships. You have those kinds of trade things throughout life as a landscape architect. After lunch, I'd get back to work and maybe have a discussion with my business partner on a human resource issue. Maybe I just received an e-mail from an employee who needs an extra vacation. Or maybe an employee is not handling his or her workload appropriately. And so we could talk human resources for probably an hour. Then I'd get back to that park project and turn off my phone and lock the door and get a little work done. You pretty much have to shut it down and turn off the phone and just say "Ok, I am unavailable." And so you wrap up the day finishing that work and answering the key e-mails that you get throughout the day.

If you could give advice to a young person who wants to work in this career field someday, what would you tell them? How can they best groom themselves for this field?
Step number one is to create that conviction for creating incredible spaces for people to live in. That's what drives me. I don't want to leave a project until I've done my best to create a great space. Step number two is drawing skills, which are very important. The computer is huge, but for me, my mind doesn't come out onto a computer very well. My mind comes through my hands on paper, so the drawing skills are critical. And then at an early stage, you need to make yourself somewhat of a specialist of some sort so you can become valuable to somebody. And that value can place you in an early job. Specialties might include becoming an irrigation specialist, a plant specialist, a restoration specialist or a technical person really skilled in computer graphics.

What kind of career advancement opportunities can one expect in this field? What kind of salary range would reflect that career path (from entry-level to the more advanced position)?

You might get started as a technician, which means you'd need to know your computer. You'd need to know AutoCAD, Photoshop, Excel, Word and preferably SketchUp — a 3-D drawing tool. Those are the main programs that are used. Then from a technician, you'd grow yourself into a landscape designer. So you move up from drafting what other people give you to doing some of your own designs. And then you begin to manage some projects with the project manager over your shoulder, and then at some point you become the project manager on a small commercial project. Then you might eventually become a full-time project manager, which means you're meeting with the client, you're designing the project, and now you're making all the phone calls and making sure everything is getting done and getting billed. So your responsibility level grows and grows. When you're a top-level project manager, you have full contact with the client and you write the contract and the principle is really taken out of the deal. And the less I work on your project, the more money you're going to make. With our firm, a technician usually starts somewhere between $12 and $15 per hour. Then we have a six-month review and an annual review after that. So as each year goes by, if you are relieving the project managers of their duties, then you get more money. A typical increase would be a dollar a year or fifty cents — depending how you perform. My project managers can make up to about $25 per hour. After that, we generally take care of them with bonuses. That's because, when times get slow, like in today's market, I want to be able to have my payroll low, and the bonuses can be null and void because there's no extra money in the pot. I think starting salaries in the San Francisco Bay Area are more like $20 per hour and can work up to something like a $75,000–$80,000 annual salary.

In your opinion, what are some of the best schools, degrees and certificates for jobs in this career field, including green-specific training?
My knowledge of schools is probably limited to the West Coast. Cal Poly, San Luis Obispo, does a wonderful job. I went to UC Davis, and I like their program. Also, the University of Arizona has a great program. Then there's Harvard and all the other ones that I don't really have any experience with.

Resources from Q&A
Cal Poly, San Luis Obispo: calpoly.edu
California State University, Chico: csuchico.edu
Land Image: elandimage.com
University of Arizona School of Architecture: architecture.arizona.edu
University of California, Davis: ucdavis.edu

 **CARL JENSEN**
Director of Design–Build, Wildlands, Inc.,
from an interview with Jim in 2008

How did you get into this career field? What was your education and experience, including any green-related training or certification?
I attended the University of California, Davis, where I got my degree in landscape architecture. Part of the instruction covered the different aspects of the landscape architecture profession, which includes habitat and ecosystem restoration. This type of work aligned much more closely with my interests and personal beliefs compared to traditional landscape architecture, so I decided to look into it professionally after I graduated. My first job was with the environmental consulting firm of Jones & Stokes, after which I came to Wildlands, Inc. where I am currently employed.

What is your current job title and how would you describe the work you do in a typical day? What are your most common tasks, including those that make yours a green job?
I am the director of design-build and a senior landscape architect. I oversee a staff of four people, including two landscape architects. Aside from the administrative tasks of running a team of four people, I coordinate all of the habitat restoration design and construction work at the company. I prepare concept designs for projects; work on construction drawing packages, which may include grading plans, planting plans, erosion control plans and construction details; I coordinate with construction contractors and take clients and regulatory staff on site visits. Some of the other tasks my staff may work on include gathering topographic data for base map preparation and construction oversight during project implementation.

If you could give advice to a young person who wants to work in this career field someday, what would you tell them? How can they best groom themselves for this field?
First, get a four-year degree in a field related to habitat restoration — such as landscape architecture, ecology or engineering. Second, learn to use Auto-CAD proficiently. AutoCAD is the industry standard for drafting and design software. Most entry-level positions will require a working knowledge of this software. Third, become knowledgeable in native plants in your geographic region and how they are used in restoration projects. Fourth, become involved

with local professional organizations related to the field of habitat restoration. This will not only allow you to learn from peers, but also to network with other professionals in the field. A good organization like this in California is SERCAL — the California Society for Ecological Restoration.

What kind of career advancement opportunities can one expect in this field? What kind of salary range would reflect that career path (from entry-level to the more advanced position)?
There are lots of opportunities for advancement in this field. For people who are hard working, ambitious and good communicators, the sky is the limit. The regulatory environment in California is fairly strict and is likely to get only more so as time goes on and natural resources come under more pressure. This means that there will likely be more work for people in the field of habitat restoration as compensatory mitigation is required under most state and federal regulatory permits. Starting salaries for landscape architects usually begin around $35,000 per year, with senior landscape architects making upwards of $90,000 per year.

In your opinion, what are some of the best schools, degrees and certificates for jobs in this career field, including green-specific training?
Degrees in landscape architecture or engineering are probably the most useful for habitat restoration careers. UC Davis, UC Berkeley and Cal Poly, San Luis Obispo have excellent programs in landscape architecture and engineering.

How does someone without previous experience in this career field land a job? What are the best strategies for job-hunting in this field?
A four-year degree is a must for this industry. Most companies, mine included, won't even consider a candidate for a technical position if they don't have a four-year degree. The degree shows that a candidate is serious about the chosen profession, and there are a lot of design and engineering basics that can be learned most effectively in an academic setting. As I said before, learning AutoCAD is a must for anyone seeking an entry-level position. Any entry-level design position will be focused on preparing figures and construction drawings using CAD.

Are there any professional associations that you would recommend joining?
SERCAL is a great organization if you work in California. The American Society of Landscape Architects is a good professional organization for landscape architects, but it is heavily focused on traditional landscape architecture and will have limited benefits for those who are practicing habitat restoration.

What emerging careers do you see developing now and into the future for this career field? What new technologies will have the greatest impact on this field? Computer-aided design software is becoming more and more powerful, allowing designers to do their work with more accuracy and detail. The integration of landscape architecture, design software and GPS technology is also allowing grading and layout plans to be directly utilized by construction equipment via GPS equipment control. This allows projects to be constructed more accurately, quickly and efficiently than before.

Resources from Q&A

American Society of Landscape Architects (ASLA): asla.org
Cal Poly, San Luis Obispo: calpoly.edu
California Society for Ecological Restoration (SERCAL): sercal.org
University of California, Berkeley: berkeley.edu
University of California, Davis: ucdavis.edu
Wildlands, Inc.: wildlandsinc.com

Landscaping and Groundskeeping Workers (Eco-friendly)

Landscaping and groundskeeping workers landscape or maintain grounds of property using hand or power tools or equipment. Workers typically perform a variety of tasks, which may include any combination of the following: sod laying, mowing, trimming, planting, watering, fertilizing, digging, raking, sprinkler installation and installation of mortarless segmental concrete masonry wall units.

Habitat restoration landscaping workers work under the direction of specialists who incorporate the use of biological systems and engineering principles to restore aquatic and terrestrial habitats suffering from erosion and industrial damage. Their duties may also include monitoring habitats for signs of decay, counting flora and fauna, testing water and soil for chemicals and pollution and reintroducing plants and animals.

Qualifications and Advancement

There usually are no minimum education requirements for this occupation, as most workers are trained on the job. Landscaping supervisors or contractors who own their own business usually need some formal training in landscape design, horticulture, arboriculture or business. A bachelor's degree may be needed for those who want to become specialists. Certifications are available.

Workers who demonstrate a willingness to work hard and quickly, have good communication skills and take an interest in the business may advance to crew leader or other supervisory positions within a few years.

Salary Survey
Median salary: $21,260 (very low)
Typical range: $17,430 to $26,860

Job Outlook and Employment
Faster than average growth is projected for this general occupation in the US, estimated from 1,220,054 jobs in 2006 to 1,441,326 in 2016. More workers will be needed to keep up with increasing demand for lawn care and landscaping services. Construction of office buildings, shopping malls, residential housing, highways and parks is expected to increase demand for these workers. In addition, the upkeep and renovation of existing landscaping and grounds are continuing sources of demand for grounds maintenance workers. Habitat restoration is also a growing field, so there should be favorable opportunities for those want to specialize in this type of work.

Where the Jobs Are
Landscaping services (36.82%); Local government (6.79%); Self-employed: 17.3%

Resources
International Society of Arboriculture (ISA): isa–arbor.com
O*NET OnLine: online.onetcenter.org (see landscaping and groundskeeping
    workers)
PLANET, the Professional Landcare Network: landcarenetwork.org
Professional Grounds Management Society (PGMS): pgms.org
Society for Ecological Restoration (SER): ser.org
Tree Care Industry Association (TCIA): treecareindustry.org
US Dept. of Labor, Bureau of Labor Statistics: bls.gov/oco/ocos172.htm

Green Business
and Enterprising Group

- Accountants, including Environmental Accountants
- Financial Analysts, including Sustainability and Sustainable Investment Analysts
- Green Entrepreneurs and Consultants
- Marketing Managers, including Environmental Marketing Specialists
- Refuse and Recyclable Material Collectors, including Recycling Technicians
- Sales Representatives, including Renewable Energy and Natural/Organic Products Sales Reps
- Sustainability Coordinators and Officers
- Travel Guides, including Ecotourism Guides and Operators

Accountants, including Environmental Accountants

Accountants analyze financial information and prepare financial reports to determine or maintain record of assets, liabilities, profit and loss, tax liability or other financial activities within an organization.

Environmental accountants help corporations and nations understand environmental costs and help find ways to save money through environmental protection measures.

Qualifications and Advancement
A bachelor's degree in accounting is the typical education requirement. Some employers prefer applicants with a master's degree in accounting or a master's degree in business administration with a concentration in accounting. Accountants must be good at working with people and with business systems and computers. Accountants should be familiar with basic accounting software packages. Environmental accountants also need to have considerable knowledge of environmental regulations as well as special environmental accounting procedures.

Some begin their careers as accountants and some as auditors. Some others begin as bookkeepers or accounting/auditing clerks. Some accountants become licensed as Certified Public Accountants (CPAs). In general, internal auditors, public accountants and management accountants have much occupational mobility. Advancement may lead to positions of greater responsibility or to supervisory/management positions. Other possibilities include chief cost accountant, budget director, manager of internal auditing, controller, treasurer, financial vice president and chief financial officer. Some become self-employed. Some others become partners in an established accounting firm.

Salary Survey

Median salary: $54,630 (very high)
Typical range: $42,520 to $71,960

Job Outlook and Employment

Faster than average growth is projected for the general occupation of accountant in the US, from 1,274,357 jobs in 2006 to 1,499,932 in 2016. However, there are no reliable statistics (yet) on the specific occupation of environmental accountants. Nevertheless, the overall job outlook for accountants is good, due to expected job growth and the need to replace accountants who retire or transfer to other occupations.

Where the Jobs Are

Professional, scientific and technical services, including accounting firms (27.21%); Finance/insurance (8.63%); Government. (8.29%); Self-employed 9.5%

Resources

American Institute of Certified Public Accountants (AICPA): aicpa.org
National Association of State Boards of Accountancy (NASBA): nasba.org
O*NET OnLine: online.onetcenter.org (see accountants)
US Dept. of Labor, Bureau of Labor Statistics: bls.gov/oco/ocos001.htm
US Environmental Protection Agency (EPA) Environmental Accounting Resources:
  epa.gov/oppt/library/pubs/archive/acct–archive/resources.htm

 JOE MUSCAT, Director of Clean Tech/Environmental Accounting, Ernst & Young, from an interview with Alice in 2008

How did you get into this career field? What was your education and experience, including any green-related training or certification?

I have a bachelor's degree in accounting and graduate work toward a CPA license, along with engineering aptitudes and an interest in science.

What is your current job title?
I'm director of clean tech, environmental accounting, Ernst & Young. I work with green and environmental accounting rules and standards.

If you could give advice to a young person who wants to work in this career field someday, what would you tell them?
Learn the fundamentals of accounting first. Understand accounting basics: where information is sourced, how reliable information is produced and presented, and understand what the user will need to do with your information. Because green or environmental accounting standards and rules are still being developed. You need to be flexible. One needs to collaborate and partner/team with people to evaluate a situation.

What kind of career advancement opportunities can one expect in this field?
The field of environmental accounting is limitless. A person can move into an "executive officer of sustainability" position or can report to the COO or the CFO in environmental accounting.

How does someone without previous experience in this career field land a job?
Internships are sometimes available. Fundamental accounting knowledge is critical first, then having an interest in the environment and education in science, too, is ideal.

Are there any professional associations that you would recommend joining?
Joining an association in your industry — "green building" and also in your function — "accounting" — would be best.

Resources from Q&A
Ernst & Young: ey.com

Financial Analysts, including Sustainability and Sustainable Investment Analysts

Financial analysts conduct quantitative analyses of information affecting investment programs of public or private institutions.

Qualifications and Advancement
A bachelor's degree in business administration, accounting, statistics or finance is the typical education requirement. However, a master's degree in

business administration (MBA) is desirable and may be necessary for career advancement. Regardless of the degree, knowledge of accounting policies and procedures, corporate budgeting and financial analysis methods is important. Advanced knowledge of options pricing, bond valuation and risk management are also important.

Financial analysts can benefit from previous work experience in an accounting office, with a securities firm or in a bank. Work as a research assistant in a brokerage house is also good experience for this career. As experience and knowledge is gained, financial analysts may advance to portfolio or financial manager, directing the investment portfolios of companies or clients. Those interested in sales may become securities agents. Some financial analysts become consultants or open their own firms.

Salary Survey
Median salary: $66,590 (very high)
Typical range: $50,700 to $90,690

Job Outlook and Employment
Much faster than average growth is projected for this occupation in the US, from 220,568 jobs in 2006 to 295,157 in 2016. Primary factors for this growth are increasing complexity of investments and growth in the industry. As the number and type of mutual funds and the amount of assets invested in these funds increase, mutual fund companies will need more financial analysts to research and recommend investments.

Where the Jobs Are
Other financial investment activities (12.23%); Management of companies and enterprises (10.11%); Securities and commodity contracts, brokerages and exchanges (9.55%); Depository credit intermediation (7.68%); Accounting, tax preparation, bookkeeping and payroll services (3.87%); Management, scientific and technical consulting services (3.32%); Self-employed: 7.82%

Resources
American Academy of Financial Management (AAFM): aafm.org
Chartered Financial Analyst (CFA) Institute: cfainstitute.org
Financial Industry Regulatory Authority (FINRA): finra.org
O*NET OnLine: online.onetcenter.org (see financial analysts)
Securities Industry and Financial Markets Association (SIFMA): sifma.org
US Dept. of Labor, Bureau of Labor Statistics: bls.gov/oco/ocos259.htm

Green Entrepreneurs and Consultants

Green entrepreneurs are the founders of businesses that produce or provide green/sustainable products and services. Some specialize in business start-ups and tend to move on to new business challenges once the business is established. Others help get the business established and then continue on as part of the management team.

Green consultants are individuals with extensive knowledge and experience in a specific profession or industry and provide their expertise and consulting services to paying clients.

What is a sustainable business? — At a minimum, a sustainable business is committed to conserving energy, preventing pollution, reducing waste and conserving water. The greening of buildings and the extensive use of renewable energy are also important aspects of a sustainable business. An even-higher standard is for a business to hold itself accountable for both the environmental and human rights impacts of its activities.

Qualifications and Advancement

Because green entrepreneurs and consultants head their own organizations or work as partners, they aren't usually subject to any formal education or experience requirements. (The exception to this is when a business or business owner's occupation is regulated by law — such as an attorney.) In some cases, entrepreneurs and consultants are self-taught people who are very intelligent, highly motivated and uninterested in pursuing a formal education when they could be starting/running a new business. Nevertheless, a successful entrepreneur or consultant generally has extensive experience and a comprehensive skill set that usually requires some formal education or training. Not coincidentally, an increasing number of public and private colleges are now offering "green MBA" programs that are already producing a new generation of green entrepreneurs. An MBA is a master's degree in business administration. A green MBA has sustainability integrated throughout the curriculum.

Advancement for entrepreneurs and consultants usually takes the form of growing as the company grows or moving on to bigger or more satisfying business projects. Some will take advantage of opportunities to return to the workforce as employees of some other organization where their skills will be highly valued and compensated.

Key skills and abilities include judgment and decision-making; oral expression and comprehension; management of financial resources; written expression and comprehension; solving problems; researching and getting information; communicating with supervisors, peers or subordinates.

Salary/Compensation

The earnings for entrepreneurs and consultants range from little or nothing to well over $100,000 per year. Some business owners and chief executive officers make millions of dollars in salaries and other benefits, but it is important to remember that many others are living on the thin line between profit and loss, and between success and failure. Especially during the start-up phase of a business, an owner may not be able to draw a salary, or perhaps only a partial salary. And when an established business goes through a difficult period, the owner may once again have to sacrifice their salary for the benefit of the business and its employees (who, rightly so, *always* expect to be paid). A business owner also has to expect to invest a good sum of money into their business. Getting a business loan or venture capital to start a business is virtually impossible without having your own significant monetary investment in the business. And being undercapitalized is a recipe for failure.

Resources

GreenBiz (news and resources): greenbiz.com
GreenBusiness.net (message board for eco-entrepreneurs): greenbusiness.net
O*NET OnLine: online.onetcenter.org (see chief executives)
Sustainable Business magazine: edie.net/magazines/
US Dept. of Labor, Bureau of Labor Statistics: bls.gov/oco/ocos012.htm
US Green Building Council/LEED AP Certification: usgbc.org

Q&A with 12 Green Entrepreneurs

- Scott Blunk, President, GreenBuilt Construction
- Josh Daniels, Owner, Green Sacramento (environmental building and design products)
- Jon Dougal, Green Building Consultant, Publisher, GreenSage eNewsLetter
- Rona Fried, SustainableBusiness.com
- Steve Heckeroth, Homestead Enterprises
- Hunter Lovins, Esq., President/Founder, Natural Capitalism, Inc.
- Ed Murray, President, Aztec Solar, Inc.
- Les Nelson, Western Renewables Group

- Debora (Debe) Overhaug, President/CEO, PRC Technologies (soy-based print cartridges)
- Lee Reich, Horticultural Consultant and Writer
- Jim Steinmetz, Reusable Lumber Company
- Fred Wood, Greenlight Magazine/Pattiwood Productions

Q&A   **SCOTT BLUNK**
President, GreenBuilt Construction, Inc., from an interview with Jim in 2008

How did you get into this career field? What was your education and experience?
I graduated as a mechanical engineer from Purdue University, served three years in the Peace Corps and then got an MBA. But I got into green building by accident. I started GreenBuilt Construction because I was tired of the drudgery of the PhD program I was enrolled in. I had read a lot on the real estate industry over the previous decade just out of my own interest, so I started buying and selling homes and fixing them myself. I got annoyed at real estate agents, so I became a real estate broker myself. As I got busier, I began hiring people to help flip the homes, and I realized I was building a useful skill set. So I got my contractors license. Just my way of life makes me a green real estate agent or a green construction manager or whatever I'm doing. When I used to work at Ford Motor Company, I was a green engineer, but only in the fact that the way I impacted the environment was in the forefront of my mind at all times. So in starting my construction company, I always have my environmental "glasses" on. And so it was to be — by my nature — a green company. As green became popular, it gave me a niche to fit.

What is your current job title and how would you describe the work you do in a typical day? What are your most common tasks?
I am President of GreenBuilt Construction. My work involves all aspects of leadership in a small company: hiring, finance, marketing, sales.

If you could give advice to a young person who wants to work in this career field someday, what would you tell them? How can they best groom themselves for this field?
Live it. Always be learning. Follow your interests and learn about them. Live your life according to your principles. Get involved in your interests, such

as clubs, social groups, etc., and someday, probably not as soon as you'd like, you'll be in the profession you desire.

Being self-employed, how do you look at career advancement? Does it generally take the form of growing/expanding your business, or is self-employment part of a career track that may lead to something else down the road?
I haven't been an employee for someone else since 1997. I cannot work for others. My future is expanding my own business. The only other option for me would be a position at another company with almost total autonomy. The great thing about growing and expanding my own business is that there are so many possibilities for growth that I can move in so many directions. I can choose to start up a new arm of my business that interests me just because I see an opportunity to learn, make money or better position the company. I think this will keep me stimulated for quite some time.

Can you suggest a salary range that someone could expect if they were to pursue work in your career field?
My employees' salaries range from $30,000 to $60,000 per year. This is much less than any of them deserve, but they see the possibilities they have here in terms of their own careers, potential income and impact on the environment. We are a great group of individuals that have fun together, work hard together and push each other to learn and grow even more green.

In your opinion, what are some of the best schools, degrees and certificates for jobs in this career field?
The better the reputation of the school, the better the chances of the job applicant. I see the candidate, but it is also the overall reputation of the school that makes a difference. Not the school's green or environmental reputation, as there really aren't any schools out there with a reputation in this new field. I would highly value candidates with a math/science background for the majority of the positions in my company. Of course, getting your LEED AP certification helps, as it shows dedication and desire to work in the green building industry. There are also local organizations, like Build It Green in our area, that have training and certification opportunities that would also show a serious interest in the industry.

How much experience is necessary before a person should venture into self-employment in your field? What positions should that experience be in?
As little as possible — it is scary out here. I would have never done this had I known how difficult it would be. If you find the opportunity, just do it. Don't think about it or research how to do it. Of course you need to know something

about your field, but don't get caught up in being an expert first. If you've worked for years in the industry you start your company in, then you will most likely just do things the same way everyone else in your industry does them. With less experience, you come with a more open mind about how to do things. This has been both a benefit and a hindrance to my own success. However, as I've said, if I knew the difficulty I would have prior to starting the company, I wouldn't have done it. And I love what I am doing now.

Are there any professional associations that you would recommend joining?
Your local chapter of the US Green Building Council (USGBC) and, for the new people in the field, a group inside the USGBC called the Emerging Green Builders.

What emerging or high-growth careers do you see developing now and into the future for this career field? What new technologies will have the greatest impact on this field?
All electrical generation fields will see huge growth. The creation of an alternative to the internal combustion engine will see a flurry of activity. There will also be tremendous growth in the conversion/upgrade of existing buildings to green standards. Particularly, energy efficiency in the existing built environment has the largest potential for both job growth and reduction in green house gases.

Resources from Q&A
Build It Green: builditgreen.org
GreenBuilt Construction, Inc.: greenbuilt.com
US Green Building Council/LEED AP Certification: usgbc.org

 Josh Daniels, Owner, Green Sacramento (environmental building and design products), from an interview with Jim in 2008

How did you get into this career field? What was your education and experience, including any green-related training or certification?
I was in the wine business for seven years before this, working for the family business in sales and marketing. We represented about 32 wineries and had about 70 employees. The problem was, I like wine, but I didn't have a passion for it, and it didn't fit into my value set very well. And as the company started getting more and more corporate, I decided to get out. In 2003, I went back to school at the New College of San Francisco. It started as an activism school back in the late 60s, initially one of those "fight the power" types, but it became more solution–oriented in the 80s. I ended up getting an education centered

on problem-solving and finding alternatives. I studied ecology, culture and the whole dwelling process in general, so when I moved to Sacramento and we wanted to remodel the house, I tried to do so in a more environmentally friendly and health-conscious way. As we were looking at the products and services available, I came to think, "There must be a better way to do this." And it just clicked — that was my next step. It took me about a year to do all the research and financing, and then I opened my business.

What is your current job title and how would you describe the work you do in a typical day? What are your most common tasks?

I am the owner of a retail store selling environmentally friendly and home-healthy building materials. I do everything from cleaning bathrooms and stocking materials, to managing employees and dealing with customers and vendors and choosing products. I'd say my primary task is working directly with customers; we're a retail business, so we're all about sales. Second would probably be marketing — making sure people know who we are, where we are and what we do. And then managing products and making sure everything gets ordered and followed through in a timely manner.

If you could give advice to a young person who wants to work in this career field someday, what would you tell them? How can they best groom themselves for this field?

First and foremost, you really have to be interested in and passionate about working in the green industry. It has to matter to you. I'm not a salesman — I hate being a salesman — but I don't have to act like one because I'm passionate about the products I carry, and that just comes through. The second thing is, get the right education. Understand what you're doing and why you're doing it, and what the principles are behind green services and products. I think the key is to be able to appreciate the larger social context of what you're doing — how it affects the economy, how it affects the environment, how it affects human health and how it affects the larger society in general.

What kind of career advancement opportunities can one expect in this field? What kind of salary range would reflect that career path (from entry-level to the more advanced position)?

At this point, that's dependent on growing the business. That could be by increasing the size of my business itself, increasing the size of my market, but mainly furthering the education of the public so that more people are using products that are sustainable and healthier in the home. I want to increase the employment in the area and grow my business to a size where I'm comfortable, so I can show that you can make money and still maintain high values and standards. But I don't think people can, or should, expect a business to grow forever. It's an unsustainable concept. The important thing is sustaining a business, while continuing to grow the concepts of green building and sustainability and a healthy society.

In your opinion, what are some of the best schools, degrees and certificates for jobs in this career field, including green-specific training?
I know of two green MBA programs specifically: one is at Presidio School of Management in San Francisco, and the other is at Dominican University in Marin. Those are both really good MBA programs because they take into account the larger context of business in society. In Northern California, there's also Build It Green, which has several certification processes. And of course, there's LEED certification from the US Green Building Council (USGBC). At least for me, that's going to become more and more important for employees to have as they start getting into LEED for home building in the upcoming years.

How does someone without previous experience in this career field land a job? What are the best strategies for job-hunting in this field?
That passion has to come through. So if somebody isn't really living a green lifestyle, if they're not convincing in that they believe in it and that they understand the concepts, then they're just not going to succeed. Or if they've got lots of perfume and makeup on, it's an instant sign that they don't get it. But more than anything, they need to have passion. After that, they need to have good people skills and good organizational skills.

Are there any professional associations that you would recommend joining?
Definitely the USGBC — that's key. The retail stores have been trying for the last two years to start some sort of a green building retailers association. But we're all starting new businesses right now, and we don't have the time or money.

What emerging careers do you see developing now and into the future for this career field? What new technologies will have the greatest impact on this field?
There's a lot of room for growth and development and innovation and ingenuity in green building and design. Energy is what's driving green technology: reductions in energy usage and finding new sustainable forms of energy. But key is the reduction of energy usage and how we improve our processes: shipping, extracting, manufacturing, etc. Water efficiency is probably as important

to energy efficiency as it is to water conservation because of the amount of energy that goes into maintaining waterways and water systems. So there is a lot going on with water and energy efficiency.

Resources from Q&A

Build It Green: builditgreen.org
Dominican University of California: dominican.edu
Presidio School of Management: presidiomba.org
US Green Building Council/LEED AP Certification: usgbc:org

Q&A **JON DOUGAL**
Executive Director,
US Green Real Estate Council,
Sustainable Development/Green
Building Consultant and Educator;
Publisher and Editor, GreenMotion.org
and GreenSage eNewsletters,
from an interview with Jim in 2008

How did you get into this career field? What
was your education and experience?

I had no experience in the field when I began, and I began by accident. I was an HVAC contractor and was getting increasingly interested in hazardous materials as they relate to asbestos, CFCs, used hydronics, waste, etc. So I started to plug into various organizations that had educational workshops, mostly in the Silicon Valley area, where phosphate and chlorine-containing cleaners were polluting the Bay from chip manufacturing and military base waste. One group asked me to take over when the previous chair moved on. I then founded the Roundtable on the Environment for the San Francisco Chamber of Commerce. We put on the first green building conference in the nation in the new sustainably built San Francisco Main Library. And I went to every meeting, workshop, conference and lecture that I could find that had anything to do with green. In many cases, I had to infer what was green — because they didn't label them as such. I eventually went to work as an architectural representative for a major flooring company and gave green lunchtime talks to introduce green materials. Eventually I became the national sustainable initiatives manager for Armstrong World Industries. But they didn't see the market and, to this day, lost out on the largest paradigm shift in the construction industry in 100 years. They are just now getting their act together on that level.

What is your current job title and how would you describe the work you do in a typical day? What are your most common tasks?

I'm the executive director of the US Green Real Estate Council and am currently involved in furthering the efforts of the real estate industry to understand the value-added proposition of green buildings. I'm also one of the founding board members of the Inland Empire Chapter of the US Green Building Council, which is fastest growing chapter in the US. I'm also a consultant and educator for sustainable development and green building, and I continue to publish e-newsletters on alternative fuels and energy.

If you could give advice to a young person who wants to work in this career field someday, what would you tell them? How can they best groom themselves for this field?

They should learn everything they can learn, speak the talk, and — mostly — live the speak. Consciousness toward the subject goes a long way. We call it heart. If you believe that it is just one planet and we are all in the effort to save tomorrow's generations, sharing information becomes paramount, and money secondary. Learn the value of networking. Connections made today may not bear fruit for ten years, but keep in touch with people over time, remember their names, collect their cards and send e-mails to stay in touch. Share your values and do them favors with no quid pro quo in mind. Call and e-mail them with opportunities you may have heard of. Offer to share rides so you can talk. Go on the tours of green installations at conferences.

What kind of career advancement opportunities can one expect in this field? What kind of salary range would reflect that career path (from entry-level to the more advanced position)?

Entry-level may be as a volunteer or intern — as these are pathways to show commitment and have a place to learn. You can't just read a book and become green. It's an ever-evolving discipline. Jobs for LEED APs are now in demand and will eventually be required of every construction company in the US. It's a big claim, but it will happen. Salaries are running from $75,000–$140,000 per year for LEED AP project managers.

In your opinion, what are some of the best schools, degrees and certificates for jobs in this career field?

Many schools that were not offering courses a short while ago now see that it is mandatory to have a curriculum on green or sustainability. All real estate professionals are boning up on what makes a building green. Community colleges and universities and engineering schools are behind the curve, but gearing up to meet the demand. We've got 40,000 new jobs in solar alone just in California. The wind industry is going to produce 20% of our US energy demand in ten years. There needs to be a workforce to install and maintain new energy systems. Testing and performance protocols will demand technicians and new testing criteria.

How does someone without previous experience in this career field land a job? What are the best strategies for job-hunting in this field?
No experience, no job. Networking is the ultimate fail-proof job-hunting mechanism in this field. It is not what you know, but evermore important "who you know" and who can give you the recommendation. Volunteer with a green builder, or with Habitat for Humanity, as all affordable housing is going green. Get on-the-job training at any level and get experience of any kind.

Are there any professional associations that you would recommend joining?
Many, many national, and many local, and all can be found through Google — USGBC/LEED, GBI, BigGreen, BIA, NAHB. Look 'em up and drill down.

What emerging or high-growth careers do you see developing now and into the future for this career field? What new technologies will have the greatest impact on this field?
Testing and materials certifications, green home inspectors–auditors–appraisers, wind and geothermal engineering, water conservation, biodiesel and all its ancillaries — seed pressing, importing oils, custom house brokers, plant operations and monitoring, landfill gas reclamation and monitoring.

Resources from Q&A

Armstrong World Industries: armstrong.com
BigGreen Discussion Group (sustainable design and construction): biggreen.org
Building Industry Association (BIA): bia.net
Green Building Initiative (GBI): thegbi.org
Habitat for Humanity: habitat.org
National Association of Home Builders (NAHB): nahb.org
San Francisco Chamber of Commerce: sfchamber.com
US Green Building Council/LEED AP Certification: usgbc.org
US Green Real Estate Council (USGREC): usgrec.org

 **RONA FRIED**
President and CEO, SustainableBusiness.com,
from an interview with Jim in 2008

*How did you get into this career field? What was your
education and experience?*
I have a doctorate degree in social/organizational psychology, but about two-thirds of the way through getting my degree, I realized that I really wanted to do
environmental work. But I didn't want to start over again on a new degree. So
I had my own business doing organizational consulting for about ten years,
but I was always trolling, looking to see how I could switch careers. Back then
there really wasn't a way to do environmental work unless you were an engineer or scientist or a non-profit organizer type. And I wasn't any of those
things. I was more business oriented. Then in 1991 when the Exxon Valdez
crashed, that was really the beginning of green business. Out of that came a
small opening, a window in time, where the population in the US became
interested in greening their lifestyle. It was really pretty miraculous. A book
came out at that time, called *365 Ways to Change the World*, which sold millions of copies. So I switched careers and opened Earthwares, one of the first
green retail stores in the country, selling alternative products to every kind of
consumer product that there was, from gifts to clothes to bedding to house-
wares to paints and stains. My next business was selling green products to natural food stores all over the country. After a few years, I realized that it wasn't
the lifestyle that I was looking for, so I went through a revisioning process and
thought about what my skills really were, and what I really wanted to be doing.
I came up with SustainableBusiness.com in 1996. It seemed like a great way to
bring people together with shared values who were all over the world.

*What is your current job title and how would you describe the work you do in a
typical day? What are your most common tasks?*
I'm president and CEO. A typical day involves the usual administration that it
takes to run a business, supervising employees, working on new services and
partnerships and generally working to grow the business. On the content side,
I produce *Progressive Investor*, which is a green investing newsletter. I do all
the research and writing and marketing and everything else for that.

*If you could give advice to a young person who wants to work in this career field
someday, what would you tell them? How can they best groom themselves for
this field?*

The first thing is to green your own lifestyle. Join some green non-profits like the Sierra Club, NRDC (Natural Resources Defense Council) — there are hundreds of excellent groups doing important work. Get involved, read their magazines, learn about the issues. Take courses at your school. Figure out which areas interest you and where there might be ways for you to build a career. Go to conferences, meet people, learn who's doing what, especially near where you live.

If you want to start your own business, you'll need the same skills to start a green business as any other business — plus a passion and deep knowledge about the particular business topic. You'll need to understand the difficulties of starting a new business, the money it takes, how long it takes and what kind of resources you need to get the business off the ground.

Being self-employed, how do you look at career advancement? Does it generally take the form of growing/expanding your business, or is self-employment part of a career track that may lead to something else down the road?
Growing your own business is a huge endeavor. It takes an enormous variety of skills and lots of determination and persistence. I consider career advancement as expanding my business and my ability to have impact on my field. I'm very mission-oriented — I don't want to just make more money; I want to make an impact through my work. As my business grows, I have more opportunities to do that by serving on boards, writing books, developing new services and seeing my services being successful and helping people. Many people sell their business at some point or move on to other things like consulting while their business continues running. Or they might expand by acquiring other businesses. There are many ways to go — it's far from static.

Can you suggest a salary range that someone could expect if they were to pursue work in your career field?
Like any other business, there's a trajectory from earning practically nothing to earning substantial amounts as your business grows or as you develop your career. The green industry is becoming very big now and will be huge in the coming years — people should expect to earn the same or more than in conventional industries.

In your opinion, what are some of the best schools, degrees and certificates for jobs in this career field?
For many years, few schools and universities offered much in the way of green business. Now, most of the major universities — like Harvard, University of Michigan, University of North Carolina — have excellent courses on the topic.

There are also schools that specialize in sustainable MBAs, such as Bainbridge Graduate Institute, and many training programs in wind, solar and renewable energy in general.

How much experience is necessary before a person should venture into self-employment in your field? What positions should that experience be in?
That depends on the person. There's always going to be those young, feisty entrepreneurs that can do it without any experience. But for most people, learning how to develop a business takes time and experience. Many people work for companies as employees before they strike out on their own. My business, which entails running a portal on green business, requires knowledge of how to develop an Internet-based business in addition to deep knowledge about the industry and about the environmental issues we cover. Like any other industry, you need to know how to build a business and you need in-depth knowledge of the field you're involved in.

Are there any professional associations that you would recommend joining?
Each segment of green business has professional associations — The Solar Energy Industries Association, American Wind Energy Association, US Green Building Council are examples. There are many hundreds of conferences each year — most of which are listed in the Events section of our website.

What emerging or high growth careers do you see developing now and into the future for this career field? What new technologies will have the greatest impact on this field?
Since we run Green Dream Jobs, we can easily track the growth in green jobs by the kinds of jobs that are posted at our site. We've seen huge growth in all kinds of green jobs, but the top areas right now are green building and solar energy. The non-profit sector has lots of jobs — they're real job engines. They have lots of different kinds of jobs from research to policy, from developing financial instruments to advocacy for people with a wide range of skills. Yes, there are definitely emerging fields that didn't exist before. For example, carbon trading will be very big. We're seeing announcements of new technologies almost every week that promise to clean up the environment and provide us with clean, inexpensive energy. We're looking at transitioning society to a new way of doing things — the change will be massive and will generate many millions of jobs and new businesses.

Resources from Q&A
American Wind Energy Association: awea.org
Bainbridge Graduate Institute: bgiedu.org

Green Dream Jobs: greendreamjobs.com
Harvard University: harvard.edu
Natural Resources Defense Council (NRDC): nrdc.org
Progressive Investor: progressiveinvestor.com
Solar Energy Industries Association: seia.org
SustainableBusiness.com: sustainablebusiness.com
US Green Building Council/LEED AP Certification: usgbc.org
University of Michigan: umich.edu
University of North Carolina: northcarolina.edu

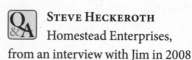 **STEVE HECKEROTH**
Homestead Enterprises,
from an interview with Jim in 2008

How did you get into this career field? What was your education and experience?
I participated in the first Earth Day in 1970 while studying architecture at Arizona State University. After getting my degree, I began designing and building passive solar homes.
I received a national award from the Energy Efficient Building Association and the Northeast Sustainable Energy Association for the design and construction of a home on the Northern California coast in 1992. I've also done a lot of teaching, including community college courses and programs for other education/training providers such as the Solar Living Institute and the American Solar Energy Society. I'm also a contributing editor to *Mother Earth News* magazine.

What is your current job title and how would you describe the work you do in a typical day? What are your most common tasks?
I am self-employed as the owner of Homestead Enterprises, a company I founded in 1975 to design and build renewable energy systems. As the owner, I spend a lot of time on the computer, answering e-mails from people interested in renewables, sourcing and ordering components and being involved in non-profit organizations. I am also doing design work, both on paper and hands-on in the shop.

If you could give advice to a young person who wants to work in this career field someday, what would you tell them? How can they best groom themselves for this field?

Make "what you believe" how you make your living. Practical hands-on experience is essential, but it is also important to have basic business knowledge. Students should look for someone in their field of interest and do an apprenticeship.

Being self-employed, how do you look at career advancement? Does it generally take the form of growing/expanding your business, or is self-employment part of a career track that may lead to something else down the road?
If your business is successful and growing, many different directions will become available. You may sell your business, keep expanding, or you may be offered an interesting job in a larger company. I worked for myself for many years before working at ECD-Ovonics as Director of Building Integrated Photovoltaic (BIPV) products. Then, after a number of years, I returned to run my own company again.

Can you suggest a salary range that someone could expect if they were to pursue work in your career field?
$40,000 to $120,000 per year.

In your opinion, what are some of the best schools, degrees and certificates for jobs in this career field?
New College in Santa Rosa, California; Humboldt State University in California; Solar Living Institute workshops in Hopland, California; and Solar Energy International workshops in Colorado.

How much experience is necessary before a person should venture into self-employment in your field? What positions should that experience be in?
At least a two- to five-year apprenticeship with businesses that are doing the same thing you want to pursue with your own business. Take architecture for example: An architect should work in construction for several years before they design buildings.

Are there any professional associations that you would recommend joining?
American Solar Energy Society, Electric Auto Association and Solar Living Institute.

What emerging or high growth careers do you see developing now and into the future for this career field? What new technologies will have the greatest impact on this field?
Manufacturing, product development, installing and marketing of building integrated photovoltaics; designing, building and marketing plug-in electric

and electric vehicles. The greatest impacts will come from flexible thin-film PV and advance battery technology.

Resources from Q&A

American Solar Energy Society (ASES): ases.org

Electric Auto Association: eaaev.org

Homestead Enterprises: renewables.com

Humboldt State University: humboldt.edu

Solar Energy International: solarenergy.org

Solar Living Institute: solarliving.org

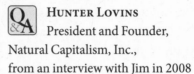

HUNTER LOVINS
President and Founder,
Natural Capitalism, Inc.,
from an interview with Jim in 2008

Hunter Lovins (far right)

How did you get into this career field? What was your education and experience, including any green-related training or certification?

My folks were always involved with trying to make the world a better place. My mother was a union organizer in the coal fields of West Virginia with John L. Lewis. My dad helped mentor César Chávez and Martin Luther King when I was growing up. So, I'm not sure I had a whole lot of choice. I worked for various groups and organizations on issues like anti-nuclear weapons, fair housing and civil rights. And then I planted trees for the first Earth Day, which, by the way, are still there! I worked with David Brower, who was the first executive director of the Sierra Club. When they fired him, I migrated with Dave to Friends of the Earth. And somewhere in there I took a couple of undergraduate degrees in sociology and political studies — with an emphasis on the environment. Then I went to law school and became a lawyer because I thought that would be a good way of achieving social change. But it turns out to be a lousy way, so I quit that. I helped create Tree People in Southern California and became their assistant director — which lasted for about six years. I did work for the United Nations. Amory Lovins and I became partners, took up traveling and worked in about 15 countries based out of London. In 1982 we created the Rocky Mountain Institute, and I ran that for about 20 years. After that I created Natural Capitalism, and here we are.

What is your current job title and how would you describe the work you do in a typical day? What are your most common tasks, including those that make yours a green job?

I'm the president of Natural Capitalism, Inc. We have someone who handles the day-to-day operations, and we run the place as a partnership. We're very collaborative in our decision-making and very collaborative with the staff. Our director of research and various other staff are generally involved in any significant decision. So, in terms of what I do, I roam the planet and try to help people implement solutions to major challenges that are facing us. It seems like we're losing every major ecosystem on the planet, and we're in a global climate crisis. We have very scary population demographics! Economic fragility. Water is going to be an even greater crisis than energy. All of our infrastructure is vulnerable. And then we have what I call the "Sustainability Imperative" — which answers such questions as Why is Wal-Mart going green? Short answer: they don't have a choice. So I work with companies, countries and communities to help them solve whatever problem is facing them at the time. As a result, I consult for everything from Wal-Mart to the government of Afghanistan.

If you could give advice to a young person who wants to work in this career field someday, what would you tell them? How can they best groom themselves for this field?

Find what you really care about and live a life that shows it. Study everything. When people tell you that you have to pick one major, tell them that half the jobs that are going to exist in 2015 haven't been invented yet. And what really matters are the interconnections between disciplines, not post-holing yourself into any one of them. Learn how to work with people and how to communicate. But before that, learn how to think. Always assume that every theory you're working on could well be wrong. And you're going to have to reinvent whatever your approach is or whatever your position is. And just be comfortable with that. There is an old Hebrew saying, "If you want to see God smile, make a plan." Hence, I literally do not know on a given day, waking up, what it is I'm going to be doing that day. I can make plans about it, but generally the universe catches me by surprise.

Now, if you want to get into the consulting biz, just as if you want to get into the writing or speaking biz, the best way to do it is to do it. The next best way is to get with somebody who is good at it and apprentice yourself with them and learn how it's done right. But, for the most part, the only way you're going to learn how to do it is to do it.

In your opinion, what are some of the best schools, degrees and certificates for jobs in this career field, including green–specific training?
Study with the people who are doing the work that you want to do. And they can appear in the tiniest of universities on the planet. A big famous university with tenure may have a more difficult time shaking up their programs and integrating sustainability, but that's not always the case. I know some wonderful professors at the Kabul University (in Afghanistan). I'm also rather fond of the place where I teach — the Presidio School of Management in San Francisco, California. If you want a business degree, I'd highly recommend that one. Our green MBA program was one of the first in the country and actually the first one to be accredited.

Are there any professional associations that you would recommend joining?
There are a growing number of associations. If you're in green building, you have the US Green Building Council. If you're in renewable energy, you have the Solar Energy Society and many others to choose from. I just joined the International Society of Sustainability Professionals. They seem to be doing a pretty good job of putting on seminars for this topic. I would advise people to get on a whole bunch of mailing lists, look around to see who's offering what, and if they don't cost too much, join them. Give it a go and if you aren't getting what you need, quit and join something else.

What emerging careers do you see developing now and into the future for this career field? What new technologies will have the greatest impact on this field?
A whole bunch. Every company and educational institution is going to need a sustainability coordinator. If your passion is engineering, engineering for sustainability is a rapidly growing field. The whole green building field is just exploding. Everything from architects to general contractors. The public policy field is also exploding. Increasingly, politicians need somebody on their staff who understands this stuff. It really is only the beginning. If what you want is to get your hands dirty, there are green-collar jobs. We're going to need people everywhere in the nation implementing energy efficiency, water efficiency and installing solar energy systems. Every community is going to need people who understand these issues. With the rising price of oil, the whole notion of what is a viable career could come apart at the seams pretty quickly. And then the careers that matter could be farming and vehicle repair. Or maybe wagon repair. The ability to be light on your feet, not very deep in debt and have a useful career is pretty darn important.

Resources from Q&A

American Solar Energy Society (ASES): ases.org

Friends of the Earth: foe.org

International Society of Sustainability Professionals (ISSP):
    sustainabilityprofessionals.org

International Solar Energy Society (ISES): www.ises.org

Natural Capitalism, Inc.: natcapinc.com

Presidio School of Management: presidiomba.org

Rocky Mountain Institute: rmi.org

Tree People: treepeople.org

US Green Building Council/LEED AP Certification: usgbc.org

 ED MURRAY, President, Aztec Solar, Inc.,
from an interview with Jim in 2008

How did you get into this career field? What was your education and experience, including any green-related training or certification?

I moved here from Boston in 1977 and was working on a degree in business administration and working at a lumber yard. One day a customer came in to the lumber yard and asked me to work on the weekend for the company he was working for. It was called Natural Heating Systems and was based out of West Sacramento, California. So I took him up on the offer. Since then I've had many trainings, including NABCEP certified, and I'm a general contractor and a solar contractor in the State of California.

What is your current job title and how would you describe the work you do in a typical day? What are your most common tasks?

I'm the president of Aztec Solar. I manage day-to-day operations for a solar contracting firm, and I also have a wholesale distribution company. My most common tasks include overseeing the P&L and accounts receivables. I make financial decisions on a daily basis, including the procurement of financing and distribution agreements with suppliers. I'm the final say as financial dealings go. I'm also involved in customer relations and oversee employees, although I'm the last step in the management chain. I'm also the treasurer for the California Solar Energy Industries Association (CALSEIA).

If you could give advice to a young person who wants to work in this career field someday, what would you tell them? How can they best groom themselves for this field?

Well, I have a perfect example: my general manager. When I hired him, he was going to high school, and during the summers, he'd work for me doing installation services, including installing hot water and pool heaters. Then he went to college, but again during the summers, he came to work for us. Then he did his senior thesis on the company itself. So I thought he'd be a prime candidate for my general manager because he knew the business from the ground up. And he's been here ever since. Now he's even got his MBA degree — which helps our company.

What kind of career advancement opportunities can one expect in this field? What kind of salary range would reflect that career path (from entry-level to the more advanced position)?
The entry level would be parts runner — picking up parts for the job. From there, installation of the solar heaters. And then crew chief of the solar installations. And then installation manager — overseeing all installations. You could also be a service technician, if you have enough experience and can repair the systems. And that's a pretty good job in itself. And then you can go into operations management. In California, today's starting-level installer would be somewhere around $12 an hour and then tip up toward $16 an hour for experienced installers. Crew chief is $17 to $20 an hour. Service technicians make up to $25 an hour, and operations managers are somewhere around $25 an hour.

As the owner of the company, career advancement takes on a whole new meaning. For example, in 2007 I sold my company to a large German firm. I sold it because I thought that I wanted to grow into a nationwide business. I was making a pretty good living, but I wanted to grow the company even further. So the company I sold it to made me the director of their solar thermal division. Then, later that year, they decided that they were opting out of the solar thermal business. They put my old company up for sale, and I purchased it back again. From this experience, I learned more than I ever wanted to know about the corporate world and more than I ever wanted to know about Microsoft Excel and PowerPoint.

In your opinion, what are some of the best schools, degrees and certificates for jobs in this career field, including green–specific training?
Schools in our communities are looking for funding to get programs for solar installers in place, so I think the community colleges would be the first place I'd look. I'm on the technical committee for the Solar Rating and Certification Corporation (SRCC), and there are many schools in the community — from colleges to universities — popping up with new curriculum on solar. So there's a renewed interest, and it's becoming popular again, which is refreshing.

How does someone without previous experience in this career field land a job? What are the best strategies for job-hunting in this field?
We just advertised for a crew leader this week in the newspaper, and we use all forms of advertising. But I would say Craigslist and newspaper advertisements. If you were in the upper echelon of management, you could talk to the headhunters. We also use temp agency employees, so we might occasionally find an installer through a temp agency and keep them for the long term.

Are there any professional associations that you would recommend joining?
NABCEP, or the North American Board of Certified Energy Practitioners. I would recommend getting the curriculum and testing for that certification. That would get you a leg up on other installers. You might also look into your "local" Solar Energy Association.

What emerging careers do you see developing now and into the future for this career field? What new technologies will have the greatest impact on this field?
The latest technology for solar is the thin-film roll-roofing type of material that would be for applying solar to commercial buildings on a roofing application. So the people that have both the roofing knowledge and the solar knowledge will be more likely to get work in the future. And that technology will probably be full born by 2011.

Resources from Q&A

Aztec Solar, Inc.: AztecSolar.com
California Solar Energy Industries Association (CALSEIA): calseia.org
Craigslist: craigslist.org
North American Board of Certified Energy Practitioners (NABCEP):
    nabcep.org
Solar Rating and Certification Corporation (SRCC): solar–rating.org

LES NELSON
Western Renewables Group,
from an interview with Jim in 2008

How did you get into this career field? What was your education and experience?
I entered this field directly out of high school and got started by doing rote mathematical calculations for a start-up solar thermal or water and space heating manufacturer in 1972. I also helped construct prototype solar collectors for

testing purposes. I had no special schooling beyond somewhat of an aptitude for mathematics and scale model building.

What is your current job title and how would you describe the work you do in a typical day? What are your most common tasks?
I have several job titles, the foremost being executive director of one entity, as well as treasurer of another, director of two more and subcontractor for a government contract. I would characterize my most common tasks as interacting with others in the solar industry by phone and e-mail, writing reports, performing advocacy work for solar energy in general at the state and federal levels and educating individuals in various state and federal agencies about the energy conservation and emission reduction capabilities of solar energy.

If you could give advice to a young person who wants to work in this career field someday, what would you tell them? How can they best groom themselves for this field?
I would recommend that a young person become involved in the day-to-day operation of a solar energy contracting company, either as an installer apprentice or in a dispatcher or customer relations position. This way the person will begin to understand the reality of interacting with the public — who ultimately has to purchase solar energy in order for all contractors and manufacturers to be successful. The next step would be sales directly with end users.

Being self-employed, how do you look at career advancement? Does it generally take the form of growing/expanding your business, or is self-employment part of a career track that may lead to something else down the road?
I view career advancement as keeping busy with contract assignments that I am paid to fulfill. There are many entities that would have you work for them on a volunteer basis, and I have at least three such engagements at this time. However, volunteer assignments do not pay bills, although they may enhance your chances of acquiring contracts with remuneration. Personally, I am not interested in becoming employed by someone else; I prefer self-employment. I am not interested in substantially increasing the size of my business, which would entail employing and managing others. I prefer to manage the size of my business to allow for me to set my own schedule. I prefer to explore and take on contractual opportunities as I see fit.

Can you suggest a salary range that someone could expect if they were to pursue work in your career field?
As a consultant in the solar energy field, with adequate experience in a given specialty or sector of the industry, it would not be unreasonable to expect to

generate a net income of $100,000 to $150,000 in the early years. This would not, however, be a salary; it would be on a contractual basis.

In your opinion, what are some of the best schools, degrees and certificates for jobs in this career field?
Several items come to mind: a contractor's license in some jurisdiction; NABCEP certified from the North American Board of Certified Energy Practitioners; solar training courses from SEI (Solar Energy International); and a degree in project financing and development or economic analysis.

How much experience is necessary before a person should venture into self-employment in your field? What positions should that experience be in?
I would say at least ten years in a position which enabled the accumulation of experience in hands-on solar activities, which would allow one to speak with some authority when dealing with policy development activities. I would urge that entry-level people begin by either taking a job as an installer of solar equipment or in an administrative role with a contractor to accumulate first-hand knowledge of the sales and installation of solar equipment, as well as a working knowledge of how it functions. Alternatively, if an individual is suited to direct sales, adequate knowledge can be accumulated quickly to allow for rapid entry into the industry. Anecdotally, some of the best solar sales people have no prior knowledge of solar technology.

Are there any professional associations that you would recommend joining?
The Solar Energy Industries Association and the American Solar Energy Society.

What emerging or high-growth careers do you see developing now and into the future for this career field? What new technologies will have the greatest impact on this field?
Photovoltaics (PV) are the hot item, although solar thermal is much more affordable. The promise of lower costs for PV has been promised for many years; however it has not transitioned into lower-cost products in the marketplace. Installation and/or sales in either technology will grow in the future, although since it is essentially a home or small business improvement item, sales track the economy in terms of locating interested customers with disposable income.

Resources from Q&A
American Solar Energy Society: ases.org
North American Board of Certified Energy Practitioners (NABCEP):
    nabcep.org

Solar Energy Industries Association: seia.org
Solar Energy International (SEI): solarenergy.org

 DEBORA (DEBE) OVERHAUG
President and CEO, PRC
Technologies (soy-based print cartridges),
from an interview with Alice in 2008

*How did you get into this career field? What
was your education and experience, including
any green-related training or certification?*
I have a bachelor of science in finance, and
I've spent my career in finance and manage-
ment. My company introduced a new toner cartridge using toner powder
from soybeans instead of oil. PRC was started in 1992 by a Maine state trooper
re–inking ribbons in his basement. I took over the company in 2005. I am very
excited about SoyPrint, our soy-based cartridges.

*What is your current job title and how would you describe the work you do in a
typical day? What are your most common tasks, including those that make yours
a green job?*
As president and CEO, my job consists of developing the big picture of where
PRC should be five years from now, putting the plan in place and removing
the roadblocks for my employees. Although my job itself is not particularly
green, it's our product and how we sell it that makes us green. We are bringing
this soy-based toner cartridge to market first because we paid attention when
the first article about soy toner came out in 2006. We immediately saw the potential for this product. We followed up with people, worked hard to bring the
toner manufacturer and cartridge manufacturer together so they could produce a product for us to sell. I helped to coordinate this effort and invested
time and resources in a new product. I believe our success was dependent on
determination, creativity and boldness.

*If you could give advice to a young person who wants to work in this career field
someday, what would you tell them? How can they best groom themselves for
this field?*
My advice is to do something you are passionate about. Then it doesn't seem
so much like work! In our field, determination, persistence and the ability to
understand customer needs are the most critical skills.

What kind of career advancement opportunities can one expect in this field? What kind of salary range would reflect that career path (from entry-level to the more advanced position)?

We have positions in customer service, sales and account management. We also employ two printer service technicians who service printers. Sales and account management positions work directly with customers. These positions start out at $40,000 to $50,000. Commissions might be paid as well. Customer service is an hourly position paying $25,000 to $30,000 per year. A customer service rep could transition into sales. For me, career advancement is different. Advancement is going to come if the company grows. But self-employment is risky and is not for everyone. You don't always know how you are going to make payroll or whether a new venture will take off. For the president, the final decision is yours — win or lose. That's scary and not everyone likes it.

In your opinion, what are some of the best schools, degrees and certificates for jobs in this career field, including green–specific training?

I have come to value a liberal arts education more and more. This gives students a broad perspective as they move forward. There are numerous wonderful schools with this type of degree.

How does someone without previous experience in this career field land a job? What are the best strategies for job-hunting in this field?

The cover letter is the most important part of job-hunting. Use it to explain how your experience fits with the job requirements. Don't be afraid to stand out and be different. Let the employer know YOU are the best person for this job and convey what you'll do better than anyone else.

How much experience is necessary before a person should venture into self-employment in your field? What positions should that experience be in?

If someone wanted to sell toner cartridges, their best experience would be in sales. Alternatively, they could work for a manufacturer, learning about the product from the inside. They could then apply this knowledge as they moved into the marketplace.

Are there any professional associations that you would recommend joining?

International Imaging Technology Council (Int'l ITC).

What emerging careers do you see developing now and into the future for this career field? What new technologies will have the greatest impact on this field?

All tech companies are trying to find ways to be greener. They have changed the packaging and packing materials. We've changed the toner. Many are starting to recycle empty cartridges. We have to find creative ways to reuse materials instead of simply throwing everything into landfills.

Resources from Q&A

International Imaging Technology Council (Int'l ITC): i-itc.org
PRC Technologies: soyprint.net

Q&A LEE REICH,
Horticultural Consultant and Writer,
from an interview with Jim in 2008

How did you get into this career field? What was your education and experience, including any green-related training or certification?
I was studying chemistry in graduate school and then stopped and went into horticulture. I got three degrees in soils and horticulture, including a doctoral degree. Then I started working for Cornell University doing research on fruit crops. I guess in the back of my mind I always thought I'd like to work from home, for myself and write for a living. I don't know why I thought that, because I never particularly liked to write when I was in school, and I was never a particularly good writer. But I did start writing a little while I was with Cornell, and when that job ended, I started writing a little more. I always had a lot of enthusiasm for gardening and horticulture and agriculture and soils. So I just started writing more. I think most garden writers start out as journalists, where they just happen to be backyard gardeners. But I had all these degrees, and so I just started writing more and more, and then in conjunction with that, I was giving a lot of lectures and doing some degree of consulting.

What is your current job title and how would you describe the work you do in a typical day? What are your most common tasks?
I guess I could call myself a horticulturalist, or I could call myself a garden writer. On my business card, it says I'm a "garden and orchard consultant." But what I do depends on the season. This time of year, I do some amount of writing, some amount of gardening and perhaps some traveling somewhere to give a talk. And when I say writing, that includes related stuff like editing and research. I write for a lot of different publications, including weekly columns for local newspapers, biweekly columns for the Associated Press, magazine articles for a number of publications, and I've written books. In the last

few years, I've also been doing a lot of photography. And, of course, I garden like a maniac!

If you could give advice to a young person who wants to work in this career field someday, what would you tell them? How can they best groom themselves for this field?
The first thing I would say is "don't do it!" After that, I would say "academics." Especially in this field, the experts usually just have a lot of experience. But I don't really think that cuts it. I think you've got to go to some — perhaps — "dry books" to get the information and to know the subject. As a writer, you also need to get used to rejection, because writers get a lot of rejection, and you need to learn to not take it personally. And while I think the college degree is really important, you don't necessarily have to have a college degree to be a published garden writer or consultant. You may not be able to make a living at it, but maybe you could. It would depend on the person.

In your opinion, what are some of the best schools, degrees and certificates for jobs in this career field, including green-specific training?
The usual top horticulture schools in the nation: Cornell, Michigan, UC Davis — there's a lot of them. But it depends more on the person and how much enthusiasm they can put into it. I've seen people come out of some of those programs, and I've been amazed at how little they know. So I think it depends more on their enthusiasm. I may be unique because of my advanced degrees, but I'm constantly reading the popular press and scientific papers to acquire new information.

Are there any professional associations that you would recommend joining?
I belong to the American Society for Horticulture Science, which I would not necessarily recommend to someone who just wants to be a garden writer, but I like it because I get the journals which are at the cutting edge of the science part. So I like to read the source science journals so I can evaluate some of the research. Since food crops are one of my main interests, I belong to a group called the North American Fruit Explorers, or NAFEX. I also belong to the California Rare Fruit Growers, even though I don't live in California. But on occasion, I'll write for them. I also belong to the Garden Writers Association — which has been most useful to me, especially when I did my first book about 20 years ago.

What emerging careers do you see developing now and into the future for this career field? What new technologies will have the greatest impact on this field?

There are always new technologies being promoted, but with my science background, I'm not usually all that wowed by any new technology. Drip irrigation is not really a new technology, but it's not widely used outside of California, and I think it's a great thing to use almost anywhere, even in the East, if you're going to water. Because it saves water, it's better for the plant and better for the soil. Another technology to watch is organic techniques, which are growing in popularity. Better for the environment and better for people's health. And a new thing I've been researching is the use of vinegar as a herbicide. I told the USDA about it — whom I also used to work for — and it turns out they've been researching it, too. Except that they've been using concentrated vinegar, which I don't think is necessary. Just use regular vinegar and mix it with a little soap and vegetable oil to help it stick better.

Resources from Q&A
American Society for Horticulture Science (ASHS): ashs.org
California Rare Fruit Growers: crfg.org
Cornell University: cornell.edu
Garden Writers Association: gardenwriters.org
LeeReich.com: leereich.com
Michigan State University: msu.edu
North American Fruit Explorers (NAFEX): nafex.org
US Department of Agriculture (USDA): usda.gov
University of California, Davis: ucdavis.edu

Jim Steinmetz

Q&A   JIM STEINMETZ
President, Reusable Lumber Company,
from an interview with Alice in 2008

How did you get into this career field? What was your education and experience, including any green-related training or certification?
I spent seven years working in an environmental action non-profit organization. After two years as executive co-director there, I left to found this company. During college and the seven years at non-profits, I supplemented my income by working in the construction industry.

What is your current job title and how would you describe the work you do in a typical day? What are your most common tasks, including those that make yours a green job?

My title is business owner. I deconstruct buildings and reclaim building materials for reuse, from both demolition and new construction, all manner of lumber, masonry, metals, windows and other building components. Transporting, remilling, reprocessing, remarketing and selling the materials we have collected, in both the wholesale and retail markets.

What makes it a green job? We're helping to keep industry out of the forest and to keep resource out of landfills; our larger goals are to shrink the size of recycling loops and to minimize the carbon footprint of the construction industry.

If you could give advice to a young person who wants to work in this career field someday, what would you tell them? How can they best groom themselves for this field?
Get hands-on experience in the sustainable construction industry/movement. Get experience with any kind of demolition — the wider the variety the better — so you can observe how truly wasteful conventional demolition practices are. Garner an understanding of the global economy and your own region's economy, and how they're embracing and incorporating new sustainable practices into day-to-day business procedures. Get an internship; identify a new market niche. Do not be afraid to try new solutions and lose money or fail in the process. That risk is part of the learning curve; that approach keeps you on the cutting edge.

What kind of career advancement opportunities can one expect in this field? What kind of salary range would reflect that career path (from entry-level to the more advanced position)?
The industry of deconstruction and material reclamation is still in its infancy, relative to what it will be. It's been estimated that only two to ten percent of all demolition debris are reclaimed. There's a lot of room to grow. However, entry-level positions are sometimes hard to come by. But the industry is growing exponentially right now, due partly to new waste reduction regulations and the need to reduce GHG (greenhouse gas) emissions. The salary range for unskilled deconstruction work is $12.50 to $25 per hour in California. Highly skilled laborers with special tools and abilities can earn $25 to $50 per hour. If you own your own business in a smaller market area, your annual income would vary between $40,000 and $90,000. In a larger market, the sky is the limit: $100,000 to $500,000. Plenty of people have tried this line of work and have left; it isn't easy; be prepared to suffer.

Being self-employed, I don't think of my occupation as a career. I look at it as my lifestyle — a path I'm on in life. I consider myself an artist, and this is where I'm doing my creative work right now. Personally speaking, I enjoy a high level of autonomy and personal creative operating freedom; I won't give that up unless forced or compensated handsomely.

In your opinion, what are some of the best schools, degrees and certificates for jobs in this career field, including green-specific training?
Apply for the top schools in the nation. Make connections; follow green technologies; use every bit of energy and influence that you develop to spur this expanding industry; put your foot in every single door. Relevant majors include: civil engineering, business, construction management, marketing and natural resource management.

How does someone without previous experience in this career field land a job? What are the best strategies for job-hunting in this field?
Do your research. Find out what's going on in your area; if there's no work in your area, look to the next closest region. Be entrepreneurial. Make a trial run and see what happens. If you like it, then give it a shot. Your first effort could be something as small as using weathered fence boards to make rustic birdhouses. Learn by doing.

How much experience is necessary before a person should venture into self-employment in your field? What positions should that experience be in?
Two to three years in construction, demolition or a construction-related industry. Experience with green development or resale of anything would be good, too. Start small and build up; don't quit your day job during the first few years.

Are there any professional associations that you would recommend joining?
LEED certification is helpful to have these days. But I'm more of a doer; I like to set an example by doing, rather than joining yet another organization or getting another certification. I'm not against them; I just think maybe there are too many out there. I'm more focused on tangible solutions.

What emerging careers do you see developing now and into the future for this career field? What new technologies will have the greatest impact on this field?
Deconstruction as a construction trade and career is expanding, and it's not just lumber that is being salvaged. There's a lot of opportunity to increase the portion of concrete, steel, gypsum board and other materials that get recycled.

The future of the profession: Managing the redistribution and reprocessing of reclaimed materials on a large scale, from building components to bricks and steel. The new trends that will have greatest impact:

a) New methods and ways of managing hazardous materials encountered in demolition, such as lead-based paint and PCBs (polychlorinated biphenyls). Better ways of integrating hazardous material remediation with building material salvage will increase efficiencies.

b) Locating a construction salvage yard next to a cogeneration plant or anaerobic digester, so that otherwise unusable organic waste can be converted to energy and fuel.

c) Paradigm change: Garbage will no longer be seen as a waste problem; rather it will be seen as a raw natural resource.

Resources from Q&A

US Green Building Council/LEED AP Certification: usgbc.org
Reusable Lumber Company: reusablelumber.com

Q&A   FRED WOOD
Greenlight Magazine and
Pattiwood Productions,
from an interview with Alice in 2008

How did you get into this career field? What was your education and experience, including any green-related training or certification?
I graduated from the University of Pennsylvania with a bachelor of arts degree in communications. I was interested in film, but took the first "media-related" job I could find, which at that time was for a 200-year-old textbook publisher named J. B. Lippincott. I've been working in media ever since, usually for myself or for established book or magazine publishers, for over 20 years now. Starting a magazine seemed like a natural next step after working for years on magazine titles for which I had little personal interest. But I have also started with others a book publishing company called Delancey Press in Philadelphia, a marketing consultancy in San Francisco called Next Steps Marketing and then, solo, a media marketing agency called Pattiwood Productions.

What is your current job title and how would you describe the work you do in a typical day? What are your most common tasks?
I'm the CFO of Greenlight Magazine, but that is more of a vocation. The job that pays my bills is as a business consultant for media and software companies where I'm the founder and CEO. One of the things we learned in publishing *Greenlight* was how difficult it is to produce a break-even publication in an

emerging market, like the green space. So my work for the magazine typically involves writing and editing and production for a period and then nothing for awhile, until we do it all again. A typical day for me is desk-work related to serving my Pattiwood Productions clients' needs through e-mail and phone (I work from home). I work on relationship building, spreadsheet creation, promotional writing, business presentations and within software designed for research and publishing.

If you could give advice to a young person who wants to work in this career field someday, what would you tell them? How can they best groom themselves for this field?

In publishing or "media," which is a better word these days to describe the business in a post-Internet world, it's really a catch-all career for folks who are not good at anything else. There are so many niches where the person with quirky career needs can be met. Copy editing is an example. Some copy editors rarely meet up with another human and are quite successful and happy. Of course, other media professionals, like Anderson Cooper for example, are stars, so there's a huge range of careers under a very broad umbrella. I suppose the advice for a young person is the same for this career as any other: follow your dreams; do what appeals to you; take advantage of opportunity when it is placed in front of you and move on when it starts to hurt.

Being self-employed, how do you look at career advancement? Does it generally take the form of growing/expanding your business, or is self-employment part of a career track that may lead to something else down the road?

Being self-employed is just a choice to create your own career life, instead of choosing one that is designed for you by others. Entrepreneurs are a certain type of person who is comfortable with challenges, uncertainty and like to lead. Career advancement isn't really applicable to an entrepreneur. You put your energies into making your businesses thrive and enjoy taking ideas you have and turning them into living entities. A corporation is a separately taxed entity in the eyes of the law, so, legally, you are actually giving birth when you incorporate. Self-employment can give you the opportunity to build a different set of skills from the ones you might end up with after being an employee, and some people can successfully move back and forth from employment to self-employment, and back again.

Can you suggest a salary range that someone could expect if they were to pursue work in your career field?

That's impossible to answer. Many self-employed people make only enough to survive — that's the reason they are self-employed: to give themselves complete control over their own time. My brother, who is self-employed, works six months a year as a landscape designer and takes six months off each year to "winter" in South America. Other self-employed people, like one of my other brothers who is a chiropractor, are very well off. After ten years, he has substantial savings, a paid-off home, a 30-foot boat and much more. So think of it as a potential range from a living wage to being a billionaire.

In your opinion, what are some of the best schools, degrees and certificates for jobs in this career field?

Interestingly enough, many entrepreneurs are not college graduates, or they have degrees that don't always linearly suggest their business success. I suppose an MBA would provide one with business training that is beneficial in understanding the fiscal aspects of business success, but sales training might be just as helpful. Of course there are some pretty clear graduate school paths that can often lead to self-employment, such as a degree in medicine, dentistry or law. It's more important to find out if you're the right personality type for self-employment/entrepreneurship than going out and getting a certain type of education under your belt. Myers-Briggs type personality tests can help, but just talking to others who have started businesses on their own is the best education.

How much experience is necessary before a person should venture into self-employment in your field? What positions should that experience be in?

I think entrepreneurs just go for it when they're ready. I worked in traditional corporate jobs for 15 years before going out on my own, so that was helpful to me in terms of learning management skills and finding out what a P/L (profit and loss) is. But, my brother the chiropractor always intended to work on his own and apprenticed with another professional right out of school. Over time he bought into the business and became an owner. My third brother, so far unmentioned, is doing the same thing in the field of law. So, it depends on the person and their personality type and ambitions. It probably also falls in the area of luck and chance fairly often: I started my second business, Next Steps Marketing, mainly because I had been swept into unemployment by the tech downturn of 2000, and it seemed unlikely I'd get another job soon. I also had a severance package to live off of until my partners and I really got the business going.

Are there any professional associations that you would recommend joining?
I think business consultants can be more successful if they are well-known in the community they serve and join a professional organization (or many) that represents the people they would like to be their clients. This provides the opportunity for networking and a higher likelihood of new business derived from business listings or referrals. Associations usually provide opportunities to speak at conferences and trade shows, which also goes a long way towards raising one's profile and bringing in new client business.

What emerging or high-growth careers do you see developing now and into the future for this career field? What new technologies will have the greatest impact on this field?
The Internet will fuel careers for many young people who want to work outside of the traditional range of careers. It also allows people to have multiple careers, fueled by the low cost of entry provided by marketing through the Internet. If more people realized how easy it is to set up a new business, and how cost-effective and targeted advertising on the Internet is becoming, more would move into the ranks of the self-employed. If the recession worsens in 2009 and more people are laid off, we may find many more Americans have the entrepreneur spirit than we imagined.

Resources from Q&A
Pattiwood Productions: pattiwoodpro.com
University of Pennsylvania (Penn): upenn.edu

Marketing Managers, including Environmental Marketing Specialists

Marketing managers determine the demand for products and services offered by a firm and its competitors and identify potential customers. Develop pricing strategies with the goal of maximizing the firm's profits or share of the market while ensuring the firm's customers are satisfied. Oversee product development or monitor trends that indicate the need for new products and services.

Qualifications and Advancement
A bachelor's degree or higher in business administration, management or marketing, plus extensive experience in related occupations, is the typical requirement. In highly technical industries, employers prefer a bachelor's degree in engineering or science, combined with a master's degree in business administration (MBA).

Most marketing managers gain experience in the occupation by working for several years as product or brand specialists. Because of the importance and high visibility of their jobs, marketing managers often are prime candidates for advancement to the highest ranks. Some may work as consultants or open their own business.

Salary Survey
Median salary: $98,720 (very high)
Typical range: $70,080 to $136,710

Job Outlook and Employment
Faster than average growth is projected for this occupation in the US, from 167,464 jobs in 2006 to 191,549 in 2016. Job growth will be spurred by intense domestic and global competition in products and services offered to consumers and increasing activity in television, radio and outdoor advertising.

Where the Jobs Are
Management of companies and enterprises (11.87%); Computer systems design/related services (4.78%); Depository credit intermediation (3.25%); Management, scientific and technical consulting services (3.24%); Self-employed: 2.33%

Resources
American Marketing Association (AMA): marketingpower.com
O*NET OnLine: online.onetcenter.org (see marketing managers)
Sales & Marketing Executives International (SMEI): smei.org
US Dept. of Labor, Bureau of Labor Statistics: bls.gov/oco/ocos020.htm

Q&A ANDREA GRAY
Director of Marketing and Public Relations,
Acterra: Action for a Sustainable Earth,
from an interview with Alice in 2008

How did you get into this career field? What was your education and experience, including any green-related training or certification?

My education was a bachelor's degree in physical education — completely unrelated to anything I have ever done professionally. I was recruited by P&G (Procter & Gamble) as a brand manager and worked in marketing for six years. I developed strong consumer marketing, strategy and project management experience. Then I worked at a number of start-ups in product marketing and learned to work in small-budget organizations. I have no professional green related training; just a personal interest.

What is your current job title and how would you describe the work you do in a typical day? What are your most common tasks, including those that make yours a green job?
Social marketing, getting people to change their behaviors to live more sustainably. Program development, partnership opportunities, publicity, branding strategies and community outreach.

If you could give advice to a young person who wants to work in this career field someday, what would you tell them? How can they best groom themselves for this field?
All experience counts. Marketing green products/services is no different than marketing non-green products/services; it is just more exciting to market something that makes the world a better place. It is important to understand the terminology, trends and issues in any field in which you are working and "green" is no exception.

What kind of career advancement opportunities can one expect in this field? What kind of salary range would reflect that career path (from entry-level to the more advanced position)?
It depends on the type of organization, such as for-profit or non-profit, and how big a role marketing plays in the organization.

How does someone without previous experience in this career field land a job? What are the best strategies for job-hunting in this field?
Focus on how your previous job experience will help you market and manage a project. Be informed on the issues to demonstrate that you can acquire the technical knowledge.

Are there any professional associations that you would recommend joining?
Not really. Volunteer with some environmental organizations, join some advocacy groups — this is the best way to understand what is going on and what the public is thinking on different issues. This knowledge is always helpful to a marketer.

What emerging careers do you see developing now and into the future for this career field? What new technologies will have the greatest impact on this field?
Social networking tools, new online communication tools. These are great and green ways to get our environmental messages out.

Resources from Q&A
Acterra: Action for a Sustainable Earth: acterra.org
Procter & Gamble: pg.com

Refuse and Recyclable Material Collectors, including Recycling Technicians

Refuse and recyclable material collectors collect and dump refuse or recyclable materials from containers into truck. May drive truck.

Qualifications and Advancement
Recycling collectors and technicians generally learn skills informally, on the job, from more experienced workers or their supervisors. Some employers prefer applicants with a high-school diploma, but most simply require workers to be at least 18 years old and physically able to perform the work. Workers who use industrial trucks must receive specialized training in safety awareness and procedures. Many of the training requirements are standardized through the US Occupational Safety and Health Administration. This training is usually provided by the employer.

Advancement may lead to supervisory positions.

Salary Survey
Median salary: $28,970 (low/moderate)
Typical range: $21,550 to $38,490

Job Outlook and Employment
Average growth is projected for this general occupation in the US, from 135,970 jobs in 2006 to 146,047 in 2016. In addition, job openings for this occupation should be plentiful due to the fact that there will be many openings created by the need to replace workers who transfer to other occupations or who retire or leave the labor force for other reasons — characteristic of occupations requiring little or no formal training prior to employment.

Where the Jobs Are
Waste collection (32.5%); Waste treatment and disposal (15.26%); Self-employment: 5.78%

Resources
National Recycling Coalition (NRC): nrc–recycle.org
O*NET OnLine: online.onetcenter.org (see refuse and recyclable material collectors)

Recycler's World: recycle.net
Solid Waste Association of North America (SWANA): swana.org
US Dept. of Labor, Bureau of Labor Statistics: bls.gov/oco/ocos243.htm

Q&A John P. Ryan
Recycling Facility Manager,
Waste Connections, Inc.,
from an interview with Alice in 2008

How did you get into this career field? What was your education and experience, including any green-related training or certification?
My undergraduate through post-graduate work was all done at Colorado State University in zoology, parasitology and protozology. I needed a career change and opted out of the cyclical construction industry. A friend said he needed help in setting up a state-mandated recycling program, so I signed on in 1989.

What is your current job title and how would you describe the work you do in a typical day? What are your most common tasks, including those that make yours a green job?
I'm the facility manager at the Cold Canyon Processing Facility, a Waste Connections, Inc. company. A typical day in the office involves administration, overseeing operations and marketing of 160 tons per day of single-stream commercial and residential curbside recycling. We keep it out of the Cold Canyon Landfill, so it doesn't get any greener than that!

If you could give advice to a young person who wants to work in this career field someday, what would you tell them? How can they best groom themselves for this field?
For a career in recycling management, go to college and get a degree in plant management/business administration — preferably a master's degree.

What kind of career advancement opportunities can one expect in this field? What kind of salary range would reflect that career path (from entry-level to the more advanced position)?
A person with an affinity for running a facility like this can expect to start out at $52,000 a year and go up to $120,000 a year, depending on the size of the facility and the part of this country it's located in. Getting on with larger Wall

Street companies like Waste Connections, Allied, Republic or Waste Management allows incredible advancement opportunities.

In your opinion, what are some of the best schools, degrees and certificates for jobs in this career field, including green–specific training?
On the West Coast, I like Cal Poly, San Luis Obispo, UC Santa Barbara and UC Davis. Because this is a field that is much in demand, there are many good universities offering great programs in the field of environmental engineering.

How does someone without previous experience in this career field land a job? What are the best strategies for job-hunting in this field?
Go to work for a garbage company that has a MRF (Materials Recovery Facility). Start out as a driver or an equipment operator.

Are there any professional associations that you would recommend joining?
Maybe SWANA (Solid Waste Association of North America).

What emerging careers do you see developing now and into the future for this career field? What new technologies will have the greatest impact on this field?
I think mechanical and electrical engineering will factor into this field in a big way. International business will be important because of the global market. Any kind of manufacturing disciplines will be of great value in this type of processing.

Resources from Q&A
Allied Waste Industries, Inc.: alliedwaste.com
Cal Poly, San Luis Obispo: calpoly.edu
Republic Services, Inc.: republicservices.com
Solid Waste Association of North America (SWANA): swana.org
University of California, Davis: ucdavis.edu
University of California, Santa Barbara: ucsb.edu
Waste Connections, Inc.: wasteconnections.com
Waste Management, Inc.: wm.com

Sales Representatives, including Renewable Energy and Natural/Organic Products Sales Reps

Sales representatives (wholesale and manufacturing, technical and scientific products) sell goods for wholesalers or manufacturers where technical or scientific knowledge is required in such areas as biology, engineering, chemistry and electronics.

Qualifications and Advancement

There is no formal educational requirement for sales representative, so the education and training requirements vary by industry, employer and product. However, a bachelor's degree can be highly desirable, especially for sales reps who work with technical and scientific products. About one in four sales reps have a bachelor's degree, and many others have completed some college. Many sales reps attend seminars to enhance their sales skills and product knowledge. Often, companies have formal training programs for beginning sales reps that can last up to two years.

Advancement often takes the form of an assignment to a larger account or territory where commissions are likely to be greater. Those with good sales records and leadership ability may advance to higher-level positions such as sales supervisor or sales manager. Others find opportunities in purchasing, advertising or marketing research.

Salary Survey

Median salary: $64,440 (very high)

Typical range: $45,630 to $91,090

Job Outlook and Employment

Average growth is projected for this occupation in the US, from 410,948 jobs in 2006 to 461,852 in 2016. Employment growth will be greatest in independent sales companies as manufacturers and wholesalers continue to outsource sales activities to independent agents rather than using in-house or direct sales workers. Independent agent companies are paid only if they sell, a practice that reduces the overhead cost to their clients. Also, by using agents who usually contract their services to more than one company, companies can share the costs of agents with each other. As the customers of independent agents continue to merge with other companies, independent agent companies and other wholesale trade firms will also merge with each other in response to better serve their clients.

Where the Jobs Are

Professional and commercial equipment and supplies merchant wholesalers (14.12%); Wholesale electronic markets and agents and brokers (11.21%); Drugs and druggists' sundries merchant wholesalers (10.67%); Electrical and electronic goods merchant wholesalers (6.47%); Computer systems design and related services (6.04%); Self-employed 3.53%

Resources

Manufacturers' Agents National Association (MANA): manaonline.org

Manufacturers' Representatives Educational Research Foundation (MRERF): mrerf.org

O*NET OnLine: online.onetcenter.org (see sales representatives, wholesale and manufacturing, technical and scientific products)

Solar Energy International (SEI): solarenergy.org

Solar Living Institute: solarliving.org

US Dept. of Labor, Bureau of Labor Statistics: bls.gov/oco/ocos119.htm

Chris Masys with customer Tyson Schmidt.

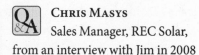

CHRIS MASYS
Sales Manager, REC Solar,
from an interview with Jim in 2008

How did you get into this career field? What was your education and experience, including any green-related training or certification?

I entered this career field three years ago, which doesn't sound like that long, but at that point the industry was basically just emerging. My education was a bachelor's degree in industrial technology from Cal Poly, San Luis Obispo. I worked as a manufacturing engineer immediately after college, then began to work in sales in another industry, and then I went to work for REC Solar. The company was started by two Cal Poly alumni back when I was still going to school there, so there are some strong alumni affiliations. At least that's what probably opened the door for me. At that point, the amount of available green-related training was pretty slim pickings. But what worked for me was having a technical background along with the sales skills. I was employee number 29, and just to illustrate the difference between then and now, today we're pushing 300 employees. So a huge amount of growth, along with a very defined training process that didn't exist back then.

What is your current job title and how would you describe the work you do in a typical day? What are your most common tasks?

My job title is Northern California Sales Manager. I've been aggressively pursuing my upward career mobility whenever possible. I started out as a residential solar consultant in the home territory of San Luis Obispo, California, for REC. Then I moved up to Sacramento and started up our operations literally as the first and only person on the ground for close to six months. I helped build that operation to a fully functioning level with a total of about 30 employees. So setting all that up probably greased the wheels for further career advancement, and subsequently I took over the management of the entire Northern California region. Now, my career path is not necessarily what I would espouse for everyone. I can't remember the last time I had a 40-hour work week. For me, it's more like an 80-hour work week is a short one. But I'm not complaining. I love what I do, and I've been very successful at doing it. But it does represent just one potential track, and I think if people were to just look at my experience, it would scare them off. Because not all jobs in renewable energy are like mine. But this industry is in its infancy, and we've had such rapid growth. Even at this point, we've only reached the tip of the iceberg. So for people who are very motivated to progress rapidly in their career and grow a business, there's very much that opportunity available. In my present position, I don't often deal directly with customers. I do have a total of ten sales reps that report directly to me, as well as five marketing staff. And then I have cross-departmental relationships with the other parts of our company. Probably my number one responsibility is making sure that revenue expectations are being met and will be met. And in as pro-active a manner as possible, making sure that we're applying the correct marketing methodology to bring in the types of leads that we need. Another strategic function of mine is to keep tabs on what's going on in the industry regarding our competitors. I'd say my third function is public speaking engagements. And a fourth one is human resources, because we're growing so quickly that job titles and responsibilities are being invented on a daily basis. So recruiting, interviewing, hiring and training — I have aspects of that in my daily work as well.

If you could give advice to a young person who wants to work in this career field someday, what would you tell them? How can they best groom themselves for this field?

For the reputable organizations, I don't think it's possible for someone to start out in solar sales without previous sales experience. I get resumés from people who call themselves sales people, but they're basically just account reps or customer service people. They're just taking care of people, and that's a lot different than closing a sale on a technical product in someone's home. What I'm generally looking for in my sales staff are people with a business or engineering background, but with sales experience in a B to C (business to consumer) capacity rather than B to B (business to business) capacity. And if they have any sort of additional environmental credentials in terms of their own hobbies, volunteer work or education, that would definitely make someone stand out because it shows that they're taking steps on their own.

What kind of career advancement opportunities can one expect in this field?
I would say that other (non-sales) positions lend themselves better to the entry level than sales. For example, a solar installer tends to be a blue-collar and construction-related career. We generally look for folks that have some electrical and mechanical expertise. A senior-level installer would have quite a bit of construction experience as well as solar installation experience. The foremen/supervisors of our crews are all journeymen electricians. So it's generally the third or fourth crew member who is building their experience and could be considered an entry-level role. I wouldn't say that it's an insurmountable barrier, but when you start out in a blue-collar capacity, it can be difficult to jump over to the white-collar side. Some sales reps specialize in residential solar, as it tends to be a simpler sale, although not always an easier sale. The commercial solar side is generally dealing with a more sophisticated client. There are typically multiple levels within an organization, and so one has to be able to speak to anyone in the organization, up to and including the CEO and the CFO. As far as career advancement goes, sales reps who get promoted generally go vertically into management. Others continue to develop and hone their sales skills and take on increasingly greater numbers of clients or higher-profile clients and higher-stakes systems. But if someone finds that sales is not for them, they might end up going to a marketing position or going into inside sales.

In your opinion, what are some of the best schools, degrees and certificates for jobs in this career field, including green-specific training?
I would suggest majoring in an engineering field at any highly regarded four year university.

How does someone without previous experience in this career field land a job? What are the best strategies for job-hunting in this field?
Take classes specific to solar, such as those given by the Solar Living Institute, or pursue some level of certification. Also, folks that have volunteered with local organizations such as Habitat for Humanity can gain valuable experience. Environmental credentials are good, but folks often fall for the trap of thinking that's all it takes. And in my opinion, most environmental studies curriculums are actually quite light in terms of their technical content and their

business content. If I were applying for a job, I would use the Internet. But I would remind myself that personal networking is crucially important. Find local trade events. A good way to start is find the places where solar companies are selling. Go to a home show and talk to everyone. Get to know some of the people by asking about their backgrounds. Be active in local organizations, such as the California Chapter of the Solar Energy Industries Association. Environmental groups such as the Sierra Club would sort of be secondary to that. I'm really looking for people focused on solar energy. There are a lot of ways that you can make a favorable environmental impact. It could be in the energy area. It could be geothermal. It could be wind. It could be working with businesses on their sustainability measures. It could be a reduction of pollutions from industrial applications. There are just a million different things. So, someone's who's just purely environmentally motivated doesn't necessarily speak to me, because they're not nearly as focused as we are.

Are there any professional associations that you would recommend joining?
The one professional association that would make sense would be NABCEP, or the North American Board of Certified Energy Practitioners.

What emerging careers do you see developing now and into the future for this career field? What new technologies will have the greatest impact on this field?
In a ten-year timeframe, new cell technologies will bring down the price point and perhaps increase efficiency. In the meantime, we need well-educated folks that can communicate very well and that have sales skills to be able to get in front of people. Up until the point that going solar is simply about placing an order, there should remain a strong need for sales reps. And, as our businesses grow, we'll need more marketing people, more accounting people, more payroll people, more of everything.

Resources from Q&A
Cal Poly, San Luis Obispo: calpoly.edu
California Solar Energy Industries Association (CALSEIA): calseia.org
Habitat for Humanity: habitat.org
North American Board of Certified Energy Practitioners (NABCEP): nabcep.org
REC Solar: recsolar.com
Sierra Club: sierraclub.org
Solar Living Institute: solarliving.org

Melissa Lucia (far right) with her coworkers.

 MELISSA LUCIA
National Sales Manager,
Dancing Deer Baking Company,
from an interview with Jim in 2008

How did you get into this career field? What was your education and experience, including any green-related training or certification?
I got recruited into leadership (management) for the Whole Foods Market in Berkeley, California, in 1995. At that point, I had over ten years of management experience in retail clothing. But basic management/leadership skills in retail clothing can translate to food pretty easily.

What is your current job title and how would you describe the work you do in a typical day? What are your most common tasks?
I left Whole Foods Market last year to become the national sales manager for a small natural food manufacturer based out of Boston, Massachusetts, called the Dancing Deer Baking Company. I coordinate getting products to different parts of the United States and to different retailers, such as Whole Foods Market, Crate and Barrel, Pier 1 and some other large retailers. I work with people on logistics, product development, promotions, programs and selling products. I work with the retailers to help them sell our products more effectively. I also help them do store start-ups.

If you could give advice to a young person who wants to work in this career field someday, what would you tell them? How can they best groom themselves for this field?
I would recommend getting into some sort of culinary program to learn about food. But you can also get a really good foundation through a nutrition program, a pastry program or a hotel and restaurant management program. If your goal is specifically food manufacturing, then you'd want to get into a food science program. These can be certificate or degree programs, but I would recommend a bachelor's degree, if not a master's degree.

What kind of career advancement opportunities can one expect in this field? What kind of salary range would reflect that career path (from entry-level to the more advanced position)?
The career path for food products sales reps can go in a couple of different directions. Some friends of mine have become brokers — where they represent

different food manufacturers. Or you can become a principal — where you represent a single food product company. Or you can stay with your employer and move up to a sales manager position or even become a vice president. You could also branch off and get into distribution, as some of my friends have done. The salary in this business can range anywhere from $75,000 to $200,000 per year, depending on the position and the company. Some of the salaries in this industry are based partly on commissions. So this field can be pretty lucrative if you've got the necessary relationships and connections — especially with large retailers.

In your opinion, what are some of the best schools, degrees and certificates for jobs in this career field, including green-specific training?
The culinary program I would recommend is the Culinary Institute in St. Helena, in Napa, California. If you're interested in a business management program, there are a lot of schools around the country with great programs.

How does someone without previous experience in this career field land a job? What are the best strategies for job-hunting in this field?
To get into the natural foods business, go to job fairs and network. The Whole Foods Market holds its own job fairs, as do some of the other large businesses. So that's a great way to come out and apply for a job. But networking is huge, too. Talk to people and someone may eventually be able to help you with a job.

Are there any professional associations that you would recommend joining?
No, but a lot of people in this business do volunteer work, and some eventually serve as board members for non-profit organizations. Another great thing for networking is joining LinkedIn. It's given me the opportunity to meet CEOs and distributors, and even a headhunter recently contacted me about a job through that group.

What emerging careers do you see developing now and into the future for this career field? What new technologies will have the greatest impact on this field?
Some of the larger natural foods companies now have energy efficiency coordinators or managers to help with store development and renewable energy initiatives. Also, there's a big push these days for locally grown foods, so that's a good thing for local vendors.

Resources from Q&A

Crate and Barrel: crateandbarrel.com
Culinary Institute of America at Greystone: ciachef.edu/california/
Dancing Deer Baking Company: dancingdeer.com

LinkedIn: linkedin.com
Pier 1 Imports: pier1.com
Whole Foods Market: wholefoodsmarket.com

Sustainability Coordinators and Officers

Sustainability coordinators and officers are new and emerging occupations that can be found in virtually all industries, although not yet in most organizations. Depending on the organization, the occupation may be considered a management position or not. The primary function of a sustainability coordinator or officer is to help an organization become more sustainable and more environmentally responsible. However, jobs in this career field can range from being a consultant or advisor to upper management, to being a recycling program coordinator. Many sustainability coordinators and officers have evolving job descriptions. Sometimes sustainability coordinator or officer is an additional job hat worn by an existing employee or manager. Sustainability coordinators and officers, especially those in the higher education sector, generally have a major responsibility for educating people about sustainability issues and best-practices. Sometimes they coordinate sustainable or green-related events. Sometimes they coordinate specific projects or programs, such as recycling or energy savings initiatives. Sometimes they participate in the planning and design of green buildings and facilities or in the greening of a company's fleet of vehicles, trucks or equipment. For a non-green business that wants to become more sustainable, sometimes the first step is to hire a sustainability professional to do an evaluation and make recommendations. Evaluations usually include conducting or coordinating energy audits of buildings and doing cost-benefit analyses. In the public sector, some sustainability coordinators are focused on green business and economic development or on green construction planning or on transportation planning. Others are focused on policy development.

What is a sustainable business or organization? — At a minimum, a sustainable business or organization is committed to conserving energy, preventing pollution, reducing waste, and conserving water. The greening of buildings and the extensive use of renewable energy are also important aspects of a sustainable business or organization. An even higher standard is for a business or organization to hold itself accountable for both the environmental and human rights impacts of its activities.

Qualifications and Advancement

The majority of job openings for sustainability coordinator or officer require a bachelor's or master's degree. In higher education, a master's degree is typically required. However, because this is a new occupation with a wide range of job responsibilities, a program of study is not yet standardized. Some major in environmental studies, environmental science or a related field, and some major in green business — such as a green MBA program. (An MBA is a master's degree in business administration, while a green MBA has sustainability integrated throughout the curriculum.) There are also jobs in which the focus is on the applicant's knowledge and experience rather than on a specific college degree. No doubt there are some sustainability coordinators who are self-taught and never attended college. Others have a college degree, but in a completely unrelated field.

It's too early in the evolution of this occupation to see a typical career path. However, generically speaking, coordinators — whether they are considered managers or not — are usually people in a lead position. And so advancement for coordinators usually means moving to a management position or to a higher-level management position. Some will take on increased responsibilities without being promoted, while others will move on to jobs with other organizations that offer greater opportunities. Some private firms have recently begun creating an executive position called a chief sustainability officer (CSO). This would be the position to aspire to for sustainability coordinators who want to advance to upper management.

Salary/Compensation

No occupational data or statistics exist (yet) for this specific occupation, so any wage information should be flagged as such. However, by assessing current job postings (online), it would appear that jobs for sustainability coordinators typically range from $30,000 to $80,000 per year, with a few earning substantially more. One limited survey found an average annual salary of $51,000. Another older survey of sustainability coordinators in the higher education sector (only) found an average annual salary of $44,200 for those with five years or less of experience, and $58,800 for those with six to ten years of experience.

Resources

Association for the Advancement of Sustainability in Higher Education
    (AASHE): aashe.org
Certified Sustainable Development Professional (CSDP) Program:
    aeecenter.org/certification/csdppage.htm

Green Wombat (blog): greenwombat.blogs.fortune.cnn.com

GreenBiz (news and resources): greenbiz.com

International Society of Sustainability Professionals (ISSP):
    sustainabilityprofessionals.org

National Sustainable Building Advisor Program (NaSBAP): nasbap.org

Sustainable Business magazine: edie.net/magazines/

Sustainable Industries: sustainableindustries.com

US Green Building Council/LEED AP Certification: usgbc.org

Steve Attinger

Q&A **STEVE ATTINGER**
Environmental Sustainability
Coordinator, City of Mountain View,
from an interview with Jim in 2008

How did you get into this career field? What was your education and experience, including any green–related training or certification?
I have a unique MBA (master's degree in business administration), focused specifically in sustainable management. At the time I enrolled at Presidio School of Management, it was one of only a few schools in the country that took the traditional MBA curriculum and integrated the principles of sustainability into every course. Prior to that, my education was in information and communication studies. I grew up in a family that was very environmentally and socially conscious, so the whole concept of sustainability is something that has always run through my veins. But about six years ago, I went through a period of deep introspection and made a significant career transition from more of a mainstream career in high-tech product management and marketing to a career in sustainability. Once I discovered that sustainability was the intersection between business, environment and society, that's when I knew I'd found my home. My first professional sustainability experience was a consulting engagement with a Swedish organization called The Natural Step, which had an office in San Francisco. Then I began volunteering with, and was later hired by, the Business and Sustainability Group in Palo Alto, where I worked while attending the Presidio MBA program. Also, just recently I became a Certified Green Building Professional (CGBP) through Build It Green's training program.

What is your current job title and how would you describe the work you do in a typical day? What are your most common tasks?

My job is environmental sustainability coordinator for the City of Mountain View, California. When the City Council funded this position, they weren't ready to make this a permanent position. So, although my position has been extended beyond the initial 12-month term, it is still considered a limited term position. By its definition, sustainability covers everything from soup to nuts. The biggest piece of my job has been coordinating our citizen-based Environmental Sustainability Task Force. This is a group of 60 citizens who live or work in Mountain View and have volunteered a significant amount of their time to develop a series of recommendations for the City Council on how to make Mountain View more sustainable and how to address California's AB32 legislation that is aimed at reducing greenhouse gas emissions. In addition to my Task Force work, I'm also leading an internal Green Team of 20 employees — which represents one person from virtually all city departments. Whereas the Task Force has focused on community-wide sustainability issues and solutions, the Green Team is focused on those issues and solutions from a city facilities and operations perspective. One of the first things I did this year was to develop a quantitative methodology by which the city council can evaluate different kinds of potential sustainability projects from a cost-benefit perspective. For example, would the city gain more by increasing their fleet of hybrid vehicles, or by installing more energy efficient lighting in city buildings? When we run the numbers for a potential project, it shows — among other quantitative data — the cost or savings associated with avoiding a ton of CO_2 per year over the project's life. I've also been doing research to introduce a new green building policy to the city council and am responsible for finding grants that the city can apply for to pay for some of these projects or to help pay for my position. I also helped develop an Environmentally Preferable Purchasing Policy, which was approved by the City Council. And I've also been working with the International Council on Local Environmental Initiatives (ICLEI) to conduct our city greenhouse gas inventory.

If you could give advice to a young person who wants to work in this career field someday, what would you tell them? How can they best groom themselves for this field?

Outside of the academics, there are going to be a number of different professional associations in a geographic area that are generally free and that you can get connected into that would enable you to network with all of the movers and shakers in that area, including sustainability professionals. Get to know the people and do informational interviews with them. And, one of the single best ways of gaining professional experience is to volunteer or intern with a private, government or nonprofit organization. I can't stress this enough. Also, help put on environmental events and get engaged in sustainability work.

What kind of career advancement opportunities can one expect in this field? What kind of salary range would reflect that career path (from entry-level to the more advanced position)?

In the public sector, the career path could mean starting out as a recycling analyst and then eventually moving up to be the solid waste manager. Then perhaps make a lateral move into a sustainability type of role. Another option, if you have the experience, is to come in as a sustainability coordinator — like I did. In the non-profit sector, depending on your experience, you could begin as an intern, as a researcher or as a project coordinator of some kind. Then work and gain experience and begin to move up in that non-profit world. There are enormous opportunities for someone interested in sustainability in the non-profit field. In the private sector, it's a little more difficult. One option is to start working in a company's Environmental, Health and Safety (EHS) group. Even medium-sized companies are going to have EHS people, and that's where you can learn about environmental compliance, worker safety and those kinds of things. Then you can move up in EHS and perhaps make a lateral move to a sustainability position. You could also move up from a recycling position, which — depending on the company — might be part of the facilities management department. Or, with more experience, you can get hired directly by a company as an environmental manager, director or sustainability officer. These positions are still few and far between in the private sector, but the number of such positions has increased significantly in the last two years, and will continue to do so.

In your opinion, what are some of the best schools, degrees and certificates for jobs in this career field, including green-specific training?

If a person is really serious about wanting to get a business focused education taught through the lens of sustainability, I would recommend schools like Presidio School of Management in San Francisco or Bainbridge Graduate Institute in Washington State. If you want to go to a more recognized school, I would encourage you to look at: University of California, Berkeley; University of North Carolina at Chapel Hill; University of Michigan; and Yale University. Also, Beyond Grey Pinstripes is a sustainability-oriented survey and ranking of business schools. You can use it to look at how much each of the schools has incorporated sustainability into their curriculum. But keep in mind that newer schools like Presidio School of Management may not show up in that ranked system.

How does someone without previous experience in this career field land a job? What are the best strategies for job-hunting in this field?

Use all the above, including networking and personal contact through volunteering and interning and through your involvement with professional associations. In today's day and age, you would want to use the online job boards as well. Use "sustainability" and "environmental" as your keywords. Use mainstream sites like HotJobs and Monster, but focus more of your time on the sustainability job sites such as Green Dream Jobs, GreenBiz, TreeHugger, Eco Jobs.com and EnvironmentalCareer.com. There are a few recruiters who focus on sustainability positions, such as Martha Montag Brown and Ellen Weinreb Recruiting, but even some of the more traditional job recruitment firms are beginning to see sustainability jobs coming through.

Are there any professional associations that you would recommend joining?

Net Impact is one of the foremost professional associations for people in my field, and they even have student groups at colleges and universities all across the country. The annual Net Impact conference is a fantastic way to learn and network, where you can meet professionals working directly in the field. They also put on all kinds of local events where they have interesting guest speakers and networking opportunities.

Are there any new technologies that will impact your job — either in the near or distant future? How will they affect your job and your career field?

New technologies are constantly affecting my job. This includes environmental technologies such as the ever-evolving discipline of "building science" (related to green building), thin-film solar and solar concentrators, greenhouse gas mitigation technologies, environmentally friendly household products and cradle-to-cradle product design, to name just a few. There are also Web 2.0/social networking technologies such as blogging, LinkedIn, Facebook and MySpace. And finally, there are mobile phone/device applications that enable access to real-time information about environmental products and services. For environmental technologies, someone in this field needs to be able to keep up with and take advantage of new sustainability-focused technologies, which are being created at a pace that exceeds innovation in most other industries. Someone would also be very wise to make use of the numerous social networking and mobile-enabled technologies for conveying information to employees, customers, the local community, faith groups, shareholders, the general public, etc. These areas are revolutionizing the way people access information, and thus are key tools for enabling people to connect, dialogue, take action/exert pressure and model the change they wish to see in the world.

Resources from Q&A

Bainbridge Graduate Institute: bgiedu.org

Beyond Grey Pinstripes: beyondgreypinstripes.org

Ellen Weinreb Recruiting: ellenweinreb.com

Environmental Career Opportunities: ecojobs.com

GreenBiz: greenbiz.com

Green Dream Jobs: sustainablebusiness.com/jobs

International Council on Local Environmental Initiatives: icleiusa.org

Martha Montag Brown: marthamontagbrown.com

Monster.com: monster.com

The Natural Step: naturalstep.org

Net Impact: netimpact.org

Presidio School of Management: presidiomba.org

TreeHugger: treehugger.com

University of California, Berkeley: berkeley.edu

University of Michigan: umich.edu

University of North Carolina at Chapel Hill: unc.edu

Yahoo! HotJobs.com: hotjobs.yahoo.com

Yale University: yale.edu

Tom Badrick (on left) with recycling crew.

Q&A **TOM BADRICK**
Sustainability Coordinator,
Legacy Health System,
from an interview with Jim in 2008

How did you get into this career field? What was your education and experience, including any green-related training or certification?

I was an environmental safety manager at a couple of different companies. One was a biotech/chemical company, and the other was an electronics manufacturing company. Then, after a layoff, I was looking for a job, and one came up running a recycling program for Legacy Health System. My educational background is a not-quite-finished science/genetics degree from the University of Oregon, which is an incredibly helpful tool to have here. Before coming to work for Legacy, I had not worked in healthcare. So I had to learn about healthcare. But I found that one of the real benefits of working in healthcare is that, at a bare minimum, about 80% of the people working in this field deliberately chose a career to help people. You have nurses and doctors and allied health professionals who have gone to school just so they can learn how to help people. And that's a very different environment.

What is your current job title and how would you describe the work you do in a typical day? What are your most common tasks?

I'm the sustainability coordinator. In any given one-hour period, I could literally be having a conversation with the CEO about what we need to do as an organization, and 20 minutes later, I could be moving some garbage cart because of some crisis going on. It's pretty much all over the map. I develop policies. I help fix things. I respond to small disasters here at work. In theory, a lot of what I focus on here is waste management. What I love doing the most is: I started our "green teams" here and we have one for each campus. A green team is an opportunity to engage a lot of employees in a process where, instead of one person looking at how to be green, you have a team of people. And then they can go back and be ambassadors to their area. The green teams are entirely voluntary based. These are regular line employees, and I'm getting real, honest feedback about what is and isn't working. And for them, it's an incredibly empowering experience. Instead of wondering who to talk to about a sustainability issue, they can go back to their area and be the person that others talk to. In terms of managing the waste stream, the trick is to have good data and then share the information. So finance people love me because every year I can identify not only what we recycled, but how much and what the cost impact on that is. And it's not so much about income, but about avoiding disposal costs. For example, we make about $15,000 per year on income from recycling, but we avoid spending a half million dollars a year on garbage. Triaging problems is the other main part of my job. How do you best implement something in a way that benefits the maximum number of people? It's basically strategic planning. For example, I look at things like document destruction with a five-year vision instead of tomorrow vision.

If you could give advice to a young person who wants to work in this career field someday, what would you tell them? How can they best groom themselves for this field?

Don't try and learn everything before you do it. Sometimes you just need to dive in. A lot of sustainability coordinators are really willing to help others, including those who are just getting started. Probably the most important thing is having good people and customer service skills. And science and chemistry in high school and college would be really helpful. Also any class you can take that's going to help you understand energy management. If you were going to start a sustainability program for an organization from scratch and didn't have any restrictions on what you should do, the very first thing you should work on is energy management because that's the big ticket. It is huge amounts of money. We're all heading down that road where we need to measure our carbon footprint. And that's not something you can just go do. So you either hire a consultant or you learn how to do it yourself. And even if you're going to hire a consultant, you should learn enough about it to know whether you've got a good consultant.

What kind of career advancement opportunities can one expect in this field? What kind of salary range would reflect that career path (from entry-level to the more advanced position)?
In the healthcare world, you might start out in housekeeping or environmental services. Or you might start out in the facilities management department. A lot of times, people in facilities management are doing this kind of work, but they just don't get recognized for it. In healthcare, there aren't many of us (sustainability coordinators or officers) yet, so there isn't really any path that leads to something above us. In a corporate world, you would hope to have a chief sustainability officer at the executive level. From what I've seen, the salary range for a sustainability coordinator is from $25,000 to $100,000 per year.

In your opinion, what are some of the best schools, degrees and certificates for jobs in this career field, including green-specific training?
I think it's too early in the evolution of this occupation to have a list of top schools. I would start by looking at the non-profit organizations working on sustainability to see what they're doing and what degrees and certificates they would recommend. Myself, I point more to reading material, and I'm a big fan of Paul Hawken. Also, *Omnivore's Dilemma* by Michael Pollan is a great book to get into.

How does someone without previous experience in this career field land a job? What are the best strategies for job-hunting in this field?
I'd network. Networking is a really valuable tool, and I use it all the time.

Are there any professional associations that you would recommend joining?
I'm a charter member of the International Society of Sustainability Professionals (ISSP), so, of course, I like that one. In healthcare, there's Practice Greenhealth. Most states have recycling associations — which is a good avenue for understanding the waste side of the business. Anything you can learn about LEED and green building would be good, and not just for engineers and architects.

What emerging careers do you see developing now and into the future for this career field? What new technologies will have the greatest impact on this field?
It's not new technology, but data-tracking tools. If you look at what I do, that's 4,200 tons of recycling and 25 different types of materials. I've got maybe 100 different places in our facility where things are picked up and where I need to have information on how much it is. Some of it's measurable, and some of it's estimatable. But being able to track your data effectively and efficiently is important — as is just about any technology that allows you to be reached 24/7.

Resources from Q&A
International Society of Sustainability Professionals (ISSP): sustainabilityprofessionals.org
Legacy Health System: legacyhealth.org
Omnivore's Dilemma by Michael Pollan: michaelpollan.com/omnivore.php
Paul Hawken: paulhawken.com
Practice Greenhealth: practicegreenhealth.org
US Green Building Council/LEED AP Certification: usgbc.org

 JILLIAN K. BUCKHOLZ
Sustainability Coordinator,
California State University, Chico,
from an interview with Alice in 2008

How did you get into this career field? What was your education and experience, including any green–related training or certification?
I became interested in environmental issues when curbside recycling started in my neighborhood. I was in elementary school, and I will never forget when my dad mounted a can crusher on the wall and how much I enjoyed using it! I continued to be a recycler through high school, even though my high school didn't have a recycling infrastructure. I was also the recycling advocate in college, making sure to advise my resident hall friends on how to properly use the receptacles in their rooms. As the college years passed, I found myself involved with different environmentally focused groups like the Ohio University Waste Busters, Recyclemania and Ecolympics. Having received my bachelor's degree in environmental geography from Ohio University, I decided to pursue a graduate degree from the Department of Geography and Planning at Chico State University. My thesis was called "Energy Use in

the CSU System: A Geographical Analysis of Policy." It argued that energy policies for the California State University system should be developed for its universities based on climate zone and bioregional data of the specific area they are located. While working on my thesis, I was moving up in the ranks at the Bidwell Environmental Institute (BEI), the umbrella non-profit green organization at Chico State. From student assistant to taxonomy lab manager to assistant director, I was gaining hands-on experience of the inner workings of the university regarding environmental projects and programs. This experience through BEI, along with my knowledge of the CSU system from working on my thesis, made me a great candidate for the new sustainability coordinator position at Chico State.

How would you describe the work you do in a typical day? What are the most common tasks?
From day to day, I never know what may land on my plate at the office. However, I try to stick to certain general objectives, like being a connector for students, working to institutionalize sustainability, doing research and coordinating green events. As a connector for students, when students have an idea of how they would like to make the campus more sustainable, I plug them into the department on campus where they can accomplish their goals. For example, two years ago, a student wondered why the university farm didn't grow organic produce to sell to the AS Food Service on campus. I plugged her into the College of Agriculture, and just this spring, we planted the first crop of organic lettuce that will be sold to the AS Food Service. I also work with a team of people, called the Institute for Sustainable Development, to create ways to institutionalize sustainability. From curriculum to internships to the creation of policy, we try to create ways to engage students and our campus community in sustainability efforts. I also try to stay connected with other sustainability coordinators, sustainability listservs and other information regarding sustainability in higher education. I then take this knowledge of what other universities are working on and share that with the administration at Chico State. This way our campus can continue to be a leader in sustainability in higher education, stay connected in the local community and learn from others about best practices.

If you could give advice to a young person who wants to work in this career field someday, what would you tell them? How can they best groom themselves for this field?
Get involved! Being a stellar student in academics is great, but it is real experience that is going to help you break into this newly emerging field.

Sustainability isn't usually something you can major in, and every sustainability coordinator I have worked with has different job duties and expectations. My advice would be to find the green issue you are most passionate about and try to gain as much experience as possible in that area so that you can prove you are knowledgeable and can easily share information with others.

What promotional and advancement opportunities exist in this field? What salaries could one expect (entry-level to advanced top level.)?
Advancement for my type of position really depends upon the university structure. I would imagine I could move from a coordinator to a director position and eventually supervise staff. AASHE.org has a chart regarding salaries of sustainability professionals. I would suggest accessing this information for an accurate view of compensation for a sustainability coordinator position.

In your opinion, what are some of the best schools, degrees and certificates that are most marketable for jobs in this career field?
As far as degrees and certificates, this will vary from engineering to social sciences, depending on an individual's interest. I am a strong believer that it doesn't matter what school you go to or what degree/certificate you get. What matters is how you embrace your education while you are in school and the real world experiences you are able to obtain while working on your degree.

How does someone without previous experience in this career field land a job? What are the best strategies for job-hunting in this field?
I would suggest doing informational interviews with professionals that are already working in the field. That's a good way to educate yourself on how to obtain a similar position. Job-hunting can be done through several eco-job listing sites on the Web.

Are there any professional associations that you would recommend joining?
SCUP, AASHE, Greenschool listserv and Sustainability Journal.

What emerging or high growth careers do you see developing in the future for this career field?
Directors of sustainability offices on all college campuses, sustainability professionals that are specific to campus needs and who specialize in specific areas such as transportation, buildings, energy, waste, purchasing. Also, I see a desire for professionals who can conduct greenhouse gas inventories for businesses as well as sustainability assessments and energy efficiency consultations. I think people know they need to be "green" but don't know how, so they are seeking professionals to teach them how they can green their organization while also saving money and resources.

Resources from Q&A

Association for the Advancement of Sustainability in Higher Education
(AASHE): aashe.org

Chico State University: csuchico.edu

Institute for Sustainable Development (formerly the Bidwell Environmental
Institute): csuchico.edu/sustainablefuture/

Recyclemania: recyclemaniacs.org

Society for College and University Planning (SCUP): scup.org

Sustainability: The Journal of Record:
liebertpub.com/publication.aspx?pub_id=252

 LONNY KNABE, Sustainable Projects Coordinator, Nike, Inc.,
from an interview with Jim in 2008

*How did you get into this career field? What was your education and experience,
including any green-related training or certification?*

I was an AmeriCorps volunteer doing recycling education in county school
districts. Nike was hiring a part-time recycling coordinator for their world
headquarters. I had actually majored in psychology when I was an undergrad,
so I didn't have any particular training when I started at Nike — other than my
AmeriCorps experience. After about a year as the recycling coordinator, I got
promoted to the sustainability coordinator. In that job, I also began looking at
sustainable cleaning products, and not long after that, I began looking at energy efficiency. I've always gone to conferences and workshops, and as far as
certifications, I'm a LEED Accredited Professional (AP) and a Certified Sustainable Building Advisor. I also just recently finished my MBA degree, which
I did while working in this job.

*What is your current job title and how would you describe the work you do in a
typical day? What are your most common tasks?*

I'm currently the sustainability manager, but I'm in the process of transitioning to a different position as the director of energy architecture for our footwear factories. Most of my job as a sustainability manager is energy and green
building for our world headquarters, our retail stores and our distribution
centers. So with this new position, I'm taking the same things that I've done
here in the US and expanding them to our footwear factories in Southeast
Asia. As the sustainability manager for Nike, I spend a lot of my time doing
return-on-investment analysis. I also do a lot of education and a lot of coordination with other groups. For example, I've been working with our retail facilities team for quite a few years doing energy efficiency projects. So I

coordinate with them and teach them about the importance of energy in their operation. I'm basically an internal consultant for sustainability. One of the things I've always tried to do as a sustainability coordinator or manager is find solutions. So with energy being one of our biggest environmental impacts, I view my job as working with the groups to find ways to reduce energy. That requires a technical understanding of energy and how it's used in the building. Then I develop "projects" to reduce energy usage. One of those projects might be a lighting project for a building. So I'll look for an appropriate lighting technology and perform a cost-benefit analysis on it.

As a sustainability professional, I think the most important thing you can do is to develop a really good understanding of everything that goes on in whatever aspect of the business impacts sustainability. For example, not just to advocate for green buildings, but to be part of the process that designs a green building and its various aspects. Not just to be a voice at the table, but to be somebody who can figure out a solution. With sustainability positions, I think there's an extra need to justify the position and your own existence. And if you can determine ways to come up with cost savings and operational benefits, then that's going to provide a lot of credibility and long-term stability to the position.

What kind of career advancement opportunities can one expect in this field? What kind of salary range would reflect that career path (from entry-level to the more advanced position)?
I think finding a career path in sustainability is fairly challenging. One of the great things about being a sustainability coordinator is you get a lot of visibility with some of the high-level managers and other people in the organization. But you may already be at the top of your organization as far as sustainability goes. So in a smaller organization, the opportunities for advancement would be limited. The other thing about sustainability is you get a very broad exposure to a lot of different aspects of the business, but you don't become a specialist in any one thing besides sustainability. So I think career advancement is challenging within sustainability.

The salary range is very wide — depending on where you are in an organization. Generally, I think if you're in a facilities-type role, you may be at the lower end. And if you're in more of a corporate responsibility or product-based sustainability position, you're going to be at the higher end. And that range can be anywhere from $30,000 to $150,000 a year.

In your opinion, what are some of the best schools, degrees and certificates for jobs in this career field, including green-specific training?

I don't know that you need an MBA, but some level of business educa
perhaps as an undergraduate — would be very helpful. The other aspect
depend on what area within sustainability you want to go into. For exa
if you were interested in designing sustainable products, you would look for
a degree program in sustainable design. If you were interested in green building, an architectural or mechanical engineering degree would be extremely
beneficial. And if you're going to be involved in facilities, I would say that
certification as a LEED AP is almost a must. Another certification program I
found interesting is Certified Sustainable Development Professional (CSDP).

Are there any professional associations that you would recommend joining?
I don't belong to one. But there is a newer one called the International Society
of Sustainability Professionals, and they may have some good resources there.

*What emerging careers do you see developing now and into the future for this
career field? What new technologies will have the greatest impact on this field?*
I think the cost of energy is going to be the biggest influencer of what goes on
in the sustainability field. As the cost of energy goes up, the number of sustainability jobs will increase. As far as technology goes, from what I've seen, most
organizations would benefit a lot from already-existing technologies such as
better building design. There have also been some pretty dramatic advancements in solar technology. Also, advanced energy monitoring is an inexpensive technology that can be used to understand the overall building energy
profile.

Resources from Q&A

AmeriCorps: americorps.org
Certified Sustainable Development Professional (CSDP) Program:
    aeecenter.org/certification/csdppage.htm
International Society of Sustainability Professionals (ISSP):
    sustainabilityprofessionals.org
National Sustainable Building Advisor Program (NaSBAP): nasbap.org
Nike, Inc.: nike.com
US Green Building Council/LEED AP Certification: usgbc.org

Travel Guides, including Ecotourism Guides and Operators

Travel guides plan, organize and conduct long-distance cruises, tours and ex-
peditions for individuals and groups.

Ecotourism is a form of tourism designed for the mutual benefit of ecologically and socially conscious travelers and natural environments and indigenous people and culture. Not all businesses that market themselves as "ecotourism" fit this criteria.

Qualifications and Advancement

The primary qualification for ecotourism guides is related knowledge and previous experience. In some cases, certifications that demonstrate the guide's knowledge of first aid or specific skills (such as whitewater rescue) are critical. For some jobs, being bilingual is essential.

So how does one get their first experience as a travel guide? By volunteering or by working for a tour company in some other capacity. As ecotourism guides gain experience and accumulate new skills, they may move on to better paying or more prestigious jobs or move into supervisory or management positions. Some may start their own ecotourism businesses.

Salary Survey

Median salary: $28,460 (low/moderate)
Typical range: $22,590 to $36,180

Job Outlook and Employment

Average growth is projected for this general occupation in the US, from 4,672 jobs in 2006 to 5,162 in 2016. However, with ecotourism growing in popularity, it is likely that jobs for ecotourism guides will grow at a faster than average rate.

Where the Jobs Are

Travel arrangement and reservation services (47.71%); Arts, entertainment and recreation (10.16%); Scenic and sightseeing transportation (3.14%); Self-employed: 26.29%

Resources

EcoBusinessLinks: ecobusinesslinks.com
Ecotourism Job Center: ecoclub.com/jobs/ (fee-based membership)
International Ecotourism Society (TIES): ecotourism.org
Leave No Trace: lnt.org
O*NET OnLine: online.onetcenter.org (see travel guides)
Planeta.com: planeta.com
Tread Lightly!: treadlightly.org
Tourism Concern: tourismconcern.org.uk
US Dept. of Labor, Bureau of Labor Statistics: bls.gov/oco/oco20055.htm (see tour guides and travel guides)

MARK FARLEY
Ecotour Operator,
Elite Land Tours, Inc.,
from an interview with Jim in 2008

How did you get into this career field? What was your education and experience, including any green-related training or certification?

Actually I was inspired by my aunt who's a paleontologist. She lives near a national park in Arizona. Now I have a master's degree as a desert naturalist. But it started a long time ago. And I've been running my own tour company for about six years now.

What is your current job title and how would you describe the work you do in a typical day? What are your most common tasks, including those that make yours a green job?

I am the owner of Elite Land Tours, and I'm also one of the tour guides. Every day is a little different, but typically I come to the office and do all the bookkeeping. I pay the bills. I might do a four-hour tour today to Joshua Tree National Park. Other days our group (employees) might go out and clean the places that we tour. We have a big problem with litter in the valley here, so we constantly have to go out and clean the places where we take people. With the population growing here and people encroaching on our area, we get more and more litter. So a big part of our job is taking care of the lands that we go to. If you're going to run an ecotour company, one of the big things is educating people. And here that means educating people on the desert. That's number one. We tell and show people how fragile the desert ecosystem is and how biodiverse it is. We give them the knowledge that the desert is not a wasteland; that it's a thriving ecosystem, and that all the animals, plants and everything are interdependent. There are lots of tour companies that call themselves ecotour companies, but many of them just use the land for their own gain. They use the land to make money without being stewards of the land. They don't pick up the litter, and they never give anything back. And we see it everyday.

If you could give advice to a young person who wants to work in this career field someday, what would you tell them? How can they best groom themselves for this field?

The first thing is they have to have a love of nature. You've got to have a passion for this, because people who think that they can walk in and get a job as a tour guide because they think it is easy are dead wrong. All of my guides are highly educated. They have a passion. I have one guide who hiked in the Pyrenees in Spain, and he just finished a hike from Mexico to Canada. You have to have a passion for this work. If you do, then you can take the word "job" out of the equation. It won't be like a traditional job. One of my other guides is a snake expert. When he takes people out, he's looking for snakes. He wants to see different species; make sure they're still part of the ecosystem and that they haven't disappeared. So you've got to have a passion for nature or else don't get into ecotourism. A formal education helps. You can find places to either take classes or get a certificate. In our area, you can get a certificate from the Living Desert University. But wherever you go, every class you take is going to add to your resumé and your knowledge base. I tell people it's like learning a language, because I learned Spanish, but I'm constantly adding words to my vocabulary. Same thing with doing the ecotours. We're constantly building on our knowledge base. I get my knowledge from so many different sources: newsletters, TV programs, classes, lectures and from the Internet. So it's one of those fields where you can really educate yourself if you have an aptitude for learning.

What kind of career advancement opportunities can one expect in this field? What kind of salary range would reflect that career path (from entry-level to the more advanced position)?

First, they should align themselves with a good company, for which there are many. Then get a job as a tour guide. That's probably the easiest way to break in. If you can't start out as a tour guide, maybe work for an outdoor company to get started. If they won't hire you as a tour guide, then find a way to hang out and become part of the group. We would love to have interns or volunteers, but it's very difficult to find people who will intern or apprentice for something like this. Everybody wants to come out of college and jump into a great-paying job. But it doesn't work that way in this field. You need to have some experience and know your way around. Even if they're a concierge at a hotel for a year — that would help to get a feel for what guests are looking for. Get familiar with tourism in general. In my company, you would get pay raises over time, but once you're a tour guide, that's pretty much what you're going to do here. If someone really impressed me, I suppose I could look at promoting them to operations manager. But we're not a big company. Much larger companies might have more opportunities for career advancement, such as tour manager and operations manager. For some tour guides, career advancement means starting your own company. When you work in a resort area, guides can sometimes make up to $6,000 a month. At the entry level it might be more like $1,500 to $2,000 a month.

In your opinion, what are some of the best schools, degrees and certificates for jobs in this career field, including green-specific training?
Aside from the Living Desert University, I really don't know of any schools to recommend. But in my opinion, tour guides should look at this as a profession. Our customers want phenomenal information from intelligent tour guides. Our customers ask about the San Andreas Fault. They want to know how much it's slipping. They want to know how the formations occurred, how old they are, how long, deep and wide! You have to be knowledgeable in many different fields: geology, botany, entomology, geography. You have to know your stuff.

How does someone without previous experience in this career field land a job? What are the best strategies for job-hunting in this field?
Search the internet for ecotour companies. Get a good resumé together that shows your skills that relate to each company you want to contact. I get resumés from all kinds of people, but I'm not looking for an IT professional. I'm looking for people with great customer service, some outdoor experience and some education in the field.

Are there any professional associations that you would recommend joining?
I belong to Tread Lightly! — a national nonprofit organization with a mission to protect recreation access and opportunities in the outdoors. And I'm a master trainer for them. I'm also a member of Leave No Trace, the International Ecotourism Society, The Living Desert, Joshua Tree National Park Association, Sierra Club and the National Audubon Society. These are all great organizations.

What emerging careers do you see developing now and into the future for this career field? What new technologies will have the greatest impact on this field?
For me, what I see emerging is lectures and seminars for all the people who can't or don't have time to get in a vehicle and go on a tour, and yet they still want to experience it through a slide show. We get a lot of seniors who stay at an elder hostel, and they hire me to go up there and talk to them. And that sort of thing has been increasing over the past couple of years. Some people come from across the country on a down-and-dirty four-day bus trip. They see a lot of places in a short amount of time. So they hire me to come down at night and talk to them about what they're going to see the following day from the window of their bus. As far as new technologies, there's a lot of great stuff

for astronomy. That's where the technology really comes in handy. And we use state-of-the-art black lights to see scorpions in the desert. We use bat detectors so you can actually hear them feeding. We also use night-vision equipment — as it doesn't disturb the wildlife, yet you can see them at night. Our customers love all that high-tech, state-of-the-art stuff.

Resources from Q&A

Elite Land Tours, Inc.: elitelandtours.com
International Ecotourism Society (TIES): ecotourism.org
Joshua Tree National Park: nps.gov/jotr
Joshua Tree National Park Association: joshuatree.org
Leave No Trace: lnt.org
The Living Desert: livingdesert.org
Living Desert University (LDU): livingdesert.org
National Audubon Society: audubon.org
Sierra Club: sierraclub.org
Tread Lightly!: treadlightly.org

Q&A   EMILIO KIFURI
Ecotour Operator, Canyon Travel, from an interview with Jim in 2008

How did you get into this career field? What was your education and experience, including any green–related training or certification?
My education was originally in biology and history, but I was in regular tourism first. This was before ecotourism was born and before we became aware of it. But as soon as I became aware of it, I stepped right into it. It's something I've always embraced. It's not only smart marketing for tour operators, but it's also the right thing to do. Besides being a tour operator, I am trying to raise the profession of a green guide to increase the salaries and make it an honorable profession. In some countries that are fortunate, like Costa Rica, you have guides that are biologists and university trained. But other countries, including Mexico, are not so fortunate. But it is slowly changing.

What is your current job title and how would you describe the work you do in a typical day? What are your most common tasks, including those that make yours a green job?

My current job title is President of Canyon Travel, a Texas corporation. I manage the operation. I deal with people who want quotes or information about our services. And that's always a pleasant thing. But beyond that, it's administrating a business that involves managing the advertising. Also, as an ecotour operator, I want to make sure that I'm giving it more than lip service. I want to make sure that I've got something really viable, and that it's preserving the environment and preserving the culture. But when you help a culture, you have to also be very careful because some cultures don't want your help. I'm all for giving them employment and giving them an opportunity to better themselves with that employment. That's what I want to offer them.

If you could give advice to a young person who wants to work in this career field someday, what would you tell them? How can they best groom themselves for this field?
You've got to know some science and history in ecotourism, because it's a matter of helping the environment. So strengthen yourself in all the sciences and in your knowledge of history. Ecotourism can also get into computer sciences, because promoting ecotourism on the Web is most important. I advertised in Smithsonian Magazine for 11 years, and it really worked out well for us. But now I don't do any magazine advertising to speak of because it's all gone to the Internet — the Web. And that's where the future lies right now.

What kind of career advancement opportunities can one expect in this field?
I don't think there is a general rule. A lot of tour guides are self-employed — they work under contract. Some also work for other companies. Some guides will start their own tour companies. When I'm stuck doing paperwork at my desk and I'm not making a profit, I wonder if I'm crazy for doing this? But I look at career advancement in terms of whether my business has a profitable year. Of course, some years are more profitable than others. But it's getting to the point where adventure ecotourism is becoming somewhat immune from downturns in the economy. I know if push came to shove, a really bad economy would definitely affect us, but it seems like more people are looking at travel as a definite essential in life. It's not a luxury anymore. It's something they need.

In your opinion, what are some of the best schools, degrees and certificates for jobs in this career field, including green-specific training?
I've looked into some of the training as far as a tour operator becoming certified. But a lot of times the certification programs just seem like ways of getting money out of you, and from here on after. And tell me, who's going to

certify the certification people? So we have all kinds of people that are experts, but sometimes they don't know anything. As far as colleges, it depends on what kind of ecotourism. I'm inclined to ecotourism on the Southwest United States; that's about as close as they get to us. And ecotourism in the Southwest US is very related to ecotourism in Northwest Mexico. I would be a terrible guide and a terrible tour operator for anything that would have to do with Ireland or England or something like that. Because I know nothing of it. But I know everything about our area, and I love our area. I'm driven with a passion for it. And so I would suggest to someone interested in ecotourism to follow the path of what they like most. If you're into scuba diving or swimming, or into birding or mountain climbing, for example. Try to find what drives you and then follow that with a passion.

How does someone without previous experience in this career field land a job? What are the best strategies for job-hunting in this field?
In my field, being bilingual in English and Spanish is all very necessary. That's one of the most important aspects. Of course, you've got to have the right personality to become a guide. You've got to like people. You've got to enjoy interchanging and sharing yourself with people. Most of our customers want to be introduced to locals. They want to see into their homes. What they're looking for is authenticity. Aside from that, a newbie may start as a helper or trail assistant. That means they get to go with the guide and listen to the guide and be around the tour. And they're assisting the guide. If we have a picnic on that trip, they carry the items and/or take responsibility for the food preparation. If you've got a college degree and some training already, or if you're a scientist or biologist, ask some of the tour operators that you're interested in. Tell them your qualifications and tell them that you're interested in the area they service and see if they're interested in you. I'd love to have a few biologists apply with me. I'm actually actively looking for that right now.

Are there any professional associations that you would recommend joining?
The International Ecotourism Society would be one. Planeta.com is not an association, but it has a wealth of information on ecotourism.

What emerging careers do you see developing now and into the future for this career field? What new technologies will have the greatest impact on this field?
As a tour operator, Web technologies are highly important in my business. I would be well served if I knew them better. Right now I just ordered a new website because I've been suffering with my old one for too long. We're not just talking about a simple website; we're talking about $15,000 plus for what we

need for this business. But that's really not very expensive when you compare it to magazine advertising. The little bitty ad I ran in the Smithsonian magazine was running almost $2,000 a month. And the new website will allow online bookings for tours. It'll be optimized with all the latest things. SEO — search engine optimization — that's a biggie in my industry.

Resources from Q&A

Canyon Travel: canyontravel.com
International Ecotourism Society (TIES): ecotourism.org
Planeta.com: planeta.com

Green Education, Communication and Law Group

○ Customer Service Representatives, including Energy Efficiency Specialists

○ Health Educators, including Environmental Health Educators and Sustainability Coordinators

○ Health Specialties Instructors, including Environmental Health Education Instructors

○ Lawyers, including Environmental and Regulatory Attorneys

○ Public Relations Specialists, including Environmental/Sustainability Specialists

○ Reporters and Correspondents, including Green Journalists

Customer Service Representatives, including Energy Efficiency Specialists

Customer service representatives interact with customers to provide information in response to inquiries about products and services and to handle and resolve complaints.

Energy efficiency specialist is generally a professional-level customer service position with electric utility companies.

Qualifications and Advancement

Most customer service representative jobs require only a high-school diploma. However, because employers are demanding a higher-skilled workforce, many of these jobs now require an associate's degree or bachelor's degree. About one in four new entrants to this occupation have completed a bachelor's degree. Another two in five have completed some college. Because of a constant need to update skills and knowledge, most customer service representatives continue to receive instruction and training throughout their career. This is particularly true of workers in industries in which products are continually changing.

Many customer service jobs are entry-level positions, which make them good points of entry into a company or industry. As skills and experience are gained, advancement may lead to supervisory or management positions or a transfer to a different type of job.

Salary Survey
Median salary: $28,330 (low/moderate)
Typical range: $22,310 to $36,190

Job Outlook and Employment
Much faster than average growth is projected for this occupation in the US, from 2.2 million jobs in 2006 to 2.7 million in 2016. Prospects for obtaining a job in this field are expected to be excellent, with more job openings than job-seekers. Bilingual jobseekers, in particular, should enjoy favorable job prospects. In addition, numerous openings will result from the need to replace experienced customer service representatives who transfer to other occupations or leave the labor force. Almost half of the utilities' workforce will be nearing retirement age within the next ten years, resulting in excellent opportunities for qualified jobseekers.

Where the Jobs Are
Telephone call centers (5.03%); Employment services (4.84%); Depository credit intermediation (4.77%); Insurance agencies and brokerages (4.41%)

Resources
International Customer Service Association (ICSA): icsa.com
O*NET OnLine: online.onetcenter.org (see customer service representatives)
Service & Support Professionals Association (SSPA): thesspa.com
US Dept. of Labor, Bureau of Labor Statistics: bls.gov/oco/ocos280.htm

Health Educators, including Environmental Health Educators

Health educators promote, maintain and improve individual and community health by assisting individuals and communities to adopt healthy behaviors. Collect and analyze data to identify community needs prior to planning, implementing, monitoring and evaluating programs designed to encourage healthy lifestyles, policies and environments. May also serve as resources to assist others or may administer fiscal resources for health education programs.

Qualifications and Advancement
A master's degree in health education or a related field is the typical education/training requirement.

Some health educators begin their careers as registered nurses. Health educators often need additional training to advance. For example, a health educator for a county health department might become a department director if they meet the educational requirements for the position. A health educator might also advance by taking a job with more responsibility in a larger organization. Some health educators become directors of a specific project or program. Others become college instructors.

Salary Survey

Median salary: $41,330 (high)
Typical range: $31,300 to $56,580

Job Outlook and Employment

Much faster than average growth is projected for this occupation in the US, from 61,546 jobs in 2006 to 77,664 in 2016. The rising cost of health care has increased the need for health educators. As healthcare costs continue to rise, insurance companies, employers and governments are finding ways to curb the cost. One option is to employ health educators to teach people how to live healthy lives and avoid costly treatments for illnesses. Awareness of illnesses such as lung cancer, HIV, heart disease and skin cancer can often be avoided with lifestyle changes that require the public to better understand the effects of their behavior on their health.

Where the Jobs Are

General medical/surgical hospitals (17.7%); Local government (11.92%); State government (8.08%); Colleges, universities and professional schools (5.1%); Federal government (4.22%); Offices of physicians (4.15%)

Resources

American Association for Health Education (AAHE): aahperd.org/aahe/
Association of Environmental Health Academic Programs (AEHAP): aehap.org
National Commission for Health Education Credentialing (NCHEC): nchec.org
National Environmental Health Association (NEHA): neha.org
O*NET OnLine: online.onetcenter.org (see health educators)
Preparing Future Faculty (PFF) program: preparing–faculty.org
Society for Public Health Education (SOPHE): sophe.org
US Dept. of Labor, Bureau of Labor Statistics: bls.gov/oco/ocos063.htm

Q&A MICHÉLE SAMARYA-TIMM
Health Educator, Franklin
Township Health Department,
from an interview with Jim in 2008

*How did you get into this career field? What
was your education and experience, including
any green-related training or certification?*
While studying biology and broadcasting
at Montclair State University, I became inspired by the content of my general education class in community health. It appealed
to my desire to work to improve the health of others, but it wasn't medicine.
It dealt instead with the determinants of health and health in populations
rather than medically treating specific individuals. To me, it was holistic, re-
alistic and had career potential. During a health education internship at a local health department, I was provided with the opportunity to see how the
system of public and environmental health correlated with the public, and it
made sense to me to pursue a career in environmental health education. So I
got both my bachelor's and master's degrees in health education from Montclair State University.

*What is your current job title and how would you describe the work you do in a
typical day? What are your most common tasks, including those that make yours
a green job?*
I'm a health educator. My professional credentials include: certified health education specialist; registered environmental health specialist; health officer;
diplomate, American Academy of Sanitarians; certified food protection manager; and lead inspector/risk assessor. The work I do on any given day varies
widely. As an environmental health educator, my responsibilities include development and implementation of effective public health education programs
related to food safety, lead poisoning, radon, wastewater disposal, air quality,
water quality and other pertinent environmental health issues. A typical day
might go as follows: 8 AM — over morning coffee, review protocols for emergency pet shelters in case of potential disasters/evacuations; 9 AM — create
a wastewater PowerPoint presentation to illustrate the importance of septic
system maintenance; 11 AM — answer a resident inquiry on potential cancer
clusters; 11:30 AM — after a brief meeting with the director of health, develop
message maps and talking points regarding a local food recall; 2 PM — a quick
lunch is followed by a visit to a local middle school to encourage students to

create ways to reduce handwashing barriers within their school community; 3:30 PM — assess a community redevelopment area for potential barriers to walking/exercise; 4 PM — return to the office to moderate a national webinar on effective modes of marketing environmental health; 5 PM — before heading home, e-mail colleague at the Centers for Disease Control to obtain free pamphlets and materials for upcoming program on youth violence prevention. Environmental health education is exciting and fast-paced, as the environment affects every person, every day.

If you could give advice to a young person who wants to work in this career field someday, what would you tell them? How can they best groom themselves for this field?

Given the wide-ranging impact of the environment on our health and our lives, there will always be a need for environmental health professionals and for environmental health education. If someone is interested in entering this field, become aware and take advantage of all opportunities. Speak to your professors and academic advisors. They should be able to provide some direction. Speak to former students who are working in environmental health — they can be great resources for career advice and local vantage points. In addition, contact your local health department and chat with the director and those working in the environmental health division. Become involved on local boards or commissions. Consider an environmental health internship, or volunteer for community events such as litter cleanups. Go where the professionals go. Environmental health and health education associations are usually welcoming to students, and many have reduced student membership rates. Read and responsibly post on environmental health listservs. Attend open public meetings or hearings on environmental health issues. Keep in contact and follow up with the environmental health professionals you meet. Read journals and e-mail the authors with related questions and comments. Find a mentor. Research the state requirements for licensure and what coursework is needed to be able to obtain or prepare you for the license. Attend a university that is accredited in environmental health or health education. Explore free online trainings such as those offered by CDC, NEHA or a federally funded public health training website. Consider summer internships and fellowships, e.g., CDC, ATSDR, NIOSH, EPA.

What kind of career advancement opportunities can one expect in this field? What kind of salary range would reflect that career path (from entry-level to the more advanced position)?

Career advancement opportunities vary widely by such factors as the licenses one holds, the region and topical expertise. Advancement opportunities are available, although one may need to switch agencies to take advantage of them. A professional would need to be flexible, as often a position focuses on areas of concern where funding is available at that time. For example, areas of concern may include environmental sustainability, bioterrorism or pandemic preparedness. Salary ranges can vary from $30,000 per year at a non-profit organization to $100,000 per year for an experienced professional in a federal or private industry position.

In your opinion, what are some of the best schools, degrees and certificates for jobs in this career field, including green-specific training?
The college should be accredited. Lists of accredited schools for environmental health can be found at the Environmental Health Accreditation Council (EHAC) website, and lists of accredited schools for health education can be found at the Association of Schools of Public Health (ASPH) website. Degrees should be science based, but also focused on what you love or enjoy — such as environmental ecology, food safety or community health.

Are there any professional associations that you would recommend joining?
Depending on focus or specialty area, there is the National Environmental Health Association, the National Association of County and City Health Officials, the Association of Food and Drug Officials, the American Public Health Association and the Society for Public Health Education. Also look for the state and local affiliates of these organizations.

What emerging careers do you see developing now and into the future for this career field? What new technologies will have the greatest impact on this field?
Emerging and re-emerging key environmental health issues including outdoor air quality, water quality, toxics and waste, healthy homes and communities, antibiotic resistant disease, infrastructure, surveillance and global environmental health. Computer-based technologies and green-collar jobs are setting the future pathways for this profession. Future areas of importance would include: environmental health law, public policy and the environment, health disparities, integrating environment and communities to improve collective and personal health, environmental justice, environmental health education for healthcare providers, environmental health faculty in academia, environmental health risk communication and environmental health literacy.

Resources from Q&A

Agency for Toxic Substances and Disease Registry (ATSDR):
www.atsdr.cdc.gov
American Academy of Sanitarians: sanitarians.org
American Public Health Association (APHA): apha.org
Association of Food and Drug Officials (AFDO): afdo.org
Association of Schools of Public Health (ASPH): asph.org
Centers for Disease Control (CDC): cdc.gov
Environmental Health Accreditation Council (EHAC): ehacoffice.org
Montclair State University: montclair.edu
National Association of County and City Health Officials (NACCHO):
naccho.org
National Environmental Health Association (NEHA): neha.org
National Institute for Occupational Safety and Health (NIOSH):
cdc.gov/NIOSH/
Society for Public Health Education (SOPHE): sophe.org
US Environmental Protection Agency (EPA): epa.gov

Health Specialties Instructors, including Environmental Health Education Instructors

Health specialties teachers, postsecondary, teach courses in health specialties, such as veterinary medicine, dentistry, pharmacy, therapy, laboratory technology and public health. Includes teachers primarily engaged in teaching and those who combine teaching and research.

Qualifications and Advancement

A doctorate degree in the subject area is the typical education requirement, although a master's degree is often adequate for positions with community colleges and some four-year colleges. However, candidates with only a master's degree will find themselves competing against others with a doctorate degree.

Instructors and professors generally begin their careers as graduate teaching assistants. Once they complete their degree, they typically find jobs as lecturers or adjunct (part-time) professors or instructors. Eventually they find a full-time position. The next step for college and university professors is to become tenured — meaning that the professor has received a permanent job contract, granted after a probationary period of several years. Advancement for tenured professors involves moving into administrative positions, such as department chairperson, dean, vice president and president.

Salary Survey

Median salary: $77,190 (very high)

Typical range: $52,500 to $118,020

Job Outlook and Employment

Much faster than average growth is projected for this occupation in the US, from 145,000 jobs in 2006 to 178,350 in 2016. Projected growth will be primarily due to increases in college and university enrollment over the next decade. This enrollment growth stems mainly from the expected increase in the population of 18- to 24-year-olds, who constitute the majority of students at postsecondary institutions, and from the increasing number of high-school graduates who choose to attend these institutions. Adults returning to college to enhance their career prospects or to update their skills also will continue to create new opportunities for postsecondary teachers, particularly at community colleges and for-profit institutions that cater to working adults.

Where the Jobs Are

Colleges, universities and professional schools (70.8%); Community colleges (21.54%); Technical and trade schools (3.04%)

Resources

American Association for Health Education (AAHE): aahperd.org/aahe/

Association of Environmental Health Academic Programs (AEHAP):
   aehap.org

National Commission for Health Education Credentialing (NCHEC):
   nchec.org

National Environmental Health Association (NEHA): neha.org

O*NET OnLine: online.onetcenter.org (see health specialties teachers,
   postsecondary)

Preparing Future Faculty (PFF) program: preparing–faculty.org

Society for Public Health Education (SOPHE): sophe.org

US Dept. of Labor, Bureau of Labor Statistics: bls.gov/oco/ocos066.htm

Lawyers, including Environmental and Regulatory Attorneys

Lawyers represent clients in criminal and civil litigation and other legal proceedings, draw up legal documents and manage or advise clients on legal transactions. May specialize in a single area or may practice broadly in many areas of law.

Qualifications and Advancement

Becoming a lawyer requires a law school degree, which generally takes three years to complete for full-time students. Law school applicants must have a bachelor's degree to qualify for admission. Although there is no recommended "prelaw" undergraduate major, prospective lawyers should develop proficiency in writing and speaking, reading, researching, analyzing and thinking logically — all skills they need to succeed both in law school and in the law.

Beginning lawyers typically start in salaried positions as associates in a law firm or as clerks working with more experienced lawyers or judges. After several years, some lawyers are admitted to partnership in their firm, or they start their own practice. Some become prosecutors for district attorneys or attorney generals, and some are nominated or elected to judgeships. Some others become law school professors.

Salary Survey

Median salary: $102,470 (very high)

Typical range: $69,910 to $150,000

Job Outlook and Employment

Average growth is projected for the general occupation of lawyer in the US, from 760,672 jobs in 2006 to 844,195 in 2016. The growth in the population and in the level of business activity is expected to create more legal transactions, civil disputes and criminal cases. Job growth among lawyers also will result from increasing demand for legal services in areas including energy and environmental law.

Where the Jobs Are

Legal services (47.56%); Local government (6.64%); State government (4.91%); Federal government, excluding postal service (4.09%); Self-employed: 25.64%

Resources

American Bar Association (ABA): abanet.org

Environmental Lawyers.com: environmentallawyers.com

Law School Admission Council (LSAC): lsac.org

lawjobs.com Career Center: law.com/jsp/law/careercenter/index.jsp

Lawyers Weekly Jobs: lawyersweeklyjobs.com

National Association for Law Placement (NALP): nalp.org

O*NET OnLine: online.onetcenter.org (see lawyers)

US Department of Justice, Environment and Natural Resources Division
    (ENRD): usdoj.gov/enrd/

US Dept. of Labor, Bureau of Labor Statistics: bls.gov/oco/ocos053.htm

Q&A CAMAS J. STEINMETZ
Land Use Attorney, Manatt,
Phelps & Phillips, LLP,
from an interview with Alice in 2008

*How did you get into this career field? What
was your education and experience, including
any green-related training or certification?*
Prior to going to law school at UC Davis, I
majored in environmental studies with an
emphasis in policy and planning at UC Santa Cruz. While at UC Santa Cruz,
I completed my thesis on the Natural Community Conservation Planning approach to preserving endangered species and worked for a non-profit, Global
Action and Information Network, tracking and analyzing environmental legislation in congress. After graduating from UC Santa Cruz, I interned with a
county planning department where I assisted in implementing the Clean Water Act by drafting ordinances and best management practices to reduce storm
water runoff pollution. I then took a position as legislative advocate for the
Committee for Green Foothills, an environmental non-profit in Silicon Valley
founded by author Wallace Stegner. We were charged with minimizing the impacts of development on our precious remaining natural resources, including
the foothills, by monitoring development applications and lobbying for general plan and zoning amendments to strengthen protection of our resources
through policies such as urban growth boundaries, density restrictions and ri-
parian buffer zones. I worked there for four years before deciding to go to law
school to pursue land use from a legal angle. My first summer after law school,
I was an intern for the Department of Justice Environmental Enforcement Division. I am now pursuing my LEED (Leadership in Energy and Environmental Design) professional accreditation to add to my green credentials.

*What is your current job title and how would you describe the work you do in a
typical day? What are your most common tasks, including those that make yours
a green job?*
I am currently a land use associate at the law firm Manatt, Phelps & Phillips,
LLP. I review development projects for compliance with the California Environmental Quality Act (CEQA) and other environmental legislation, draft
conservation easements, enroll property in the Williamson Act, which serves
to protect agricultural property from development in exchange for a property
tax reduction, assist property owners in challenging large development projects by referendum and initiative, obtain entitlements for transit-oriented and

compact infill development projects, assist developers in meeting LEED cer-tified standards and represent solar energy service providers. On a pro bono basis, I am currently representing Hidden Villa, Inc., a non-profit farm and environmental summer camp, in obtaining a use permit from Santa Clara County to allow the lease of a portion of their 1,600-acre property to Heifer International, Inc. for construction and operation of a "Global Village" to pro-mote sustainable solutions to global hunger, poverty and environmental deg-radation.

If you could give advice to a young person who wants to work in this career field someday, what would you tell them? How can they best groom themselves for this field?

I think the best way to groom for a career in the land use law field is to pursue an undergraduate degree in planning and/or environmental studies before obtaining your law degree. Because land use is largely governed by cities and counties, it is also very helpful to have some hands-on experience in planning, politics and lobbying elected officials. Maybe, most importantly, find and de-velop a relationship with a great mentor that can take you under their wing and show you the ropes and give you enough leeway to advance and develop.

What kind of career advancement opportunities can one expect in this field? What kind of salary range would reflect that career path (from entry-level to the more advanced position)?

Typically, at a law firm, you can expect to be an associate for about seven to nine years before becoming an "income partner." Then, depending on how much revenue you bring in, you could hope to become an "equity partner." Salary depends upon the size and stature of the law firm you work at and the location of your practice. Entry-level salary at the top law firms is currently $170,000, with approximately $10,000 to $20,000 raises each year. Entry-level salaries at smaller law firms are as low as $60,000.

What emerging careers do you see developing now and into the future for this career field? What new technologies will have the greatest impact on this field?

Emerging legal careers and practice areas are assisting clients in addressing climate change and the energy crisis through sustainable, compact, transit-oriented development that integrates renewable energy sources and used/re-newable building materials.

Resources from Q&A

Committee for Green Foothills: greenfoothills.org
Global Action and Information Network: gain.org/gain/

Heifer International, Inc.: heifer.org

Hidden Villa, Inc.: hiddenvilla.org

Manatt, Phelps & Phillips, LLP: manatt.com

University of California, Davis: ucdavis.edu

University of California, Santa Cruz: ucsc.edu

US Department of Justice, Environment and Natural Resources Division (ENRD): usdoj.gov/enrd/

US Green Building Council/LEED AP Certification: usgbc.org

Public Relations Specialists, including Environmental/Sustainability Specialists

Public relations specialists engage in promoting or creating goodwill for individuals, groups or organizations by writing or selecting favorable publicity material and releasing it through various communications media. May prepare and arrange displays and make speeches.

Qualifications and Advancement

A bachelor's degree in public relations, journalism, advertising or communication is the typical education requirement. A college degree combined with PR experience, usually gained through an internship, is considered excellent preparation for PR work; in fact, internships are becoming vital to obtaining employment. Some firms seek college graduates who have worked in electronic or print journalism. Others seek applicants with demonstrated communication skills and training, or experience in a field related to the firm's business.

In PR firms, recent graduates may be hired as research or account assistants. With experience, they can be promoted to account executive. From there they may become account supervisor, PR manager, vice president and then senior vice president. The career path of a PR specialist at a corporation is similar, but the position names may be different. Some experienced PR specialists start their own consulting firms.

Salary Survey

Median salary: $47,350 (high)

Typical range: $35,600 to $65,310

Job Outlook and Employment

Faster than average growth is projected for this occupation in the US, from 243,275 jobs in 2006 to 286,145 in 2016. The need for good public relations in an increasingly competitive business environment should spur demand for these workers in organizations of all types and sizes. Those with additional language capabilities are also in great demand. Employment in public relations firms should grow as firms hire contractors to provide PR services rather than support full-time staff.

Where the Jobs Are

Advertising and related services (12.05%); Colleges, universities and professional schools (7.01%); Local government (3.87%); Management of companies and enterprises (3.68%); Religious organizations (3.54%); Grant-making and -giving services (3.05%); Self-employed: 4.91%

Resources

Council of Public Relations Firms: prfirms.org
Institute for Public Relations (IPR): instituteforpr.org
International Association of Business Communicators (IABC): iabc.com
National Association for Interpretation (NAI): interpnet.com
O*NET OnLine: online.onetcenter.org (see public relations specialists)
Public Relations Society of America (PRSA): prsa.org
True Spin Conference: truespinconference.com
US Dept. of Labor, Bureau of Labor Statistics: bls.gov/oco/ocos086.htm

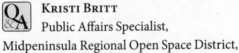
Kristi Britt
Public Affairs Specialist,
Midpeninsula Regional Open Space District,
from an interview with Alice in 2008

How did you get into this career field? What was your education and experience, including any green-related training or certification?

I wanted to have a business degree to fall back on — no matter what career path I chose. Within the business discipline, I chose what I thought would be the most creative specialty and offered the most job diversity, which for me was marketing. After having gained some general marketing experience, I wanted to apply my knowledge and skills within the preservation and enjoyment of open space. I graduated from San Jose State University with a bachelor's degree in business and marketing. I began my career in inside sales for a computer hardware distributor, then transitioned to a marketing associate position for a particle size analyzer company, and now I've worked for nearly 12 years for the Midpeninsula Regional Open Space District in the public affairs department. Although I do not have any specific green-related training or certification, I have a personal interest in the preservation of open space and communicating with the public about this valuable resource, and how they can enjoy and benefit from it.

What is your current job title and how would you describe the work you do in a typical day? What are your most common tasks, including those that make yours a green job?

As a public affairs specialist, I'm responsible for responding to the public, the media and partner agencies and getting our message out to the public through outreach activities and written communications — engaging them in low-intensity recreation, environmental education and volunteer opportunities. I'm responsible for most of our literature, including the quarterly newsletter, preserve maps and brochures; planning and leading dedication events and other large-scale public gatherings; responding to and working with the media; managing special projects, such as production of our trail guide book; production and implementation of our new logo; and creation of new public programs and resources. The aspects of my job that make it a green job are writing/communicating to help educate the public about important environmental issues and to inform the public of the historical, natural and cultural resource features of the open-space preserves. In addition, there is a sustainability greening component to my job. Related to producing the district's literature, a key district goal is to use recycled and/or post-consumer waste content materials and soy-based ink in its print materials. As the green movement is making its way further into mainstream business, such as the printing industry, there are far greater environmentally friendly production processes and product offerings available, including paper stocks. It is part of my job to be knowledgeable regarding these offerings and to ensure that we are working with environmentally aware and responsible contractors. We are also beginning to research eco-friendly caterers and environmentally friendly product alternatives to traditional cups, plates, utensils, water bottles, etc.

If you could give advice to a young person who wants to work in this career field someday, what would you tell them? How can they best groom themselves for this field?

I would highly recommend participating in an internship, research project or volunteer opportunity. The marketing/public affairs related positions for a park or open space agency are inherently more limited, as the number of agencies with this focus is limited, so participating in an internship will provide networking opportunities and an opportunity to get a foot in the door.

What kind of career advancement opportunities can one expect in this field? What kind of salary range would reflect that career path (from entry-level to the more advanced position)?

When considering career advancement opportunities, be aware of the organization's size and inherent limitations for advancement. Entry-level positions generally include marketing/public affairs administrative assistants and/ or associates and clerical, support-related tasks. Mid-level positions include marketing/public affairs or communications specialists and often include a supervisory and project management component. Marketing/public affairs department managers and directors represent middle to upper management positions.

Entry-level to a more advanced department manager position includes a range of approximately $47,000 to $116,000. A director of marketing position would likely begin around $150,000.

In your opinion, what are some of the best schools, degrees and certificates for jobs in this career field, including green-specific training?

A bachelor's degree in marketing, journalism, public relations, environmental communications, environmental studies or communications with environmental communication as a specialty.

How does someone without previous experience in this career field land a job? What are the best strategies for job-hunting in this field?

I would recommend pursuing an internship, research project or volunteer opportunity. Research open space, agricultural and other government agencies, as well as private, non-profit land trusts and partner agencies local to the area. Schedule an informational interview with the agency's marketing/public affairs staff, if possible. This will provide an opportunity to hone one's interviewing skills and provide additional real-world information. Landing a job in a green career field without previous experience takes the interest and the initiative of the person to educate and green themselves through on-the-job training and attendance at conferences/seminars.

Are there any professional associations that you would recommend joining?

CAPIO (California Association of Public Information Officials). Attend a public relations conference such as The True Spin Conference — A National PR Conference for Progressives. Also the NAI (National Association for Interpretation).

What emerging careers do you see developing now and into the future for this career field? What new technologies will have the greatest impact on this field?

Diversity specialists — as the country's population continues to become increasingly diverse, a component of the future of the environmental movement will be to reach out to these diverse communities and to diversify the environmental movement itself. In addition to providing greater attention to cultures and languages, consideration of generations and trends is an important topic. Greater attention to research of the needs and behaviors of baby boomers, generations X, Y and C, as they will be the supporters, visitors and users of parks and open space, will increasingly emerge as an area of interest. Familiarity with multimedia is also important. As the younger generations — Gen Y and Generation C — are defined as "tech generations" and value audio, video, animation, etc., the incorporation of these modes of communication to convey messages will become increasingly important to reach these audiences who will be the future voters and supporters of parks and open space.

Resources from Q&A
California Association of Public Information Officials (CAPIO): capio.org
Midpeninsula Regional Open Space District: openspace.org
National Association for Interpretation (NAI): interpnet.com
San Jose State University: sjsu.edu
True Spin Conference: truespinconference.com

Reporters and Correspondents, including Green Journalists

Reporters and correspondents collect and analyze facts about newsworthy events by interview, investigation or observation. Report and write stories for newspaper, news magazine, radio or television.

Qualifications and Advancement
A bachelor's degree in journalism is the typical education requirement. However, some employers hire graduates with other majors. They look for experience on school newspapers or with broadcasting stations and internships with news organizations. Large-city newspapers and stations sometimes prefer candidates with a degree in a subject-matter specialty such as economics, political science or business. Some large newspapers and broadcasters hire only experienced reporters.

Most reporters and correspondents start at small publications or broadcast stations as general assignment reporters or copy editors. Large publications and stations hire few recent graduates; as a rule, they require new reporters to have several years of experience. Beginning reporters cover court proceedings and civic and club meetings, summarize speeches and write obituaries. With experience, they are given more difficult assignments, cover an assigned beat or specialize in a particular field. Some advance by moving to larger newspapers or stations. A few become columnists, writers, announcers or public relations specialists. Reporters can also become editors in print journalism or program managers in broadcast journalism. Some eventually become broadcasting or publishing industry managers.

Salary Survey
Median salary: $33,470 (low/moderate)
Typical range: $24,370 to $51,700

Job Outlook and Employment
Little growth is projected for this occupation in the US, estimated from 59,212 jobs in 2006 to 59,921 in 2016. Many factors will contribute to the limited job growth. Consolidation and convergence will continue in the publishing and broadcasting industries. As a result, companies will be better able to allocate their news analysts, reporters and correspondents to cover news stories. Constantly improving technology also is allowing workers to do their jobs more efficiently and that will limit the number of workers needed. However, the continued demand for news will create some job opportunities, and many job openings will be the result of replacing workers who leave the occupation.

Where the Jobs Are
Newspaper publishers (62.36%); Television broadcasting (12.36%); Radio broadcasting (3.47%); Self-employed: 9.2%

Resources
Committee of Concerned Journalists (CCJ): concernedjournalists.org
Green Press Initiative: greenpressinitiative.org
Project for Excellence in Journalism (PEJ): journalism.org
Society of Environmental Journalists (SEJ): sej.org

Photo by Matthew T. Stallbaumer.

JOHN ROCKHOLD
Managing Editor, *Mother Earth News*,
from an interview with Jim in 2008

How did you get into this career field? What was your education and experience?
In college, I majored in English and minored in magazine journalism. My original ambition was to be a nature writer/poet, but I realized the odds of that paying the bills were slim to none. With my English education, I was able to focus on creative and nonfiction writing about nature and wildlife. I even won the university's nature writing contest two years in a row. I knew I wanted to do something with writing, editing and/or publishing nature and environmental content. The questions were how would I get such a job and what exactly would I be doing? After college, I got into the magazine industry, first as a writer, then later as an editor. Eventually I pursued a job opening with *Mother Earth News* and was fortunate enough to get my foot in the door.

What is your current job title and how would you describe the work you do in a typical day? What are your most common tasks?
I'm the managing editor for *Mother Earth News*. A typical day has me doing a little bit of everything: planning, scheduling, supervising, coordinating, editing and writing. My most common tasks are supervising our progress against deadlines, planning and coordinating content for the magazine and website and working with the editors on our staff to answer their questions and guide them. Since becoming the managing editor, I'm doing less day-to-day editing and more planning and coordinating.

If you could give advice to a young person who wants to work in this career field someday, what would you tell them? How can they best groom themselves for this field?
Dream big. Figure out what you generally want to do, and then passionately pursue it. It's a really good idea to have education in both the field you want to get into, such as journalism, and the specific topic, such as environmental issues. While you don't necessarily need two degrees, someone who has two, or at least a major and minor, in both journalism and mechanical engineering,

for example, would stand a better chance to be an editor/writer about renewable energy than someone with just a journalism degree and an interest in renewable energy. It's also important to get out there and get experience, even while you're still in school. Whether it's an internship, volunteer work or outside workshops, that hands-on experience will help you stand out from the rest of the field.

What kind of career advancement opportunities can one expect in this field? What kind of salary range would reflect that career path (from entry level to the more advanced position)?

I really believe that those who work hard and put forth their best energy will find advancement opportunities, even in areas where it seems unlikely. In the case of the media industry, there are frequent opportunities for those who earn it. Salaries vary so much based on region and specific company that I hesitate to say specifics. But don't hesitate to place a great value on having a job you love, even if it pays less than a job you wouldn't love. Also, good things come to those who earn them: if you're unhappy with an entry-level salary, work hard, be patient and earn a promotion.

In your opinion, what are some of the best schools, degrees and certificates for jobs in this career field?

It depends on what aspect of green or sustainability issues you want to get into. But definitely do your homework and try to find a school with a quality program in your area of interest, as well as a community around it that offers additional opportunities for internships, volunteer opportunities, etc.

How does someone without previous experience in this career field land a job? What are the best strategies for job-hunting in this field?

Previous experience doesn't have to be professional or education. You can learn, volunteer and do things in your personal time that would go a long way toward making you qualified for a job. As far as job-hunting, search high and low. Scour the job websites, as well as the websites of specific companies and organizations. And don't be afraid to contact a company you're interested in working for, even if they don't have any advertised openings. Your initiative will likely make a positive impression, and you might get ahead of the crowd when there is an opening.

What emerging or high-growth careers do you see developing now and into the future for this career field? What new technologies will have the greatest impact on this field?

Communication will be central to everything; the ability to convey a quick, accurate and compelling message will be paramount. And the Internet will continue to be at the heart of it all. If you're not familiar with the Internet and its capabilities, you'll be left behind.

Resources

Mother Earth News (magazine): motherearthnews.com

Natural and Land Resource Management Group

o Fish and Game Wardens, including Wildlife Officers

o Park Naturalists, including Park Rangers and Interpreters

o Range Managers, including Natural Resource Managers

Fish and Game Wardens, including Wildlife Officers

Fish and game wardens patrol assigned area to prevent fish and game law violations. Investigate reports of damage to crops or property by wildlife. Compile biological data.

Qualifications and Advancement

Requirements vary by state and agency. An associate's degree is the most common education requirement; however, over 40 percent of recent hires had at least a bachelor's degree. Combining a wildlife management major with law enforcement courses is good preparation. And yet many of the skills needed for this occupation are learned through both formal and on-the-job training, which can last up to one year.

Fish and game wardens and wildlife officers may be promoted to supervisory positions after several years of experience. They may also become wildlife inspectors or special agents, where they receive training as criminal investigators. Promotion depends on experience, training, exam scores and job performance. A bachelor's degree is sometimes required for promotion.

Salary Survey

Median salary: $43,700 (high)

Typical range: $34,380 to $52,770

Job Outlook and Employment

No growth is projected for this occupation in the US, estimated at 8,030 jobs in 2006 and projected at 8,017 jobs in 2016. The level of government spending determines the level of employment for fish and game wardens. The number of job opportunities, therefore, can vary from year to year and from place to place. Layoffs, on the other hand, are rare because retirements enable most staffing cuts to be handled through attrition.

Where the Jobs Are

State government (86.8%); Local government, excluding education and hospitals (12.29%)

Resources

North American Wildlife Enforcement Officers Association (NAWEOA):
    naweoa.org
O*NET OnLine: online.onetcenter.org (see fish and game wardens)
US Dept. of Labor, Bureau of Labor Statistics: bls.gov/oco/ocos160.htm
    (see fish and game wardens)
US Fish and Wildlife Service: fws.gov

 LORRAINE DOYLE
Fish and Game Warden,
California Department of Fish and Game,
from an interview with Jim in 2008

How did you get into this career field? What was your education and experience, including any green-related training or certification?
My father was a park ranger when I was a child. He worked for the California Department of Parks and Recreation (DPR) for over 30 years. We camped and hiked and enjoyed the outdoors. My parents had a great love of plants and wildlife, and they passed it on to me. I majored in natural sciences at Chico State University with the goal of becoming a park ranger. I began working for DPR in the summer of 1980 at Folsom Lake State Recreation Area (SRA) as a seasonal park aide. After I graduated from college, I worked another summer at Folsom Lake SRA and then applied to the California Department of Fish and Game for a seasonal position at the Sacramento National Wildlife Refuge for waterfowl season. I worked there for four seasons and another three seasons at Folsom Lake SRA. I tested for Fish and Game Warden Cadet in 1983 after seeing what wardens did, and I was hired as a cadet in December of 1984. I completed the peace officer academy in April of 1985 and began work as a warden in Long Beach, California.

What is your current job title and how would you describe the work you do in a typical day? What are your most common tasks, including those that make yours a green job?

I am a fish and game warden. There is no typical day as a warden! Unfortunately, there is paperwork to be done. Having a computer makes some of this easier, but there are still reports to write and forms to complete. A day of patrol could be driving in designated areas, often within the Sierra National Forest, looking for fish- and game-related activities. It could be a skiff patrol on a lake for anglers. Court appearances take time from patrol. But if a violation is found, a good report must be compiled and then submitted to supervisors and to the District Attorney's office and/or court. If you don't have a good report, you can't get your case filed or get a conviction.

If you could give advice to a young person who wants to work in this career field someday, what would you tell them? How can they best groom themselves for this field?

Most fish and game wardens are not in this line of work to make money. They have to be prepared to make less than other law enforcement officers who often have fewer responsibilities. I would encourage them to work on their writing skills. Experience in jobs that provide exposure to the public can be invaluable. A good background in general wildlife is helpful. The law enforcement portion of our job is taught at the academy. Currently our academy also teaches fish- and game-specific subjects, but a solid background prior to the academy is beneficial. Also, they must be in good physical condition to be hired and to complete the academy training.

What kind of career advancement opportunities can one expect in this field? What kind of salary range would reflect that career path (from entry-level to the more advanced position)?

Wardens can be promoted up the ranks. In California, the pay range is about $3,500 to $5,000 per month. The non-supervisory position of lieutenant specialist pays up to about $6,300 per month. That position is generally used for training, equipment and special investigations. Lieutenant is the first-line supervisor position, and the pay range for that is $4,770 to $6,300 per month. The next level is captain, which pays about $5,500 to $7,200 per month. Then we have assistant chiefs, a position that pays between $6,000 and $8,000 per month, and the chief who makes up to about $13,400 per month.

In your opinion, what are some of the best schools, degrees and certificates for jobs in this career field, including green-specific training?

In California, I would recommend a bachelor of arts or bachelor of science degree from any state university or University of California school. It is often hard to complete a degree once working as a warden. The department recommends biological sciences, police science or law enforcement, natural resources conservation, ecology or related fields. Completion of a bachelor's degree earns another $100 per month. Completion of a two-year associate's degree earns another $50 per month. Sixty units is the required minimum upon completion of the academy.

How does someone without previous experience in this career field land a job? What are the best strategies for job-hunting in this field?
The warden position is entry-level. Our academy gives a good base to build upon with further training during the field training period. Warden cadets should be willing to start anywhere in the state for which they apply.

Are there any professional associations that you would recommend joining?
Wardens who belong to the California Fish and Game Wardens Association also belong to the North American Wildlife Enforcement Officers Association (NAWEOA). They also have a student membership available.

What emerging careers do you see developing now and into the future for this career field? What new technologies will have the greatest impact on this field?
Unfortunately, in terms of job growth, this is a stagnant field. More often than not, positions are cut due to budget problems. In fact, we have the same number of wardens in California now as we had several decades ago. This could change with pressure from the public to increase protection for our natural resources with more positions and better pay. But these days, many prospective candidates for fish and game warden will choose other jobs that offer higher pay.

Resources from Q&A
California Department of Fish and Game: dfg.ca.gov
California Department of Parks and Recreation: parks.ca.gov
California Fish and Game Wardens Association (CFGWA):
    californiafishandgamewardens.com
Folsom Lake State Recreation Area: parks.ca.gov/?page_id=500
North American Wildlife Enforcement Officers Association (NAWEOA):
    naweoa.org
Sacramento National Wildlife Refuge: fws.gov/sacramentovalleyrefuges/
Sierra National Forest: fs.fed.us/r5/sierra/

Park Naturalists, including Park Rangers and Interpreters

Park naturalists plan, develop and conduct programs to inform public of historical, natural and scientific features of national, state or local parks.

Qualifications and Advancement

A bachelor's degree in biology, forestry, wildlife management or natural science-related fields is the typical education requirement. Some students major in education and minor in a life science program or vice versa.

Some park naturalists start their careers as volunteer naturalists until an employment opportunity comes up. New graduates tend to get jobs as park naturalists only for the summer months. As they gain experience, naturalists are able to move into year-round positions. Moving to another area of the country is another way to get a year-round job. Naturalists who have leadership skills may move into regional naturalist, visitor services or park management positions. Some agencies require a master's degree for management positions.

Salary Survey

Median salary: $54,970 (very high)
Typical range: $40,950 to $68,460

Job Outlook and Employment

Slower than average growth is projected for the general occupation of conservation scientists in the US, estimated from 19,777 jobs in 2006 to 20,830 in 2016. Federal and state budgetary constraints are expected to keep job growth to a minimum for this occupation. However, a large number of workers are expected to retire over the next decade. This is likely to create some job opportunities.

Where the Jobs Are

Park naturalists/rangers and interpreters work for federal, state and regional/local parks. Some jobs are with private agencies where fundraising or writing grants is a key part of the job.

Resources

Association of National Park Rangers (ANPR): anpr.org
Leave No Trace: lnt.org
National Association for Interpretation (NAI): interpnet.com
National Park Service: nps.gov

National Parks Conservation Association (NPCA): eparks.org
North American Association of Environmental Education (NAAEE):
    naaee.org
O*NET OnLine: online.onetcenter.org (see park naturalists)
Student Conservation Association (SCA): thesca.org
USAJOBS: www.usajobs.gov
US Dept. of Labor, Bureau of Labor Statistics: bls.gov/oco/ocos048.htm

 AMY LETHBRIDGE, Deputy Executive Officer/Chief of
Interpretation, Mountains Recreation and Conservation Authority,
from an interview with Jim in 2008

*How did you get into this career field? What was your education and experience,
including any green-related training or certification?*
I came into it sort of sideways. My degree was in political science, and I was
actually working for a state senator who represented the Malibu area. As a
member of his staff, I was able to visit some of the local interpretive programs
in the Santa Monica Mountains, specifically for inner-city kids. And I was just
really struck by how wonderful they were and how important they were, and I
had this overwhelming feeling that I wanted to be part of that. It especially af-
fected me because I was raised in a rural mountain area, and the outdoors was
an integral part of my childhood.

*What is your current job title and how would you describe the work you do in a
typical day? What are your most common tasks, including those that make yours
a green job?*
My job title is actually deputy executive officer. So I do a combination of overall agency administration, program planning and supervision. Unfortunately I
don't get to do a lot of program delivery anymore. I do a lot of work with community organizations, identifying what the needs of under-served groups are
in Los Angeles and figuring out how to make our programs meet their needs.
I also hire and do a lot of training of naturalists, interpreters and rangers. I
certainly consider the work we do green. An administrator is an administrator, but we are really fostering exposure to the outdoors and a healthy lifestyle.
Not just in terms of exercise and clean air, though that's certainly a huge part
of it, but we work to create safe, beautiful places where children can run and
play and have fun and experience traditional outdoor activities that they normally can't. And I think all of those things make both the participants and the
planet healthier and lead to better stewardship of the planet.

If you could give advice to a young person who wants to work in this career field someday, what would you tell them? How can they best groom themselves for this field?

I would tell them: be persistent, follow your dreams, volunteer. There are a lot of ways to get into fields — you just have to get involved and keep turning over every rock until you find what works for you. Education is obviously important, too. I tend to hire a lot of young people with degrees in the natural sciences or in recreation. More and more, it's difficult without at least a bachelor's degree, although I do hire some great folks who have volunteered for a long time and have on-the-ground experience. So in my part of the green world, it's possible to get in without the degree, but typically it's necessary. There are a couple of different entry paths, but starting with volunteering is pretty standard, say as an interpretive guide at a kiosk or in a visitor center handing out brochures. That's a real common entry-level place. Then you can work your way up to giving public programs that someone else has developed and eventually to developing your own interpretive programs. Then you get into planning, where you're planning the whole visitor experience at an entire site. And there's a lot of room to grow. It's never going to be a field where we make a ton of money, but it's incredibly rewarding work.

What kind of career advancement opportunities can one expect in this field? What kind of salary range would reflect that career path (from entry-level to the more advanced position)?

In California you start in the low $20,000s. If you work all the way up, and you're willing to get out of the field a little bit and take on administrative and planning roles, you could end up making $50,000 or $60,000 per year. But, of course, one of the things that happens in interpretation is that the people who want to be outside and with the people sometimes don't want to do the administration or supervision. But that is where there tends to be career growth. Now, a park ranger has to be that very special person who is both a good law enforcement officer and a terrific interpreter. All of our park rangers are certified interpretive guides. But if they find they really love the law enforcement side, then there's a lot more money to be made working for a city police department.

In your opinion, what are some of the best schools, degrees and certificates for jobs in this career field, including green-specific training?

Humboldt State University has a great program in natural resources and interpretation. That's the one that I hire a lot of people from. It's rare to even find that program somewhere, and I know I get very good people out of it. What strikes me about the Humboldt program is that I've never met anyone who didn't love it — love it there, love the experience and really come to me with great skills.

How does someone without previous experience in this career field land a job? What are the best strategies for job-hunting in this field?
Since we're out there doing public programs, in my case I would recommend going out to see some of the programs in order to get an idea of what we do and whether you really want to do it. Sometimes people really romanticize interpretation, and park rangers especially! And making a personal connection somewhere really helps. Yes, check the government websites and everything, but when someone makes a personal connection and is volunteering, or if they're in college and pursuing an internship, it says a lot to me that they're willing to put in that kind of time.

Are there any professional associations that you would recommend joining?
The National Association for Interpretation is an excellent organization, both to promote people's individual growth as an interpreter and the field of interpretation. I think they're just amazing. Also the North American Association of Environmental Education is a great organization. Those are the two that, in this sort of outdoor education field, I've used to both my own personal and program's benefit.

What emerging careers do you see developing now and into the future for this career field? What new technologies will have the greatest impact on this field?
Well I think we're all waiting to see how best to use technology. I think technology can enhance interpretive programs in a variety of ways, but I think we also have some examples of where technology for technology's sake doesn't really add anything, and at times even takes away from it. There's a big move in interpretation where you can "download the digital park ranger on your iPod" — that sort of thing. There's a lot of buzz about that, and several companies are market testing those kinds of programs. I think there's a place for everything, but I am of the belief that a personal interpreter, someone who can guide you face-to-face and give you the message of a site, is the most effective kind of interpretation. But agencies can't always afford that. So we'll see what happens with all of this digital potential we have. In Los Angeles, one of the things we struggle with all the time is how to address the multiple languages issue, and that's something that perhaps technology can help us with. So there are areas where it could potentially be really helpful. But again, I firmly believe

that a real interpreter is the best way to go. In general, we don't tend to be a very diverse field, so the other thing that means for agencies like mine is doing a better job making sure there's diversity among your staff, and making sure that interpretation is a career choice for a much more diverse group of people who might speak those other languages.

Resources from Q&A

Humboldt State University: humboldt.edu

Mountains Recreation & Conservation Authority (MRCA): mrca.ca.gov

National Association for Interpretation (NAI): interpnet.com

North American Association of Environmental Education (NAAEE):
   naaee.org

 REBECCA ALFAFARA
Park Ranger,
Zion National Park,
from an interview with Jim in 2008

How did you get into this career field? What was your education and experience, including any green-related training or certification?

I started in this career field by completing an internship through the Student Conservation Association & AmeriCorps for college credit. I also volunteered with the Volunteers-In-Parks Program at Badlands National Park in South Dakota. These positions enabled me to gain valuable experience in the field, as well as network. Often people will start off their careers in this field by volunteering or interning to get their foot in the door. My own education includes a bachelor of science degree from Michigan State University. My degree is in park recreation and tourism resources with an emphasis in natural resources. I have worked for some state parks in New Hampshire, Badlands National Park for two seasons and Zion National Park for the past two seasons. As a park ranger, I have received significant training about park resources, interpretation and environmental education, as well as Leave No Trace training.

What is your current job title and how would you describe the work you do in a typical day? What are your most common tasks?

My current job title is interpretive park ranger for the National Park Service. My typical day varies, as each day can be very different. Some tasks include presenting interpretive talks, tours and hikes; staffing visitor information desks; roving hiking trails to make contacts with visitors and cleaning up litter; working with youth for our Junior Ranger Program to help promote future park stewards, as well as various other projects. Other projects can range from composing to editing park publications and media. In my everyday activities, I try to set a good example of being sustainable and to help to get the message across to visitors whether roving on the trails or during formal programs.

If you could give advice to a young person who wants to work in this career field someday, what would you tell them? How can they best groom themselves for this field?

Be persistent and willing to volunteer. Often you need to get yourself known by interning and working hard so that you can make a name for yourself. To groom yourself for this career, I'd say go to college and gain experience working with the public, which involves public speaking and education. Take courses that you enjoy, but science, history and education classes can go a long way — even if they are not necessarily required.

What kind of career advancement opportunities can one expect in this field? What kind of salary range would reflect that career path (from entry-level to the more advanced position)?

As a park ranger, you can expect to work many years as a seasonal employee. This means you will work less than half the year in a particular position at a given park. Once you gain the much-needed experience with the National Park Service, you can compete more successfully for a permanent position. Once permanent, you will earn a higher salary, receive benefits and work year-round at the same park. Also, after working as a permanent employee, you gain status that enables you to apply for permanent positions open to status candidates only. Many rangers are not picky about their first permanent posting (park area). They are able to change parks; however, some will spend their entire careers at the same park. By gaining experience and diversifying their skills, they can climb the National Park Service ladder. Most entry-level positions within the interpretation field start as a GS–4 Park Guide or GS–5 Park Ranger. GS–7 and GS–9 positions are often lead or permanent positions. You spend a minimum of a year at each grade before qualifying for the next grade. Once you move up, rangers tend to spend less time in the field and more time supervising and doing administrative duties.

In your opinion, what are some of the best schools, degrees and certificates for jobs in this career field, including green-specific training?

Due to the fact that for my position you basically just need a bachelor's degree, I couldn't really say that there is any school that is better than another. What is important is to get a degree and gain experience with education and/or public speaking. It wouldn't hurt to have science, education and computer skills, either.

How does someone without previous experience in this career field land a job? What are the best strategies for job-hunting in this field?
Without previous experience, you can land a job by having a background in education or interpretation. If you are a student, another option would be to apply through the Student Temporary Employment Program (STEP). The National Park Service opens up a number of jobs specifically for students to gain much-needed experience. This allows students to get experience without having to compete for jobs with those who already have years of work with the National Park Service. The best strategies for job-hunting would be to check the USAJOBS.gov website often. When you find a job to your liking, read everything — maybe even twice. Often applications are disregarded for leaving out minor details. So check over your application packet thoroughly and don't follow the traditional single-page resumé rule for this agency. My resume is already 11 pages and growing!

Are there any professional associations that you would recommend joining?
There are many professional associations that park rangers belong to. For the interpretive park ranger, I would recommend the National Association of Interpretation. They also offer certifications, trainings and workshops. I also belong to the Association of National Park Rangers — which helps me keep up with the goings-on of the National Park Service. Assuming leadership roles in any such association would be beneficial. However, you are not required to belong to any associations.

What emerging careers do you see developing now and into the future for this career field? What new technologies will have the greatest impact on this field?
As far as emerging careers go, the National Park Service will be celebrating its 100th birthday in 2016, and we are already vamping up for that by bulking up staff numbers and performing much-needed maintenance to some structures, roads and trails in order to help with the celebration of our park's treasures. New technologies that will impact this field would include green technologies. Often I go to work and see new practices being implemented to improve sustainability or even new items. For instance, within the last season at Zion, my division replaced many computers with computers that use less energy and

are a fraction of the cost of regular computers. The Internet and computers
have also cut back on our paper usage, which I know will continue into the future. We also have LED lights at each desk to limit the use of our overhead fluorescent lights. These are small things that really add up. Not to mention our
hybrid vehicles, propane shuttles and our wonderful recycling program.

Resources from Q&A

AmeriCorps: americorps.org
Association of National Park Rangers (ANPR): anpr.org
Badlands National Park Volunteers in Parks (VIP) Program:
    home.nps.gov/applications/vips/volunteer.cfm?id=BADL
Leave No Trace: lnt.org
Michigan State University: msu.edu
National Association for Interpretation (NAI): interpnet.com
National Park Service: nps.gov
Student Conservation Association (SCA): thesca.org
Student Temporary Employment Program (STEP):
    opm.gov/employ/students/intro.asp
USAJOBS: usajobs.gov
Zion National Park: nps.gov/zion/

Range Managers, including Natural Resource Managers

Range managers research or study range land management practices to provide sustained production of forage, livestock and wildlife.

Qualifications and Advancement

A bachelor's degree in range management or range science is the typical education requirement. More than 30 colleges and universities offer degrees in
range management that are accredited by the Society of Range Management.
In the federal government, a combination of experience and appropriate education occasionally may substitute for a four-year range management degree.
Graduate degrees are usually required for teaching and research positions.

Some range management students may get their initial experience in this
occupation as a range technician. Recent range management graduates usually
work under the supervision of experienced senior range managers. After gaining experience, they may advance to more responsible positions. Range managers may advance to supervisor jobs in which they plan the work of others.

Those who have a master's degree or higher can become teachers or researchers. Others go into business for themselves as range management consultants or ranchers.

Salary Survey
Median salary: $54,970 (very high)
Typical range: $40,950 to $68,460

Job Outlook and Employment
Slower than average growth is projected for conservation scientists in the US, estimated from 19,777 jobs in 2006 to 20,830 in 2016. The management of storm water and coastlines has created demand for people knowledgeable about runoff and erosion on farms and in cities and suburbs. The opening of federal lands to leasing by oil and gas companies is creating a healthy demand for range managers, who are finding work with consulting companies to help write environmental impact statements. A small number of new jobs will also result from the need for range managers to provide technical assistance to owners of grazing land through the Natural Resource Conservation Service.

Where the Jobs Are
Range managers work mostly in the western states, where most of the range land is located. Most range manager jobs are with the federal government, in agencies such as the US Department of Agriculture (USDA) and the Bureau of Land Management (BLM). Some jobs are with state government agencies. Some others are with the Nature Conservancy or other such non-profit organizations that acquire and manage large tracts of land.

Resources
O*NET OnLine: online.onetcenter.org (see range managers)
Society for Range Management (SRM): rangelands.org/srm.shtml
US Dept. of Labor, Bureau of Labor Statistics: bls.gov/oco/ocos048.htm

Natural Sciences Group

- Atmospheric and Space Scientists, including Air Analysts, Environmental Meteorologists and Climatologists

- Biochemists and Biophysicists, including Toxicologists and Ecotoxicologists

- Biological Technicians, including Environmental and Wildlife Technicians

- Chemical Technicians, including Environmental and Green Chemical Technicians

- Chemists, including Environmental and Green Chemists and Forensic Toxicologists

- Earth Sciences Professors

- Environmental Science Technicians, including Lab Techs and Air Pollution Auditors

- Environmental Scientists, including Environmental Researchers, Analysts and Investigators

- Epidemiologists, including Environmental Epidemiologists

- Forest and Conservation Technicians, including Soil Conservation and Biomass Technicians

- Forest and Conservation Workers, including Conservation and Reforestation Aides/Workers

- Foresters, including Environmental Protection Foresters and Forest Pathologists

- Geoscientists, including Environmental Geologists, Hydrogeologists and Marine Geologists

- Hydrologists, including Environmental Hydrologists and Water Resources Managers

- Microbiologists, including Environmental and Public Health Microbiologists

- Physicists, including Health and Atmospheric Physicists

- Soil and Plant Scientists, including Agronomists

- Soil and Water Conservationists, including Ecologists and Erosion Specialists

- Tree Trimmers and Pruners, including Arborists

○ Water Treatment Plant Operators

○ Zoologists and Wildlife Biologists, including Marine Biologists

Atmospheric and Space Scientists, including Air Analysts, Environmental Meteorologists and Climatologists

Atmospheric and space scientists investigate atmospheric phenomena and interpret meteorological data gathered by surface and air stations, satellites and radar to prepare reports and forecasts for public and other uses.

Qualifications and Advancement

A bachelor's degree in atmospheric science or a related field is the typical education requirement. Sometimes a combination of education and experience may be substituted for a degree. Obtaining a second bachelor's degree or a master's degree enhances employment opportunities, pay and advancement potential. A master's degree is usually required for conducting applied research and development, and a doctorate degree is required for most basic research positions.

Beginning atmospheric scientists often do routine data collection, computation or analysis and some basic forecasting. Entry-level operational meteorologists in the federal government usually are placed in intern positions for training and experience. During this period, they learn about the Weather Service's forecasting equipment and procedures and rotate to different offices to learn about various weather systems. After completing the training period, they are assigned to a permanent duty station. Experienced atmospheric scientists may advance to supervisory or administrative jobs or may handle more complex forecasting jobs.

Salary Survey

Median salary: $77,150 (very high)

Typical range: $55,530 to $96,490

Job Outlook and Employment

Average growth is projected for this occupation in the US, estimated from 8,759 jobs in 2006 to 9,684 in 2016. There will continue to be demand for atmospheric scientists to analyze and monitor the dispersion of pollutants into the air to ensure compliance with federal environmental regulations, but related employment increases are expected to be small. Efforts toward making and improving global weather observations also could have a positive impact on employment.

Where the Jobs Are

Federal government, excluding postal service (36.58%); Colleges, universities and professional schools (8.46%); Management, scientific and technical consulting services (7.82%)

Resources

American Association of State Climatologists (AASC): stateclimate.org
American Geophysical Union (AGU): agu.org
American Meteorological Society (AMS): ametsoc.org
International Association of Meteorology and Atmospheric Sciences
    (IAMAS): iamas.org
National Oceanic and Atmospheric Administration (NOAA): noaa.gov
National Weather Service: nws.noaa.gov
O*NET OnLine: online.onetcenter.org (see atmospheric and space scientists)
US Dept. of Labor, Bureau of Labor Statistics: bls.gov/oco/ocos051.htm

 DAVID F. ZIERDEN, State Climatologist, Florida State University, from an interview with Jim in 2008

How did you get into this career field? What was your education and experience, including any green-related training or certification?
I attended undergraduate school here at the Florida State University Department of Meteorology. Then I pursued a master's degree here under the direction of Dr. Jim O'Brien. About the time I was finishing up my master's work, he took over a position as the Florida state climatologist. He needed help in running the State Climate Office, and so he hired me full-time upon completion of my master's degree. I then worked as the assistant state climatologist for about eight years. Then, two years ago, Dr. O'Brien retired, and I took over his position as the state climatologist. Prior to 1973, state climatologists were federal employees of a national NOAA (National Oceanic and Atmospheric Administration) program. That program was terminated in 1973 due to budget cuts, but NOAA encouraged the different states to keep the position alive and open. So here in Florida, the state climatologist's office eventually became part of Florida State University's Meteorology Department.

What is your current job title and how would you describe the work you do in a typical day? What are your most common tasks?

The first task is just answering the phone. The National Weather Service is getting more involved now, but prior to a couple of years ago, they weren't equipped or trained to give out old weather data or climate information. All their duties were in monitoring and forecasting the near-term weather. So we serve the purpose, along with our partners at the NOAA regional climate centers and the National Climatic Data Center, to provide these climate services. The list of possible users for this information is endless. It includes construction companies, insurance companies, tourism and recreation entities, health researchers — whoever needs information about climate or historical weather data. Another project we're involved in involves five other universities here in the southeast. It's a program sponsored by NOAA and the US Department of Agriculture called the Southeast Climate Consortium. We do research and applications, and our main thrust is bringing climate information — particularly seasonal climate predictions — to agriculture and forestry and water resources, enabling these sectors to really use this new information. The seasonal climate forecasts here in the southeast are especially tied to the El Niño/La Niña cycle in the Pacific Ocean, which really has a major impact on our climate here in Florida and the southeast, particularly in the winter months.

If you could give advice to a young person who wants to work in this career field someday, what would you tell them? How can they best groom themselves for this field?

Climatology is really a sub-set of atmospheric sciences or meteorology. So the first thing would be to get a good education in an established meteorology or atmospheric science program. And the first advice there is to make sure you're good at math and science, because it is a physical science, and you need lots of mathematics and physics in learning the basics of our atmospheric circulation and atmospheric dynamics — which is the background for our science. So don't shy away from the math and sciences if that's a field you're interested in.

What kind of career advancement opportunities can one expect in this field? What kind of salary range would reflect that career path (from entry-level to the more advanced position)?

It's kind of a small niche in a specialized field, but I think the two main areas for career opportunities in climatology are either in academia, in a university setting or with NOAA and one of its sponsored programs. The best way to start getting there is first get an education. A bachelor's degree won't really provide many opportunities for you in this day and age. Job opportunities are so limited that I would certainly advise in getting at least a master's degree or a PhD and also familiarize yourself with NOAA programs and the different academic settings. But every state climate office is different, in that some have more financial resources than others, and one with more resources is probably a good way to get your foot in the door.

In your opinion, what are some of the best schools, degrees and certificates for jobs in this career field, including green–specific training?
Here at Florida State University, we have a very strong program. Penn State University, University of Maryland and University of Oklahoma have very strong programs.

How does someone without previous experience in this career field land a job? What are the best strategies for job-hunting in this field?
Even more so than internships, post-doctoral programs and fellowships are the best way to get your foot in the door.

Are there any professional associations that you would recommend joining?
The American Meteorological Society is one. And for the state climatologists, we have a professional organization called the American Association of State Climatologists.

What emerging careers do you see developing now and into the future for this career field? What new technologies will have the greatest impact on this field?
The three new technologies that are really impacting our field include: one, the use of satellite observations and satellite data in climatology. Now that we have the satellites up, in some cases for 20 or 30 years, we can do climate studies with satellite data that was previously impossible. Two, as computer power and capability continues to grow, computer modeling of the atmosphere and climate models are going to become more refined and more useful as tools. And three is geographic information systems, or GIS. The analyses and display of climate information through GIS systems is really expanding, and there's some opportunity there.

Resources from Q&A

American Association of State Climatologists (AASC): stateclimate.org
American Meteorological Society (AMS): ametsoc.org
Florida State University Meteorology Department: met.fsu.edu
National Oceanic and Atmospheric Administration (NOAA): noaa.gov
Pennsylvania (Penn) State University: psu.edu
University of Maryland: umd.edu
University of Oklahoma: ou.edu

PETER FELSCH
Warning Coordination
Meteorologist, National Weather Service,
from an interview with Alice in 2008

How did you get into this career field? What was your education and experience, including any green-related training or certification?

My interest in weather began while observing thunderstorms and heavy snow events at our vacation home at Lake Tahoe, California. I received a bachelor's degree in meteorology at San Jose State University, graduating in 1986. I began my career as an intern with the National Weather Service (NWS) then became an agricultural meteorologist in 1990. I was then promoted to meteorologist in charge of the Santa Maria office. In 1994, I was promoted to my current position as warning coordination meteorologist at the Missoula, Montana, office.

What is your current job title and how would you describe the work you do in a typical day? What are your most common tasks, including those that make yours a green job?

As warning coordination meteorologist (WCM) of the National Weather Service, I am the liaison officer between the NWS and its customers — coordinating with emergency responders, county and state emergency coordinators, sheriffs and 911 coordinators on planning and response to hazardous weather. That's a large portion of the WCM job description. A WCM also keeps this group of customers, as well as the media, informed of new technologies and NWS products to receive weather warnings effectively and as quickly as possible. A WCM also leads the outreach program of a NWS office. The local NWS office will attend and host booths at county fairs and educators' conferences, provide presentations to civic groups and schools, as well as promote office tours of its facilities. A WCM will work around 25% of forecast shifts. Presentations on La Niña, El Niña, climate change and global warming are common to all customers.

If you could give advice to a young person who wants to work in this career field someday, what would you tell them? How can they best groom themselves for this field?

Courses in physics and mathematics are highly encouraged in high school and college. Look for colleges that have meteorology programs. I would also recommend visiting a local NWS office and taking a tour of the facility and possibly request a job shadow.

What kind of career advancement opportunities can one expect in this field? What kind of salary range would reflect that career path (from entry-level to the more advanced position)?
To pursue a position as a meteorologist requires a bachelor's degree in meteorology. A typical progression of working in the NWS is, first, an internship, followed by a general forecaster position, then senior forecaster, which requires shift work, i.e., working around the clock. Each job advancement requires a competitive bidding process. Management positions include science operations officer, warning coordination meteorologist and service hydrologist. The "meteorologist in charge" is the officer manager. NWS salaries range from starting around $45,000, with senior forecasters and management positions ranging from $90,000 to $107,000.

In your opinion, what are some of the best schools, degrees and certificates for jobs in this career field, including green-specific training?
University of Utah, San Jose State University, San Francisco State University, Penn State University and University of Oklahoma.

How does someone without previous experience in this career field land a job? What are the best strategies for job-hunting in this field?
A degree in meteorology is highly recommended. However, students pursuing degrees in hydrology or meteorology are considered for summer positions.

What emerging careers do you see developing now and into the future for this career field? What new technologies will have the greatest impact on this field?
PDAs, cellphones, pagers, GPS units, etc. are all becoming more sophisticated and are now beginning to utilize weather radar and weather warning information to protect life and property. And this is the mission of the NWS — to protect life and property.

Resources from Q&A
National Weather Service: nws.noaa.gov
Pennsylvania State University (Penn State): psu.edu
San Francisco State University: sfsu.edu
San Jose State University: sjsu.edu
University of Oklahoma: ou.edu
University of Utah: utah.edu

Biochemists and Biophysicists, including Toxicologists and Ecotoxicologists

Biochemists and biophysicists study the chemical composition and physical principles of living cells and organisms, their electrical and mechanical energy and related phenomena. May conduct research to further understanding of the complex chemical combinations and reactions involved in metabolism, reproduction, growth and heredity. May determine the effects of foods, drugs, serums, hormones and other substances on tissues and vital processes of living organisms.

Qualifications and Advancement

A doctorate degree in biochemistry or biophysics is the typical education requirement. The doctorate degree is required for independent research, research administration and for most college and university faculty positions. Those with only a master's degree are somewhat limited to jobs in applied research, management or as instructors at community colleges and some four-year colleges.

Biochemists and biophysicists often gain experience while in college by working as research or laboratory assistants. With a bachelor's degree, they can usually work as laboratory assistants or technicians or in some non-research jobs. With the appropriate teaching credential, they may also find jobs as high school teachers. Those with a master's degree may qualify for some jobs in basic research or applied research.

Salary Survey

Median salary: $76,320 (very high)
Typical range: $53,390 to $100,060

Job Outlook and Employment

Average growth is projected for this occupation in the US, from 20,131 jobs in 2006 to 23,326 in 2016. Efforts to discover new and improved ways to clean up and preserve the environment will continue to add to job growth. However, the increase in federal spending on basic research has slowed substantially and is not expected to match its past growth over the 2006–2016 projection period. This may result in a competitive environment for obtaining and renewing research grants.

Where the Jobs Are

Research and development in the physical, engineering and life sciences

(44.81%); Pharmaceutical and medicine manufacturing (20.75%); Colleges, universities and professional schools (8.66%); Self-employed: 2.07%

Resources

American Chemical Society (ACS): portal.acs.org

American Society for Biochemistry and Molecular Biology (ASBMB): asbmb.org

Biophysical Society: biophysics.org

O*NET OnLine: online.onetcenter.org (see biochemists and biophysicists)

Society of Environmental Toxicology and Chemistry (SETAC): setac.org

Society of Toxicology (ST): toxicology.org

US Dept. of Labor, Bureau of Labor Statistics: bls.gov/oco/ocos047.htm

US Environmental Protection Agency (EPA): epa.gov

Q&A ANNIE WEISBROD
Toxicologist, The Procter & Gamble Company, from an interview with Jim in 2008

How did you get into this career field? What was your education and experience, including any green-related training or certification?

I started with a bachelor's degree in genetics and limnology from the University of Wisconsin–Madison and worked as a lab tech in insect research (pests exposed to natural tree toxins) for 1.5 years. From there, I went to work for a large international, student nonprofit organization called AIESEC for about a year in New York City. It's basically a peace organization; they organize student internships around the world and have ties to the United Nations. It was 1990, and they were just starting to teach business students about sustainable development, so I became their only scientist on staff to plan sustainability-related education. I also learned marketing, fundraising and strategy development. Then I moved to Helsinki, Finland, to take an environmental communications internship with a large company, Outokumpu Oy. When that visa ran out, I switched to a student visa and worked for a year in an aquatic toxicology lab at the Helsinki University of Technology. It was the Outokumpu job that really opened my eyes to what people do in the environmental sciences in industry and what kind of positive impact is possible at that level. So I decided to pursue a PhD program. I ended up at North Carolina State University in Raleigh, Department of Toxicology, where I studied the bioaccumulation of organic contaminants in whales and their food through a joint program with Woods Hole Oceanographic Institution in Massachusetts.

What is your current job title and how would you describe the work you do in a typical day? What are your most common tasks?

I am currently a senior scientist in product safety and regulatory affairs, and I'm becoming a sustainability specialist. I've worked for Procter & Gamble for ten years now, and this is really the third job I've had here. The first was an environmental risk assessor, which means I collected data and ran tests to understand and predict the environmental fate and effects of newly invented chemicals — after they are released by consumers when they dispose of the product. Obviously, if there is any safety concern with a chemical, that chemical isn't used. My second job was more related to environmental communications — I essentially worked in technical external policy, leading cross-sector teams with SETAC and other institutions to develop new methods for assessing bioaccumulation. Persistence, bioaccumulation and toxicity are three of the critical endpoints that governments use to assess the safety profile of a chemical for humans and wildlife. My current job is to guide and assess the sustainability of new products, materials and processes. I do that by collecting internal data and working with external experts, like at the US Environmental Protection Agency (EPA), to develop the calculations and computer models that we use to assess whether something is more sustainable or not. It is important not only to look at carbon footprints, but also to examine how a material or process might affect biodiversity or habitat, water availability and cleanliness, smog formation, eutrophication, etc. All the environmental information that we communicate to the public is approved by me and lawyers, to ensure we are accurate and not misleading. No greenwashing!

If you could give advice to a young person who wants to work in this career field someday, what would you tell them? How can they best groom themselves for this field?

Get a technical degree; don't major in business or politics if you want to do environmental work. Major in the environmental sciences and get at least a master's degree, because in most cases, you need that much information just to be useful. Get involved in professional societies and create a network of peers. The planet doesn't present simple problems, so you'll need to rely on various skill sets and work in a team in order to solve complex problems. So, good collaboration and communication skills are important.

What kind of career advancement opportunities can one expect in this field? What kind of salary range would reflect that career path (from entry-level to the more advanced position)?

If you only have a bachelor's degree, you're probably going to be limited to laboratory or field work. Some people with master's degrees will also conduct laboratory or field research. If you have a master's and switch into related industry fields, like regulatory affairs, or if you come in with a PhD, you can either stay on the technical side as I have or you can go into management. If you become a manager, you're dealing across disciplines with human safety, environmental safety, regulatory needs, analytical chemistry and more. As a manager, you oversee people working in specific method development and technical policy, help to set priorities and communicate the information to make business decisions. On the technical side, you will also manage teams and projects, set priorities and communicate, but you don't have to guide people along their career paths and place them in new assignments. Depending on what experience you have coming in, I would say the salary for industry jobs like mine ranges from $80,000 to $120,000 per year. If you're doing lab tech work, it's probably more like $40,000 per year.

In your opinion, what are some of the best schools, degrees and certificates for jobs in this career field, including green-specific training?

The schools I went to were both excellent: North Carolina State and the University of Wisconsin. I was very well prepared for my job. Other great programs that come to mind are UC Berkeley, Michigan State, Clemson, Texas Tech and North Texas. I know there are other good schools, too. I've just met a lot of students from these programs who are very involved with SETAC. For my type of job, it is important to find a program that provides a strong background in chemistry, ecology, toxicology/biochemistry, statistics and, in general, what is involved with being "a good scientist."

How does someone without previous experience in this career field land a job? What are the best strategies for job-hunting in this field?

You have to develop a network of peers; that's why I think joining a professional association is so important.

Are there any professional associations that you would recommend joining?

For any field involving the study of pollution and sustainability, I would say the best one is the Society of Environmental Toxicology and Chemistry. And second would probably be the environmental sciences division of the American Chemical Society.

What emerging careers do you see developing now and into the future for this career field? What new technologies will have the greatest impact on this field?
The biggest thing that is going to impact environmental science is not a technology, but a concept: people's interest in sustainability. The problem I see today is that we have a lot of people talking sustainability, but not with enough scientific background to really understand how to assess it and make good long-term decisions. So, I think the job growth is going to be in the area of developing new product or process sustainability assessments, as well as broadspectrum environmental impact assessments.

Resources from Q&A
AIESEC (Association Internationale des Étudiants en Sciences Économiques et Commerciales): aiesec.org
American Chemical Society (ACS): portal.acs.org
Michigan State University: msu.edu
North Carolina State University: ncsu.edu
Procter & Gamble: pg.com
Society of Environmental Toxicology and Chemistry (SETAC): setac.org
Texas Tech University: ttu.edu
University of California, Berkeley: berkeley.edu
University of North Texas: unt.edu
University of Wisconsin–Madison: wisc.edu
US Environmental Protection Agency (EPA): epa.gov
Woods Hole Oceanographic Institution: whoi.edu

Biological Technicians, including Environmental and Wildlife Technicians

Biological technicians assist biological and medical scientists in laboratories. Set up, operate and maintain laboratory instruments and equipment, monitor experiments, make observations and calculate and record results. May analyze organic substances, such as blood, food and drugs.

Qualifications and Advancement
An associate's degree in chemistry or biology is the typical education/training requirement. However, about 60 percent of all biological technicians have a bachelor's degree or higher.

Entry-level biological technicians whose training or educational background encompasses extensive hands-on experience with a variety of laboratory equipment, including computers, usually require only a short period of on-the-job training as a research assistant or laboratory technician. As they gain experience and knowledge, technicians take on more and more responsibility and work with increasing independence. Some may become supervisors. At universities, however, biological technicians often have their career paths tied to those of the professors they work for; when those professors leave, the technicians may face uncertain employment prospects.

Salary Survey
Median salary: $35,710 (low/moderate)
Typical range: $28,580 to $45,770

Job Outlook and Employment
Faster than average growth is projected for this occupation in the US, from 78,690 jobs in 2006 to 91,288 in 2016. The growing number of agricultural and medicinal products developed with the use of biotechnology techniques boosts demand for these workers. Also, an aging population and stronger competition among pharmaceutical companies are expected to contribute to the need for innovative and improved drugs, further spurring demand. Most growth in employment will be in professional, scientific and technical services and in educational services.

Where the Jobs Are
Colleges, universities and professional schools (30.71%); Research and development in the physical, engineering and life sciences (24.89%); Federal government (15.64%); Pharmaceutical and medicine manufacturing (9.14%)

Resources
American Institute of Biological Sciences (AIBS): aibs.org
BiologyJobs.com: biologyjobs.com
O*NET OnLine: online.onetcenter.org (see biological technicians)
US Dept. of Labor, Bureau of Labor Statistics: bls.gov/oco/ocos115.htm

Chemical Technicians, including Environmental and Green Chemical Technicians

Chemical technicians conduct chemical and physical laboratory tests to assist scientists in making qualitative and quantitative analyses of solids, liquids and gaseous materials for purposes, such as research and development of new products or processes, quality control, maintenance of environmental standards and other work involving experimental, theoretical or practical application of chemistry and related sciences.

Qualifications and Advancement

Green or environmental chemical technicians are generally research technicians who work in experimental laboratories assisting chemists or chemical engineers. An associate's degree in chemistry or a related field is the typical education/training requirement. However, chemical technician positions in research and development are often filled by applicants who have a bachelor's degree.

Research technicians usually start as an assistant to a research chemist or chemical engineer. As they gain experience and knowledge, technicians are given more difficult assignments and have less supervision. Some may advance to supervisory positions, but that usually requires a graduate degree.

Salary Survey

Median salary: $39,240 (high)
Typical range: $30,640 to $49,870

Job Outlook and Employment

Slower than average growth is projected for this occupation in the US, from 61,228 jobs in 2006 to 64,793 in 2016. The slow job growth for this occupation is due to the chemical manufacturing industry that, except for pharmaceutical and medicine manufacturing, is expected to decline in overall employment as companies downsize and turn to outside contractors (in other countries) to provide specialized and lower-cost services. Employment in testing laboratories, however, is expected to grow much faster than average.

Where the Jobs Are

Testing laboratories (15.06%); Research and development in the physical, engineering and life sciences (11.53%); Pharmaceutical and medicine manufacturing (10.86%); Basic chemical manufacturing (10.58%); Resin, synthetic rubber and artificial synthetic fibers and filaments manufacturing (5.37%); Paint, coating and adhesive manufacturing (3.87%); Other chemical product and preparation manufacturing (3.81%); Colleges, universities and professional schools (3.16%)

Resources

American Chemical Society (ACS): portal.acs.org
O*NET OnLine: online.onetcenter.org (see chemical technicians)
US Dept. of Labor, Bureau of Labor Statistics: bls.gov/oco/ocos115.htm

Chemists, including Environmental and Green Chemists and Forensic Toxicologists

Chemists conduct qualitative and quantitative chemical analyses or chemical experiments in laboratories for quality or process control or to develop new products or knowledge.

Qualifications and Advancement

A doctorate degree in chemistry is the typical education requirement. However, for research positions, employers often prefer candidates who have completed a post-doctoral research fellowship or have other post-doctoral experience.

Chemists with only a bachelor's degree usually work as laboratory assistants or in non-research jobs such as product testing, quality control or technical sales. With the appropriate teaching credential, they may also find jobs as high school teachers. Chemists with a master's degree have the additional advantage of qualifying for some jobs in basic research, applied research or product development. Chemists with a doctorate degree often take temporary post-doctoral research positions that provide specialized research experience and often offer the opportunity to publish research findings. This is often essential in obtaining a permanent position in basic research or as a university professor. In private industry, some may become managers in a chemistry-related field.

Salary Survey

Median salary: $59,870 (very high)

Typical range: $44,780 to $82,610

Job Outlook and Employment

Average growth is projected for this occupation in the US, estimated from 83,697 jobs in 2006 to 91,340 in 2016. Job growth will occur in professional, scientific and technical services firms as manufacturing companies continue to outsource their R&D and testing operations to these smaller, specialized firms. There will also be job growth in pharmaceutical and biotechnology research. More chemists will be employed to develop and improve the technologies and processes used to produce chemicals for all purposes and to monitor and measure air and water pollutants to ensure compliance with local, state and federal environmental regulations. Environmental research will offer many new opportunities for chemists, as well as research into traditional and alternative energy sources.

Where the Jobs Are

Pharmaceutical/medicine manufacturing (17.29%); Testing labs (10.37%); Federal government (6.94%); Basic chemical manufacturing (4.28%); Colleges and universities (3.81%)

Resources

American Academy of Forensic Sciences (AAFS): aafs.org
American Association of Pharmaceutical Scientists (AAPS): aapspharmaceutica.com
American Chemical Society (ACS): portal.acs.org
O*NET OnLine: online.onetcenter.org (see chemists)
Pharmaceutical Research and Manufacturers of America (PhRMA): phrma.org
US Dept. of Labor, Bureau of Labor Statistics: bls.gov/oco/ocos049.htm

Q&A **VALORAN P. HANKO**
Staff Chemist, Applications, Laboratory Manager, Dionex Corporation, from an interview with Alice in 2008

How did you get into the biochemistry career field? What was your education and experience, including any green-related training or certification?
After finishing a master's degree in molecular biology, I was able to pick positions in the industry that provided a link to the betterment of humanity. All great discoveries in science come from the step-by-step advance of scientific instruments and the creative ways to use them to solve problems. My skills and talents in biochemistry for the advancement of the science of fermentation, and the conversion of biomass to renewable energy resources, are utilized well by my current employer, Dionex.

What is your current job title and how would you describe the work you do in a typical day? What are your most common tasks, including those that make yours a green job?
I am a staff chemist and the applications laboratory manager. I manage and coach junior chemists within my group and serve as consultant to customers, product managers, research and development, sales, technical specialists and service departments. I design and execute experiments in the lab for the purpose of developing new applications supporting many different fields, includ-

ing the green field. Green applications focus on the analytical techniques that solve concerns about measuring toxic chemicals in the environment, monitoring fermentation processes involved in the production of renewable energy sources derived from biomass. Another aspect of this job that makes it "green" is that the instruments produced by the company I work for have adopted solvent systems for which the instruments operate that are environmentally friendly or designed to use much less solvents. Instead of using highly toxic organic solvents for running the instruments, they typically operate using solvents that produce a waste stream consisting of sodium chloride or sodium carbonate. What that means is that analytical labs throughout the world using these instruments are not generating toxic by-products. The typical day includes interactions with junior chemists, providing guidance on their experiments in the lab and running my own experiments using chromatography instrumentation. This consists of operating or maintaining the instruments and evaluating the data produced and then reducing this data down into a summary report that can be interpreted. Ultimately, I write up this data and publish in scientific journals, company documents and orally present at scientific meetings where other scientists throughout the world can benefit from the work.

If you could give advice to a young person who wants to work in this career field someday, what would you tell them? How can they best groom themselves for this field?

My advice to a young scientist is to get clear early about the types of activities you enjoy without as much concern for the details of the job. The aspects about the activities you enjoy include whether you really like to think, analyze, work with your hands, design something new or problem-solve. Activities that help enhance performance include giving oral presentations, reading and writing well. Those ultimately going into management will benefit from having social skills. These very basic skills need to match with your passion, and you need to be comfortable alone to solve problems and make decisions that manage your daily activities. There are positions in this field that just follow defined procedures, and if that is comfortable, then opportunities exist. But generally they do not lead to fast career advancement.

What kind of career advancement opportunities can one expect in this field? What kind of salary range would reflect that career path (from entry-level to the more advanced position)?

The talent of the individual generally defines the career advancement in this field. In some organizations, the education and the degree also define this advancement, although it is clear that ultimately the innate creativity and curiosity of the individual, and their knowledge in the field, and specialized mental disciplines to analyze, focus and organize determine their success in almost every organization. Although salary is defined in an organization based on the level of scientific or technical expertise, a starting chemist in 2008 with a BS degree can expect about $55,000–60,000, while an advanced level with PhD can expect to start at about $70,000–80,000. After 20 years in the field, the degrees generally become less important than what you can show you know and are capable of doing, and the salary range becomes quite broad. Currently, experienced chemists can expect $80,000–120,000, which is about double that of a starting chemist.

In your opinion, what are some of the best schools, degrees and certificates for jobs in this career field, including green-specific training?
The most important aspects of success in this field that relate to school and training are based on their experiences, the skills learned. Research in the green-specific field is currently broad for chemists, ranging from organic, polymer, biological, inorganic specializations. My specialization in biological chemistry provides the basis for research in the fermentation processes, and my background in toxicology provides for the work engaged in environmental studies. Green-related chemists are exploring new ways to create cost-effective alternative fuels, measure environmental toxicants, explore chemical relationships of human activities to changes in the environment and impacts on life. In my experience, a BS degree is the minimal requirement, and a master's degree is highly recommended, and a doctorate to create more immediate credibility as an expert out of school.

How does someone without previous experience in this career field land a job? What are the best strategies for job-hunting in this field?
Absence of experience in this highly professional career is clearly career limiting. It is nearly impossible to get a job as a chemist without some experience doing chemistry. It is essential that extra-curricular activities in chemistry be pursued during college, most likely at the college. Taking a position as a research assistant in one of the professors' labs is one of those ways. Senior thesis work will help provide practical experience. A master's thesis involving lab studies, with a project chosen that matches some green-field occupation targeted after graduation, is another way. Post-doctoral studies are another. In all of these approaches, it is highly recommended that some publication and/or presentation at a scientific meeting for this work be pursued for inclusion in

the resumé. The involvement in this project should also lead to some networking contacts outside the school, and these relationships need to be nurtured and developed and then used near or after graduation from college.

Are there any professional associations that you would recommend joining?
American Chemical Society (ACS) is a good start, but more specific associations will depend on the exact area within chemistry one will be targeting.

What emerging careers do you see developing now and into the future for this career field? What new technologies will have the greatest impact on this field?
For the next 20 to 30 years, a major refocus onto alternative fuel sources can be expected. Solar, biomass, hydrogen and fusion are well-known alternative fuel sources, and research will require a significant increase in the number of material and process chemists to do the research and then attend to the production. The monitoring of the health of the environment, and restoring the environment back to good health, is also a developing field for chemists. Analytical chemists will be required to ensure effective monitoring and research into applications required to monitor toxicants and to develop the instrumentation by instrument manufacturers to provide the tools needed to reach higher sensitivity, greater accuracy and more robustness of the techniques. Instrumentation development may be one of the most important new technologies, leading the way to innovation in the green field, as instrumentation is almost always now, and forever more, at the heart of high-technology.

Resources from Q&A
American Chemical Society (ACS): portal.acs.org
Dionex Corporation: dionex.com

Earth Sciences Professors, Postsecondary

Atmospheric, earth, marine and space sciences teachers, postsecondary, teach courses in the physical sciences, except chemistry and physics. Includes teachers primarily engaged in teaching and those who combine teaching and research.

Biological science teachers, postsecondary, teach courses in biological sciences. Includes teachers primarily engaged in teaching and those who combine teaching and research.

Environmental science teachers, postsecondary, teach courses in environmental science. Includes teachers primarily engaged in teaching and those who combine teaching and research.

Forestry and conservation science teachers, postsecondary, teach courses in environmental and conservation science. Includes teachers primarily engaged in teaching and those who combine teaching and research.

Chemistry teachers, postsecondary, teach courses pertaining to the chemical and physical properties and compositional changes of substances. Work may include instruction in the methods of qualitative and quantitative chemical analysis. Includes teachers primarily engaged in teaching and those who combine teaching and research.

Qualifications and Advancement

A doctorate degree in the academic subject area is the typical education requirement, although a master's degree is often adequate for positions with community colleges and some four-year colleges. However, candidates with only a master's degree will find themselves competing against other candidates with a doctorate degree.

Instructors and professors generally begin their careers as graduate teaching assistants. Once they complete their degree, they typically find jobs as lecturers or adjunct (part-time) professors or instructors. Eventually they find a full-time opportunity. The next step for a college or university professor is to become tenured. This means that the professor has received a permanent job contract, granted after a probationary period of several years.

Advancement for tenured professors generally involves moving into administrative positions, such as department chair, dean, vice president and president. This often requires an additional graduate degree in education administration. Many professors have moved in and out of administrative positions — as they find greater satisfaction as teachers. Others prefer the administrative positions to the classroom.

Postsecondary Teachers' Salary Survey

Specialty	Median salary	Typical salary range
Atmospheric, Earth, Marine and Space Sciences	$69,300	$50,390 to $94,470
Biological Science	$69,210	$49,420 to $101,780
Environmental Science	$64,780	$46,500 to $89,680
Forestry and Conservation Science	$64,430	$46,900 to $84,140
Chemistry	$61,220	$46,920 to $85,550

Job Outlook and Employment

Much faster than average growth is projected for these five occupations in the US, from 1.6 million jobs in 2006 to 2 million in 2016. Projected job growth will be primarily due to increases in college and university enrollment over the next decade. This enrollment growth stems mainly from the expected increase in the population of 18- to 24-year-olds, who constitute the majority of students at postsecondary institutions, and from the increasing number of high-school graduates who choose to attend these institutions.

Where the Jobs Are

Colleges, universities and professional schools (70.8%); Community colleges (21.54%); Technical and trade schools (3.04%)

Resources

American Association for the Advancement of Science (AAAS): aaas.org
American Meteorological Society (AMS): ametsoc.org
American Society of Plant Biologists (ASPB): aspb.org
Association of Environmental Engineering and Science Professors (AEESP): aeesp.org
Association of Environmental Professionals (AEP): califaep.org
Ecological Society of America (ESA): esa.org
International Association for Ecology (INTECOL): intecol.net
International Society of Sustainability Professionals (ISSP): sustainabilityprofessionals.org
National Association of Environmental Professionals (NAEP): naep.org
O*NET OnLine: online.onetcenter.org (see any of the five occupation titles listed under earth sciences professors)
Preparing Future Faculty (PFF) program: preparing–faculty.org
US Dept. of Labor, Bureau of Labor Statistics: bls.gov/oco/ocos066.htm

Q&A **JIM PUSHNIK**
Earth Sciences Professor,
California State University, Chico,
from an interview with Jim in 2008

How did you get into this career field? What was your education and experience, including any green-related training or certification?
I grew up as a member of a military family and had moved around all my life. By the time I graduated from high school, I had attended somewhere in the neighborhood of 14 different schools. The one constant throughout all that was my connection with the places we lived — with

the outside world. And so, as my father retired and we were living in Los Angeles, I felt a sort of separation from the natural world. I initially went to a community college, and interestingly enough, a biology professor who studied cockroaches caught my attention. I was just fascinated by this individual's intense study of cockroaches, their behavior and their breeding patterns. So I took that general biology class, and his enthusiasm got me going, and it sort of reconnected me with my childhood of outdoor experiences. I ended up going to Humboldt State University, where I initially studied marine biology but ended up finding the ocean land mass and the vegetation on land more interesting. I got my PhD in biochemistry at Utah State University. I was always interested in air pollution, so for my dissertation, I studied air pollution and the impact on agriculture. I was looking at the impacts of a power generating plant's emissions on surrounding agricultural yields.

What is your current job title and how would you describe the work you do in a typical day? What are your most common tasks?
I'm a professor in the Chico State Department of Biological Sciences and currently the Rawlins Professor of Environmental Literacy. A general day usually starts out with preparation for my interactions with the students, which is a passion for me. I spend a lot of time trying to bring in contemporary information and use items out of the news to make the point that these are not just academic discussions that we are having — whether it be about water use or about microbial pathogens moving into certain areas. Much of my career has had to do with air pollution and CO_2 emissions, and that has stayed with me all through the rest of my career. So I try to bring those kinds of things in. Then I spend a couple hours a day meeting with my graduate students. Then a few hours a day in the classroom, and then I work on projects with students, which involves going out in the field to do research. In addition, there are administrative functions such as meetings and service activities.

If you could give advice to a young person who wants to work in this career field someday, what would you tell them? How can they best groom themselves for this field?
You'll want a PhD and a firm foundation in the fundamental sciences: Earth science, hydrology, biology — get a solid base of knowledge there. But also begin to explore areas that involve the social sciences and economics, because those are the factors that are coming into play. It's fine to become a specialist, but as we move into a more complex world, what we're going to need is a broader understanding of how social demands and economics are going to affect our natural resources. We've come to a point in our intellectual devel-

opment where we recognize that things like toxicology are not isolated from ecology or any discipline you can name. It's always tied to something else. What my program in environmental literacy is all about is walking the seam between various disciplines, because that's where real change can be accomplished. I can't emphasize enough the importance of understanding system dynamics — how things are connected to everything else.

What kind of career advancement opportunities can one expect in this field? What kind of salary range would reflect that career path (from entry-level to the more advanced position)?
One would start out as an associate faculty member, which means working part-time with no benefits. Within the California State University system, an incoming faculty member — an assistant professor — starts out at about $55,000 per year. Then we have a scheduled pay elevation scheme in which you would peak out at around $80,000 to $90,000 per year — depending on your discipline. Beyond that, you'd generally have to leave teaching and go into administration or get a job in the private sector.

In your opinion, what are some of the best schools, degrees and certificates for jobs in this career field, including green-specific training?
There are a lot of great schools to study environmental science. Of course, the Ivy League schools are absolutely fantastic. We also have some phenomenal ones here in California, including San Diego State and UC Berkeley. Humboldt State has a stellar program in forestry and land–ocean interface. Chico is really focused on sustainability and sustainable development practices. Cal Poly, San Luis Obispo is a good one. Arizona State has a really good program as well.

How does someone without previous experience in this career field land a job? What are the best strategies for job-hunting in this field?
Most people who get their first faculty job come to work without any prior teaching experience. I was fortunate that, having done several post-docs, I was able to teach a class in each of them. So I was the associate faculty at that point. That's how I developed my skill sets. And I think a lot of people get it that way. The other way to get experience is by doing community outreach. Give public talks. Do museum talks and Rotary Club talks, because those all help develop your teaching skills, and it connects you with a whole separate group of people. In fact, as I'm saying that, I'm also thinking that one of the most valuable things I ever did was to get on the rubber-chicken circuit where I learned to speak to people with different mindsets.

Are there any professional associations that you would recommend joining?
I belong to several professional organizations including the Ecological Society of America, the International Society of Sustainability Professionals and the American Society of Plant Biologists. Those are just my disciplinary associations. I also belong to the American Association for the Advancement of Science.

What emerging careers do you see developing now and into the future for this career field? What new technologies will have the greatest impact on this field?
I think you're going to see a huge push toward it now — the recognition is that we all live on one planet, and we don't have an escape route. We have a finite amount of energy coming in, and we know at what rate it passes through. So how we use what's left past the inputs and outputs becomes critical. And I think it's going to fall to the Earth sciences to figure out how you distribute that energy use to most efficiently provide for the human needs as well as for the needs of all the other species on our planet. I'm also really interested in hydro-ecology. We can live without most things, but we need air, water and dirt. And hydro-ecology is about the interaction of all those things. Given the rate at which global change is occurring, we need to look at larger patches of the Earth at a time. So I see a real need in the future for people that are using remote testing techniques to get at ecological processes. And that would include satellite imagery taken with satellites that have the capacity to do what's referred to as a hyperspectral analysis. From that, we can extract patterns and correlate those with physical processes taking place on the surface. And when you look at it on a larger scale, you begin to see patterns emerging, and that means you could ultimately begin to predict where you're going to have problems and become pro-active.

Resources from Q&A
American Association for the Advancement of Science (AAAS): aaas.org
American Society of Plant Biologists (ASPB): aspb.org
Arizona State University: asu.edu
Cal Poly, San Luis Obispo: calpoly.edu
Ecological Society of America (ESA): esa.org
Humboldt State University: humboldt.edu
International Society of Sustainability Professionals (ISSP):
    sustainabilityprofessionals.org
Rawlins Professor of Environmental Literacy:
    csuchico.edu/nsci/environmentalFocus/rawlins.shtml
San Diego State University: sdsu.edu

University of California, Berkeley: berkeley.edu
Utah State University: usu.edu

Environmental Science Technicians, including Lab Techs and Air Pollution Auditors

Environmental science and protection technicians (including health) perform laboratory and field tests to monitor the environment and investigate sources of pollution, including those that affect health. Under direction of an environmental scientist or specialist, may collect samples of gases, soil, water and other materials for testing and take corrective actions as assigned.

Qualifications and Advancement

An associate's degree is the typical education/training requirement. However, almost half of all environmental technicians have a bachelor's degree or higher.

Environmental technicians usually start as an assistant to an environmental scientist. As they gain experience and knowledge, technicians are given more difficult assignments and have less supervision. Some environmental technicians may advance to supervisory positions. However, a master's degree is usually the minimum requirement to become an environmental scientist.

Salary Survey

Median salary: $38,090 (high)
Typical range: $29,450 to $49,340

Job Outlook and Employment

Faster than average growth is projected for this occupation in the US, from 36,500 in 2006 jobs to 46,701 in 2016. Environmental technicians will be needed to help regulate waste products; to collect air, water and soil samples for measuring levels of pollutants; to monitor compliance with environmental regulations; and to clean up contaminated sites. Over 80 percent of this growth is expected to be in professional, scientific and technical services as environmental monitoring, management and regulatory compliance increase.

Where the Jobs Are

Local government (21.17%); Management, scientific and technical consulting services (20.89%); State government (13.14%); Testing laboratories (9.97%); Colleges, universities and professional schools (4.85%); General medical and surgical hospitals (3.68%)

Resources
Association of Environmental Professionals (AEP): califaep.org
National Association of Environmental Professionals (NAEP): naep.org
O*NET OnLine: online.onetcenter.org (see environmental science and
    protection technicians)
US Dept. of Labor, Bureau of Labor Statistics: bls.gov/oco/ocos115.htm

Environmental Scientists, including Environmental Researchers, Analysts and Investigators

Environmental scientists and specialists conduct research or perform investigation for the purpose of identifying, abating or eliminating sources of pollutants or hazards that affect either the environment or the health of the population. Utilizing knowledge of various scientific disciplines to collect, synthesize, study, report and take action based on data from measurements or observations of air, food, soil and water.

Qualifications and Advancement
A master's degree in natural science is the typical education requirement. The master's degree is the minimum educational requirement for most entry-level applied research positions. A doctorate degree is necessary for most college and university faculty positions and for most high-level research positions. A bachelor's degree may be adequate for a few entry-level positions.

Environmental scientists gain valuable experience while still in college by working in school laboratories and by doing internships. After finishing college, environmental scientists often begin their careers in field exploration or, occasionally, as research assistants or technicians. They are given more difficult assignments as they gain experience. Eventually, they may be promoted to project leader, program manager or some other management or research position.

Salary Survey
Median salary: $56,100 (very high)
Typical range: $42,840 to $74,480

Job Outlook and Employment
Much faster than average growth is projected for this occupation in the US, from 83,267 jobs in 2006 to 104,142 in 2016. Job growth for environmental scientists should be strongest in private-sector consulting firms. Much job

growth will result from a continued need to monitor the quality of the environment, to interpret the impact of human actions on terrestrial and aquatic ecosystems and to develop strategies for restoring ecosystems. In addition, environmental scientists will be needed to help planners develop and construct buildings, transportation corridors and utilities that protect water resources and reflect efficient and beneficial land use.

Where the Jobs Are

State government (23.68%); Management, scientific and technical consulting services (21.38%); Local government (11.56%); Federal government, excluding postal service (7.5%); Colleges, universities and professional schools (5.47%); Research and development in the physical, engineering and life sciences (4.38%); Testing laboratories (3.23%); Self-employed: 2.15%

Resources

Association of Environmental Professionals (AEP): califaep.org
National Association of Environmental Professionals (NAEP): naep.org
O*NET OnLine: online.onetcenter.org (see environmental scientists and
    specialists)
US Dept. of Labor, Bureau of Labor Statistics: bls.gov/oco/ocos050.htm

Q&A   ROBERT CARLSON
Resource Management Analyst,
California Integrated Waste Management Board,
from an interview with Jim in 2008

How did you get into this career field? What was your education and experience?
I have a bachelor of science degree in ecology and systematic biology with a concentration in wildlife management from Cal Poly, San Luis Obispo. I spent some time working as an environmental chemist during college, and when I graduated I worked as a seasonal biologist performing wildlife surveys. I started my full-time work shortly afterwards, performing CEQA (California Environmental Quality Act) reviews, and after realizing that regulatory work was not my cup of tea, I transferred to a position working on recycling and resource management issues.

What is your current job title and how would you describe the work you do in a typical day? What are your most common tasks?

My formal title is integrated waste management specialist, but a more descriptive title would be resource management analyst. Most of my duties focus around making it easier for people to do more eco-friendly things in their lives. My daily duties vary from discussing emerging recycling technology to educating the public on how best to reduce their environmental impacts, to researching the most effective way to solve a problem. I get to meet with experts in a wide range of specialties and be involved in discussions that help shape environmental policy. My typical day involves reviewing global news articles, reviewing legislative proposals and providing technical assistance to various entities. There are a lot of meetings with professionals from various disciplines, and writing reports, briefs or summaries are also large parts of my duties.

If you could give advice to a young person who wants to work in this career field someday, what would you tell them? How can they best groom themselves for this field?

Above all other skills and education, I would say that refining your critical-thinking and writing skills are among the highest priorities. These skills will allow you to grow and adapt, as well as effectively communicate with others. The technical skills and education are important, but there is such a wide array of topics in this field that no single educational background is vital. Public speaking and presentation skills, along with project management, are also highly useful skills for this field. Regardless of how well you've performed your analysis or how knowledgeable you are in your field, if you cannot communicate your ideas and findings to a broad range of audiences, you may not be very effective.

What kind of career advancement opportunities can one expect in this field? What kind of salary range would reflect that career path (from entry-level to the more advanced position)?

Advancement opportunities are available and fairly accessible. But there is a limit to the advancement opportunities on the technical side of this career, as most of the upward movement happens after you reach a management level. This is more true in the public sector than in the private sector; often private firms will allow for higher-level technical staff without having to shift to management. Salaries vary widely, but generally a non-management technical position will earn between $3,000 and $6,000 per month in the public sector and $3,500 to $8,000 per month in the private sector. Once you reach management levels, the salary range goes up to around $7,500 and $10,000 per month for public and private, respectively. Another benefit would be the myriad of contacts that one could acquire working in this field. These contacts could set one up for a career in the green industry for quite a while.

In your opinion, what are some of the best schools, degrees and certificates for jobs in this career field?
A bachelor's degree is almost universally required, even for an entry-level position. Usually a bachelor of science degree is preferred to a bachelor of arts degree, and oftentimes advanced degrees are preferred, particularly in the private sector. I would suggest a degree in a subject that you are interested in, since people are hired from a wide range of educational backgrounds. I work with soil scientists, wildlife biologists, geologists, civil engineers and MBAs. Multi-disciplinary degrees are also very useful and provide you with a broad background that can help you adapt to and work with a large number of topics and professionals.

How does someone without previous experience in this career field land a job? What are the best strategies for job-hunting in this field?
Well, you have to start somewhere and pre-degree experience is usually hard to come by. I would suggest working as a student assistant or intern while you're going to school in the field you think you would like to work in. Also, put a lot of thought into your school projects, such as in-class projects, or your thesis or dissertation. These projects can give your potential employer a good example of the kind of work you are capable of. My own senior thesis provided me with many contacts and the real-world experience that assisted me greatly in my future job-hunting. Looking for jobs can be difficult, but I would suggest starting your search as early as possible, particularly if you're thinking about entering the public sector where the application process can be complicated for the first-time applicant.

Are there any professional associations that you would recommend joining?
I personally do not belong to any professional associations, but there are some out there, and they each have their pros and cons. Besides the various professional organizations specific to a particular discipline, such as wildlife biologists, chemists, engineers, etc., there is the National Association of Environmental Professionals.

What emerging or high-growth careers do you see developing now and into the future for this career field? What new technologies will have the greatest impact on this field?

Currently environmental concern is growing worldwide, and that makes our profession more and more in demand. Global warming is a particularly hot topic right now and will probably experience the most growth in the coming years. To some extent, this depends on the environmental concerns specific to your local area. So if your region has a particular concern regarding water quality or erosion, those areas will likely expand quickly. Technologies related to modeling future impacts of current activities, GIS for example, has quickly become virtually universally applicable in the environmental field, which will likely play a large part in determining the focus of future environmentally related jobs. While perhaps not a technology per se, life cycle analysis is becoming a widely used and highly regarded science. Being able to conduct and/or understand life cycle analyses will be a great asset in this field.

Resources from Q&A
Cal Poly, San Luis Obispo: calpoly.edu
California Integrated Waste Management Board (CIWMB): ciwmb.ca.gov
National Association of Environmental Professionals (NAEP): naep.org

Epidemiologists, including Environmental Epidemiologists

Epidemiologists investigate and describe the determinants and distribution of disease, disability and other health outcomes and develop the means for prevention and control.

Environmental epidemiology is the branch of public health that deals with environmental conditions and hazards that may pose a risk to human health.

Qualifications and Advancement
A doctorate degree in epidemiology is the typical education requirement, although a master's degree is adequate for some positions. Epidemiologists who work in hospitals and health care centers often must have a medical degree with specific training in infectious diseases.

Epidemiologists with a doctorate degree often take temporary post-doctoral research positions that provide specialized research experience. Post-doctoral positions often offer the opportunity to publish research findings. A solid record of published research is essential in obtaining a permanent position involving basic research, especially for those seeking a permanent college or university faculty position. Some may become managers or administrators in the pharmaceutical industry.

Salary Survey
Median salary: $56,670 (high)
Typical range: $45,220 to $71,080

Job Outlook and Employment
Average growth is projected for this occupation in the US, estimated from 4,507 jobs in 2006 to 5,119 in 2016. Most new jobs will be with local government agencies.

Where the Jobs Are
State government (33.71%); Local government (23.29%); General medical and surgical hospitals (11.07%); Colleges, universities and professional schools (10.48%)

Resources
International Society for Environmental Epidemiology (ISEE): iseepi.org
Journal of Exposure Science and Environmental Epidemiology:
     nature.com/jes/
O*NET OnLine: online.onetcenter.org (see epidemiologists)
US Dept. of Labor, Bureau of Labor Statistics: bls.gov/oco/ocos008.htm

Forest and Conservation Technicians, including Soil Conservation and Biomass Technicians

Forest and conservation technicians compile data pertaining to size, content, condition and other characteristics of forest tracts, under direction of foresters; and train and lead forest workers in forest propagation, fire prevention and suppression. May assist conservation scientists in managing, improving and protecting rangelands and wildlife habitats and help provide technical assistance regarding the conservation of soil, water and related natural resources.

Qualifications and Advancement
An associate's degree in a science-related field is the typical education/training requirement. However, because employers' preferences vary, some forest and conservation technicians have a bachelor's degree in chemistry, biology or forestry. About 40 percent of new job entrants have a bachelor's degree.

Forest and conservation technicians often start by working in seasonal (summer) jobs in state and national forests. New technicians sometimes begin as helpers. Experienced technicians can advance to lead worker or supervisor. A bachelor's degree is often necessary for advancement to jobs like foresters and conservationists. Those with a master's degree or doctorate degree can choose to become researchers or college faculty.

Salary Survey
Median salary: $30,880 (low/moderate)
Typical range: $26,270 to $40,030

Job Outlook and Employment
Little or no growth is projected for this occupation in the US, estimated from 33,829 jobs in 2006 to 33,166 in 2016. The lack of job growth for this occupation is due to the federal government's budgetary constraints and continued reductions in demand for timber management on federal lands. However, there is expected to be some job growth with state and local governments within specialties such as urban forestry. In addition, an increased emphasis on specific conservation issues, such as environmental protection, preservation of water resources and control of exotic and invasive pests, may provide some employment opportunities.

Where the Jobs Are
Federal government, excluding postal service (75.99%); State government (10.2%); Local government (6.59%)

Resources
O*NET OnLine: online.onetcenter.org (see forest and conservation
    technicians)
Society of American Foresters (SAF): safnet.org
US Dept. of Labor, Bureau of Labor Statistics: bls.gov/oco/ocos115.htm

Forest and Conservation Workers, including Conservation and Reforestation Aides/Workers

Forest and conservation workers, under supervision, perform manual labor necessary to develop, maintain or protect forest, forested areas and woodlands through such activities as raising and transporting tree seedlings; combating insects, pests and diseases harmful to trees; and building erosion and water control structures and leaching of forest soil. Includes forester aides, seedling pullers and tree planters.

Qualifications and Advancement
Generally, a high-school diploma is sufficient for most forest and conservation worker jobs. Most of these workers develop their skills through on-the-job

training, learning from experienced workers. Many forest worker jobs offer only seasonal employment during warm-weather months, so many of these workers are hired to perform short-term, labor-intensive tasks, such as planting tree seedlings or conducting pre-commercial tree thinning.

Forest and conservation workers generally begin as laborers, carrying tools and equipment, clearing brush, performing equipment maintenance and loading and unloading logs and brush. Further experience may lead to jobs involving the operation of more complicated machinery and equipment and eventually to supervisory positions. An associate's degree in a science-related field is required to move into a position as a forest or conservation technician.

Salary Survey
Median salary: $20,810 (very low)
Typical range: $17,330 to $31,540

Job Outlook and Employment
Slower than average growth is projected for this occupation in the US, from 19,844 jobs in 2006 to 20,939 in 2016. Demand for forest and conservation workers will continue to increase as more land is set aside to protect natural resources and wildlife habitats. In addition, more jobs are expected to be created by federal legislation designed to prevent destructive wildfires by thinning the forests and setting controlled burns in dry regions susceptible to forest fires.

Where the Jobs Are
State government (26.46%); Crop production (18.46%); Forestry (14.61%); Local government (7.54%); Self-employed: 5.05%

Resources
O*NET OnLine: online.onetcenter.org (see forest and conservation workers)
Society of American Foresters (SAF): safnet.org
US Dept. of Labor, Bureau of Labor Statistics: bls.gov/oco/ocos178.htm

Foresters, including Environmental Protection Foresters and Forest Pathologists

Foresters manage forested lands for economic, recreational and conservation purposes. May inventory the type, amount and location of standing timber, appraise the timber's worth, negotiate the purchase and draw up contracts for procurement. May determine how to conserve wildlife habitats, creek beds, water quality and soil stability and how best to comply with environmental regulations.

Qualifications and Advancement

A bachelor's degree in forestry, range management or a related field is the typical education requirement, although some private employers may accept a combination of experience and some education. Sixteen states have licensing requirements for "professional forester." Those who wish to perform specialized research or teach at the college level should have a master's or doctorate degree.

Foresters often start as forestry technicians while still in college. Inexperienced foresters usually work under the supervision of experienced foresters. After gaining experience, they advance to positions with greater responsibility. In the federal government, most foresters start in forest resource management. Here an experienced forester may eventually supervise a ranger district and may advance to forest supervisor or regional forester. In private industry, foresters start by learning the practical and administrative aspects of the business and acquiring comprehensive technical training. They are then introduced to contract writing, timber harvesting and decision-making. Some foresters work their way up into top managerial positions within their companies.

Salary Survey

Median salary: $51,190 (high)
Typical range: $40,870 to $62,290

Job Outlook and Employment

Slower than average growth is projected for the general occupation of conservation scientists in the US, estimated from 13,188 jobs in 2006 to 13,868 in 2016. The federal government and some state governments expect a large number of foresters to retire over the next decade, which will create a large number of job openings despite the projection of slower than average job growth. However, the best opportunities for foresters may be in consulting — as governments and businesses are increasingly contracting out for forestry services.

Where the Jobs Are

State government (26.92%); Federal government (16.09%); Local government (10.79%); Sawmills/wood preservation (7.97%); Logging (5.19%); Management, scientific and technical consulting services (4.38%); Self-employed: 4.16%

Resources

Association of Consulting Foresters of America (ACF):
    www.acf–foresters.org
Forest Guild: forestguild.org
Global Association of Online Foresters (GAOF): foresters.org
O*NET OnLine: online.onetcenter.org (see foresters)
Society of American Foresters (SAF): safnet.org
US Dept. of Labor, Bureau of Labor Statistics: bls.gov/oco/ocos048.htm

 DAVID JARAMILLO, Registered Professional Forester,. Sierra Forest Legacy, from an interview with Jim in 2008

How did you get into this career field? What was your education and experience, including any green-related training or certification?

. I always knew I wanted to have a career that involved the environment and natural resources. I was influenced by several people — mainly a couple of professors at my junior college who had great views and facts regarding our natural resources and how we as a society have managed and, in many cases, mismanaged those resources. After learning about the state of our environment, I knew it was my responsibility to better educate myself in a field that would take me in a direction that would allow me to make some direct change. After looking at several universities, I decided to attend Humboldt State University where I received a bachelor of science degree in forestry conservation, as well as minors in wildlife management and environmental ethics. These degrees gave me a foundation and helped prepare me for a professional career as a forester.

What is your current job title and how would you describe the work you do in a typical day? What are your most common tasks?

I'm a registered professional forester and work with a conservation group called Sierra Forest Legacy, which is very influential on how we treat our natural resources in California. My workdays mainly involve speaking with homeowners, homeowner groups and fire-safe councils — regarding fire mitigation and how communities can better prepare themselves for wildfire, while still preserving the environment. I'm also involved in community wildfire protection plan writing, which involves a large amount of collaboration with varying interests — with the goal of making communities more prepared for wildfire. Lastly, I'm currently involving myself in fuels reduction projects that will reduce uncharacteristically high amounts of forest vegetation and restore the environment to a more natural condition. I feel that this is a green career because I am looking at environmentally friendly ways to restore an environment that has been heavily degraded by a century of fire suppression and inappropriate logging practices. My main goal is to once again have forests that can burn freely and naturally and function as an intact ecosystem. This goal is not one that I can achieve in my lifetime, but my hope is that future generations will be able to enjoy a forest that is fire resilient and full of species that today we consider endangered and/or threatened.

If you could give advice to a young person who wants to work in this career field someday, what would you tell them? How can they best groom themselves for this field?
I would tell them to pursue a degree in some kind of environmental studies such as wildlife, forestry, soil science, hydrology, etc. I would also tell them to begin developing relationships with groups that are considered environmentally friendly. The best way to groom yourself for a career in this field is to keep an open mind and expect to tailor yourself into whatever you feel you are called to do. This field is very broad, so there are not too many limitations as to what you can do if you are willing to learn and apply yourself.

What kind of career advancement opportunities can one expect in this field? What kind of salary range would reflect that career path (from entry-level to the more advanced position)?
Career advancement in this field varies, depending on what you are willing to do. In the non-profit world, advancements are limited, but the work horizon is very dynamic. Pay for a forester in a non-profit organization will range from $40,000 to $55,000 per year, depending on experience and what the organization is involved in. Although the pay is not what you could make elsewhere, the work is very satisfying.

In your opinion, what are some of the best schools, degrees and certificates for jobs in this career field, including green-specific training?
I believe that all of the forestry schools are good, but of course I am biased to Humboldt State. I feel that all of the schools will provide the basic foundation, although some will provide you with more field experience due to their proximity to forests. It is up to the student to take those fundamentals and apply them in a way that is the most environmentally friendly way possible.

How does someone without previous experience in this career field land a job? What are the best strategies for job-hunting in this field?
This is a pretty competitive workplace, and the best way to land a job is to show interest in the field and a willingness to lead. Many foresters offer sum-

mertime field work and sometimes hire people that have little or no work experience in the field. Once you get a season of field experience, you are more likely to get hired for another season and potentially gain full-time work as you build your resumé. The best way to job hunt in this field is to look for organizations that you feel you would want to work with and then begin contacting the directors and let them know of your interest. Even if a particular organization has no openings, they may point you into a direction that ends up connecting you with a job.

Are there any professional associations that you would recommend joining?
The Forest Guild.

What emerging careers do you see developing now and into the future for this career field? What new technologies will have the greatest impact on this field?
Careers in fuels reduction, forest certification, small-wood utilization, energy production and forest management for carbon sequestration are developing careers in the forestry field. Technologies that mill and add value to small-diameter trees are having the greatest impact on this field. The added value may come in the form of alternative energy or wood products that can be manufactured using small-diameter trees that perform to the same or better standard that traditional timbers do.

Resources from Q&A
Forest Guild: forestguild.org
Humboldt State University: humboldt.edu

Geoscientists, including Environmental Geologists, Hydrogeologists and Marine Geologists

Geoscientists study the composition, structure and other physical aspects of the Earth. May use geological, physics and mathematics knowledge in exploration for oil, gas, minerals or underground water or in waste disposal, land reclamation or other environmental problems.

Environmental geologists are concerned with the prevention and treatment of chemicals that adversely affect our soil and water. Hydrogeologists are concerned with groundwater, its occurrence, utilization, testing and management. Marine geologists are concerned with geophysical, geochemical, sedimentological and paleontological investigations of the ocean floor and coastal margins.

Qualifications and Advancement

A master's degree in environmental geology, hydrogeology or marine geology is the typical education requirement. This is the minimum educational requirement for most entry-level applied research positions. A doctorate degree is necessary for most college and university faculty positions and high-level research positions. A bachelor's degree may be adequate for a few entry-level positions.

Geoscientists gain valuable experience while still in college by working in research-related internship positions. After finishing college, they often begin their careers as research assistants. They are given more difficult assignments as they gain experience. Those with a graduate degree may be promoted to project/program manager. In some cases, a doctorate degree may be necessary for advancement.

Salary Survey

Median salary: $72,660 (very high)
Typical range: $51,860 to $100,650

Job Outlook and Employment

Much faster than average growth is projected for this occupation in the US, estimated from 31,061 jobs in 2006 to 37,850 in 2016. The need for energy, environmental protection and responsible land and water management will spur employment demand. Many geoscientists monitor the quality of the environment, including aquatic ecosystems, deteriorating coastal environments and rising sea levels — all activities that will spur employment growth for this occupation.

Where the Jobs Are

Oil and gas extraction (17.93%); Management, scientific and technical consulting services (16.1%); State government (9.42%); Federal government (8.38%); Support activities for mining (6.54%); Colleges/universities (4.74%); Self-employed: 2.17%

Resources

American Geological Institute (AGI): agiweb.org
American Geophysical Union (AGU): agu.org
Association of Environmental & Engineering Geologists (AEG): aegweb.org
International Association of Hydrogeologists (IAH): iah.org
Marine Geology and Geophysics at MIT:
    web.mit.edu/mit-whoi/www/research/mgg/
O*NET OnLine: online.onetcenter.org (see geoscientists)

US Dept. of Labor, Bureau of Labor Statistics: bls.gov/oco/ocos288.htm
Water Environment Federation (WEF): wef.org

Q&A   TERA CURREN
Geologist, US Forest Service,
from an interview with Jim in 2008

How did you get into this career field? What was your education and experience, including any green-related training or certification?
I got into geology in particular because I realized that I really liked math, chemistry and physics, and geology put it all together. I have a bachelor's degree in geology and also a master's degree in geology. I have about ten years experience as a geologist. Before that, I was a technician with the National Park Service and helped do studies on road rehabilitation techniques and their effectiveness, basically taking out old logging roads and restoring them to a "natural" forest environment. In terms of certificates, I'm a certified minerals administrator — which you get through the Forest Service based on experience and in-house education.

What is your current job title and how would you describe the work you do in a typical day? What are your most common tasks?
I'm a geologist. The thing I spend the most time doing is closing abandoned mines or hazardous mine openings. We do it to provide for public safety and also to enhance the habitat for bats and other critters. The next main thing I do is administer active mining claims on federal land. I make contact with mining claimants, educate them on what they can do on federal lands and inspect claims to make sure they're staying in compliance with all the federal environmental regulations. I also do some engineering geology — anything that has to do with roads or bridges. Of all of my tasks, I probably spend the most time writing NEPA (National Environmental Protection Act) documents.

If you could give advice to a young person who wants to work in this career field someday, what would you tell them? How can they best groom themselves for this field?
While in college, or during the summers, get experience with the Forest Service as an intern in one of their programs. The work may not be what you think, and to prepare for that, getting job experience is really important.

What kind of career advancement opportunities can one expect in this field? What kind of salary range would reflect that career path (from entry-level to the more advanced position)?

You can become a program manager, and from there you could rise to a manager position in a regional office. At the entry level, you would probably start out at $22,000 to $24,000 per year. As a program manager, you could make up to $70,000 or $80,000.

In your opinion, what are some of the best schools, degrees and certificates for jobs in this career field, including green-specific training?

Some people find a lot of success when they go to a school with a mining geology degree, such as the University of Nevada at Reno or the Colorado Schools of Mines. But any university with a bachelor's degree program in geology would work for a career in the Forest Service.

How does someone without previous experience in this career field land a job? What are the best strategies for job-hunting in this field?

There is a website called USAJOBS for federal jobs, so you can start your job search there. But the best thing is to not wait until you graduate from school. I think at this point the Forest Service offers better opportunities for people that are still in school with a year or two left to go, either by getting experience as an intern or by participating in the Student Career Experience Program (SCEP). That's really the best way to come into the Forest Service.

Are there any professional associations that you would recommend joining?

There are several associations that you could join, but as far as the type of geology that I do, there aren't really any associations.

What emerging careers do you see developing now and into the future for this career field? What new technologies will have the greatest impact on this field?

Most of the "ologists" that work for the Forest Service use GIS software and GPS units. But my job in particular doesn't require any new technology. Our jobs involve a lot of physical labor. Our engineers who design new facilities are using newer, more green technology to make the facilities more energy efficient. The Forest Service is bringing hybrid vehicles into our work fleet, too. There is a trend towards that in our agency.

Resources from Q&A

Colorado Schools of Mines: mines.edu

National Park Service: nps.gov

University of Nevada, Reno: unr.edu

USAJOBS: usajobs.gov

US Dept. of Agriculture, Forest Service: fs.fed.us

US Dept. of Agriculture, Forest Service, Student Career Experience Program (SCEP): fs.fed.us/fsjobs/forestservice/scep.html

Hydrologists, including Environmental Hydrologists and Water Resources Managers

Hydrologists research the distribution, circulation and physical properties of underground and surface waters; study the form and intensity of precipitation, its rate of infiltration into the soil, movement through the Earth and its return to the ocean and atmosphere.

Environmental hydrologists are usually concerned with the pollution carried by water, including oceans, rivers, streams, rain, snow and ice — and devise methods to clean and control it. Some study weather-related problems, including global warming.

Qualifications and Advancement

A bachelor's degree is the typical education requirement. However, increasingly, hydrologists need a master's degree in a natural science. This is also the minimum requirement for most applied research positions in private industry. A doctorate degree is necessary for high-level research positions.

Hydrologists usually begin working under the supervision of a more experienced hydrologist. They collect field data and process samples. As they gain experience, they are given more responsibility. They plan projects and write reports. Eventually, they may be promoted to project leader or program manager.

Salary Survey

Median salary: $66,260 (very high)

Typical range: $51,370 to $82,140

Job Outlook and Employment

Much faster than average growth is projected for this occupation in the US, estimated from 8,314 jobs in 2006 to 10,337 in 2016. Job growth should be strongest in private-sector consulting firms and will be spurred largely by the increasing demands placed on the environment and water resources by population growth. Further demand should result from the need to comply with complex environmental laws and regulations. Hydrologists are also needed to study hazardous-waste sites and determine the effect of pollutants on soil and ground water so that engineers can design remediation systems. Increased government regulations, such as those regarding the management of storm water, and issues related to water conservation, deteriorating coastal environments and rising sea levels will stimulate employment growth.

Where the Jobs Are

Federal government, excluding postal service (27.95%); Management, scientific and technical consulting services (18.41%); State government (15.36%); Local government (5.43%); Self-employed: 2.36%

Resources

American Institute of Hydrology (AIH): aihydro.org
International Association for Environmental Hydrology: hydroweb.com
O*NET OnLine: online.onetcenter.org (see hydrologists)
US Dept. of Labor, Bureau of Labor Statistics: bls.gov/oco/ocos050.htm
US Geological Survey: Water Resources of the United States: water.usgs.gov
Water Environment Federation (WEF): wef.org

Microbiologists, including Environmental and Public Health Microbiologists

Microbiologists investigate the growth, structure, development and other characteristics of microscopic organisms, such as bacteria, algae or fungi. Includes medical microbiologists who study the relationship between organisms and disease or the effects of antibiotics on micro-organisms.

Environmental microbiology is the study of the composition and physiology of microbial communities in the environment, including soil, water, air and sediments. Public health microbiology is the specialized area that detects and identifies the micro-organisms associated with infectious and communicable disease.

Qualifications and Advancement

A doctorate degree in microbiology is the typical education requirement. The doctorate degree is required for independent research, research administration and most college and university faculty positions. Those with only a master's degree are somewhat limited to jobs in applied research, management or as instructors at community colleges and some four-year colleges.

Microbiologists often gain experience while in college by working as research or laboratory assistants. With a bachelor's degree, they can usually work as laboratory assistants or technicians or in some non-research jobs. With the appropriate teaching credential, they may also find jobs as high school teachers. Microbiologists with a master's degree may qualify for some jobs in basic research or applied research.

Salary Survey
Median salary: $57,980 (very high)
Typical range: $43,850 to $80,550

Job Outlook and Employment
Average growth is projected for this occupation in the US, from 17,357 jobs in 2006 to 19,306 in 2016. Efforts to discover new and improved ways to clean up and preserve the environment will continue to add to job growth. However, the increase in federal spending on basic research has slowed substantially and is not expected to match its past growth over the 2006–2016 projection period. This may result in a competitive environment for obtaining and renewing research grants.

Where the Jobs Are
Research and development in the physical, engineering and life sciences (24.99%); Pharmaceutical and medicine manufacturing (19.08%); Federal government (15.13%); Colleges, universities and professional schools (9.31%); State government (9.25%); Local government (3.91%); Self-employed: 2.25%

Resources
American Society for Microbiology (ASM): asm.org
BiologyJobs.com: biologyjobs.com
O*NET OnLine: online.onetcenter.org (see microbiologists)
US Dept. of Labor, Bureau of Labor Statistics: bls.gov/oco/ocos047.htm

Physicists, including Health and Atmospheric Physicists

Physicists conduct research into the phases of physical phenomena, develop theories and laws on the basis of observation and experiments and devise methods to apply laws and theories to industry and other fields.

Health physics is a field of science concerned with the evaluation and control of health hazards focused on the safe use of ionizing radiation. Atmospheric physics is the application of physics to the study of the atmosphere.

Qualifications and Advancement

A doctorate degree in physics is the typical education requirement. However, for research positions, employers often prefer candidates who have completed a post-doctoral research fellowship or have other post-doctoral experience. Physicists with only a master's degree may be eligible for applied research jobs or for faculty positions at community colleges or some four-year colleges. Those with only a bachelor's degree are limited to some non-research jobs.

Physicists with a doctorate degree often take temporary post-doctoral research positions that provide specialized research experience. Post-doctoral positions often offer the opportunity to publish research findings. A solid record of published research is essential in obtaining a permanent position involving basic research, especially for those seeking a permanent college or university faculty position. In private industry, some may become managers or administrators in a physics-related field.

Salary Survey

Median salary: $94,240 (very high)
Typical range: $72,910 to $117,080

Job Outlook and Employment

Slower than average growth is projected for the general occupation of physicists in the US, from 16,516 jobs in 2006 to 17,641 in 2016. Federal research funds are the major source of funding for physics-related research. Although these expenditures are expected to increase, resulting in some job growth, the limited funds available for science research will result in competition for basic research jobs. However, biotechnology and nanotechnology research should continue to grow.

Where the Jobs Are

Research and development in the physical, engineering and life sciences (32.02%); Federal government (20.47%); Colleges, universities and professional schools (14.41%); General medical and surgical hospitals (4.95%); Navigational, measuring, electromedical and control instruments manufacturing (3.27%)

Resources

American Institute of Physics (AIP): aip.org
American Physical Society (APS): aps.org
Health Physics Society (HPS): hps.org
International Association of Meteorology and Atmospheric Sciences
    (IAMAS): iamas.org

O*NET OnLine: online.onetcenter.org (see physicists)
US Dept. of Labor, Bureau of Labor Statistics: bls.gov/oco/ocos052.htm

 LINDA SEWELL, Senior Health Physicist, Pacific, Gas and Electric, from an interview with Alice in 2008

How did you get into this career field? What was your education and experience, including any green-related training or certification?
I have a bachelor of science in biology and a master of science in health physics. I would also recommend becoming a certified health physicist, which is the credentialing program for professional health physicists. It is somewhat analogous to the professional engineer (PE) program. In my case, health physicists are a necessary component in the day-to-day workings of a nuclear power plant.

What is your current job title and how would you describe the work you do in a typical day? What are your most common tasks, including those that make yours a green job?
As a senior health physicist, a typical day may include: talk to workers about questions they may have regarding radiation exposure, perform/review calculations of radiation exposure, update computer information, review and revise procedural guidance, research technical literature, troubleshoot and repair radiation monitoring equipment and talk to the public about nuclear power as a green solution.

If you could give advice to a young person who wants to work in this career field someday, what would you tell them? How can they best groom themselves for this field?
Get a solid background in math, up to and including calculus. Get a solid background in biology, physics and chemistry. Getting exposure to those classes in high school will make college and graduate school much easier, and you'll be able to concentrate on the new things you are learning.

What kind of career advancement opportunities can one expect in this field? What kind of salary range would reflect that career path (from entry-level to the more advanced position)?
Career advancement is open-ended. The last two vice presidents and plant managers at my place of employment started out their careers as health physicists. Typically, the entry level at a power plant would be in the $50,000 to $60,000 range. Staying within health physics, the top level at a power plant

might be about $150,000. If you were to continue advancing out of health physics and up the management chain, the ceiling goes up significantly.

In your opinion, what are some of the best schools, degrees and certificates for jobs in this career field, including green-specific training?
I got my graduate degree in health physics from the University of Florida, so I am partial to that school. There are a number of other good programs at Texas A&M, Georgia Tech, Tennessee, San Diego State and University of Michigan. I know I am leaving others out of the mix, but that is a good list to start with.

How does someone without previous experience in this career field land a job? What are the best strategies for job-hunting in this field?
If you have a degree in health physics, you will have little difficulty finding a job. The employers will probably come to you if your college/university holds a job fair.

Are there any professional associations that you would recommend joining?
The Health Physics Society.

What emerging careers do you see developing now and into the future for this career field? What new technologies will have the greatest impact on this field?
The field of health physics has a number of career opportunities, both in and out of the nuclear power industry. Regarding new technologies, as is true everywhere, the advancements in computers and technology as a whole are presenting new and exciting opportunities on a regular basis.

Resources from Q&A
Georgia Institute of Technology (Georgia Tech): gatech.edu
Health Physics Society (HPS): hps.org
San Diego State University: sdsu.edu
Texas A&M University: tamu.edu
University of Florida: ufl.edu
University of Michigan: umich.edu
University of Tennessee, Knoxville: utk.edu

Soil and Plant Scientists, including Agronomists

Soil and plant scientists conduct research in breeding, physiology, production, yield and management of crops and agricultural plants, their growth in soils and control of pests; or study the chemical, physical, biological and mineralogical composition of soils as they relate to plant or crop growth. May classify and map soils and investigate effects of alternative practices on soil and crop productivity.

Qualifications and Advancement

A master's degree in agronomy or a related field is the typical education requirement. This is the minimum educational requirement for most entry-level applied research positions. A doctorate degree is necessary for college and university faculty positions and for most high-level research positions. A bachelor's degree may be adequate for a few entry-level positions.

Agronomists and soil scientists gain valuable experience while still in college by working in school laboratories and by working in summer internship positions. After finishing college, they often begin their careers as research assistants or technicians. They are given more difficult assignments as they gain experience. Certification may be important for advancement. Eventually, agronomists and soil scientists can be promoted to project leader or program manager.

Salary Survey

Median salary: $56,080 (very high)
Typical range: $42,410 to $72,020

Job Outlook and Employment

Average growth is projected for this occupation in the US, from 15,790 jobs in 2006 to 17,110 in 2016. Although past agricultural research has created higher-yielding crops, crops with better resistance to pests and plant pathogens and more effective fertilizers and pesticides, research is still necessary as insects and diseases continue to adapt to pesticides and as soil fertility and water quality continue to need improvement. This and an increasing demand for biofuels will create more jobs for agricultural scientists. Agricultural scientists will also be needed to balance increased agricultural output with protection and preservation of soil, water and ecosystems.

Where the Jobs Are

Federal government (17.45%); Colleges, universities and professional schools (12.32%); Research and development in the physical, engineering and life sciences (10.48%); Nondurable goods merchant wholesalers (8.86%); Management, scientific and technical consulting services (4.84%); Local government (3.53%); State government (3%); Self-employed: 17.72%

Resources
American Society of Agronomy (ASA): agronomy.org
California Native Plant Society (CNPS): cnps.org
O*NET OnLine: online.onetcenter.org (see soil and plant scientists)
Soil Science Society of America (SSSA): soils.org
US Dept. of Labor, Bureau of Labor Statistics: bls.gov/oco/ocos046.htm

Soil and Water Conservationists, including Ecologists and Erosion Specialists

Soil and water conservationists plan and develop coordinated practices for soil erosion control, soil and water conservation and sound land use.

Qualifications and Advancement
A bachelor's degree is the typical education requirement. Most soil and water conservationists have degrees in environmental studies, agronomy, general agriculture, hydrology or crop or soil science; a few have degrees in related fields such as wildlife biology, forestry and range management. In the federal government, a combination of experience and appropriate education occasionally may substitute for a four-year degree, but job competition makes this difficult.

Some soil and water conservationists start their careers as conservation technicians. With a combination of experience and education, they can advance to soil or water conservationists. Recent graduates usually work under the supervision of experienced conservationists. After gaining experience, they may advance to more responsible positions. Conservationists usually begin working within one county or conservation district and, with experience, may advance to the area, state, regional or national level. After several years of experience, some may become consultants.

Salary Survey
Median salary: $54,970 (very high)
Typical range: $40,950 to $68,460

Job Outlook and Employment
Slower than average growth is projected for the general occupation of conservation scientists in the US, estimated from 19,777 jobs in 2006 to 20,830 in 2016. The management of storm water and coastlines has created demand for people knowledgeable about runoff and erosion on farms and in cities and suburbs. Additionally, soil and water quality experts will still be needed as

states design initiatives to improve water resources by preventing pollution by agricultural producers and industrial plants.

Where the Jobs Are

Federal government (38.37%); Local government (18.25%); State government (16.83%); Social advocacy organizations (5.2%); Self-employed: 3.91%

Resources

California Native Plant Society (CNPS): cnps.org

National Association of Conservation Districts (NACD): nacdnet.org

Natural Resources Conservation Service (NRCS): nrcs.usda.gov

O*NET OnLine: online.onetcenter.org (see soil and water conservationists)

Soil and Water Conservation Society (SWCS): swcs.org

USAJOBS: usajobs.gov

US Dept. of Agriculture, Forest Service: fs.fed.us

US Dept. of Agriculture, National Resources Conservation Service:
    nrcs.usda.gov

US Dept. of Labor, Bureau of Labor Statistics: bls.gov/oco/ocos048.htm

Water Environment Federation (WEF): wef.org

Q&A **BOBETTE PARSONS**
Conservation Specialist,
US Dept. of Agriculture,
National Resources Conservation Service,
from an interview with Alice in 2008

How did you get into this career field? What was your education and experience?
My entering this career field stemmed from my love of the natural environment which began when I was a young child. As a junior at Humboldt State, I applied for a position as a cooperative education student with the USDA Forest Service and landed a summer position before my senior year. At that time, I had completed calculus, physics and other physical science courses which gave me a competitive edge over other students who had avoided taking these "hard" classes. These courses are the proving grounds for people going into disciplines like hydrology or soil science. After working as a hydrologist for three years, I made a decision to go back to school to get a master's degree in soil science. Most of my research has been within my area of emphasis — the protection and wise use of soil and water resources.

What is your current job title and how would you describe the work you do in a typical day? What are your most common tasks?

I'm a soil conservationist. A typical day includes some conservation planning with a private land user, some conservation practice design work and some report writing or documentation work. A general rule is about ten hours in the office for every hour in the field. Common tasks include making contacts with land users, evaluating resource problems, quantifying natural resource issues and then evaluating alternatives for future management. A soil conservationist is a catalyst for change. The goal is to promote changes that will protect natural resources and provide for a higher quality of life for generations to come.

If you could give advice to a young person who wants to work in this career field someday, what would you tell them? How can they best groom themselves for this field?

I have found that good people generally go into these "helping" fields, so almost anywhere you work in this field, you will be part of a team where you will be able to work with others having common goals. You will find it rewarding if you enjoy helping people and you like the way it feels when you know you have done something that will help protect the Earth's resources for the future. Positions in resource conservation or management usually involve large geographic areas, and travel is the general rule. I would suggest meeting with people in the various positions that look interesting and conducting informational interviews to get a feel for the culture. I always like to ask "What are your greatest rewards?" and "What do you like best about this job?"

What kind of career advancement opportunities can one expect in this field? What kind of salary range would reflect that career path (from entry-level to the more advanced position)?

Once in the federal system, transferring and promotion within the same agency becomes fairly easy. What a lot of people do not realize is that the USDA does most of its hiring at the entry level, then promotes from within. Generally the salary range for the federal government is lower than in private industry, but average for government, i.e., county, state or federal. The medical and retirement benefits are better than much of the private sector and should be taken into account as part of the compensation package. An average soil conservation position for an individual just out of college with a bachelor of science degree would be at the GS–5 level with a salary of around $25,000 a year. These positions are sometimes set up as 5–7–9, which means that the individual can promote non-competitively from the GS–5 to the GS–9 level with a year or two between promotions. Those who enter with master's degrees, or some other related experience, can often start at the GS–7 level with an annual salary of around $31,000. It will normally take a minimum of five to eight years to attain the GS–11 where the salary is around $46,000 a year. At the high end, a GS–15 makes $91,500 per year.

In your opinion, what are some of the best schools, degrees and certificates for jobs in this career field?
In my opinion, bachelor of science degrees which emphasize land use management or conservation planning are the best ones for this field. A master of science degree which focuses on a particular type of land use or natural resource discipline is also recommended. Degrees that are most useful include soil science, agricultural economics, agronomy, agricultural engineering, wildlife biology or range management. Once an individual has looked at the academic requirements for the various natural resource positions, it will be fairly easy to locate the college or university that will best prepare them for their career. Most states will have one or two programs that will best prepare the individual for work specific to that region.

How does someone without previous experience in this career field land a job? What are the best strategies for job-hunting in this field?
The best way to get into a position with the federal government in the natural resource management field is to use a combination of strategies: Use the USAJOBS or AVUE Central websites to apply for jobs that are listed by federal agencies, and make personal contacts with professionals in the offices that you would like to work in. Some agencies also have cooperative education programs or internships that may not be listed on these websites. If you are still in college, this is the best time to make your contacts and to let the people in your school's career placement center know what your goals are. I had some friends who even had professors in their departments help promote them.

Are there any professional associations that you would recommend joining?
I would recommend joining the Soil and Water Conservation Society of America. I would also recommend joining a professional society for the particular land use or discipline you are emphasizing, such as agronomy, soil science or forestry.

What emerging or high growth careers do you see developing now and into the future for this career field? What new technologies will have the greatest impact on this field?
Computer technology has had the greatest impact on this field in the past decade. This has increased the ease of information transfer between professionals

and the public. The use of computers has also facilitated conservation planning, practice design and tracking. Because this has brought about some significant changes in our day-to-day operations, individuals with communication and computer technology skills will be at an advantage in applying for most positions. There is also a demand at present for new professionals in the natural resource management field, as many of the dedicated conservationists who have served over the past 30–40 years are now retiring.

Resources from Q&A

Avue Central: avuecentral.com

Humboldt State University: humboldt.edu

Soil and Water Conservation Society (SWCS): swcs.org

USAJOBS: usajobs.gov

US Dept. of Agriculture, Forest Service: fs.fed.us

US Dept. of Agriculture, National Resources Conservation Service: nrcs.usda.gov

Tree Trimmers and Pruners, including Arborists

Tree trimmers and pruners cut away dead or excess branches from trees or shrubs to maintain right-of-way for roads, sidewalks or utilities or to improve appearance, health and value of tree. Prune or treat trees or shrubs using handsaws, pruning hooks, sheers and clippers. May use truck-mounted lifts and power pruners.

An arborist is a professional in the practice of arboriculture, the management and maintenance of trees and other perennial woody plants. Arborists are focused on the health and safety of individual trees or wooded landscapes.

Qualifications and Advancement

There usually are no minimum education requirements for this occupation, as most workers are trained on the job. To become a certified arborist, however, usually requires some formal training in arboriculture, in addition to on-the-job training. Various certifications are available through the International Society of Arboriculture (ISA).

Workers who demonstrate a willingness to work hard and quickly, have good communication skills and take an interest in the business may advance to crew leader or other supervisory positions within a few years. Some certified arborists start their own businesses after several years of experience in this occupation.

Salary Survey

Median salary: $28,250 (low/moderate)

Typical range: $22,300 to $36,150

Job Outlook and Employment

Average growth is projected for this occupation in the US, from 40,560 jobs in 2006 to 45,071 in 2016. Opportunities should increase as utility companies step up pruning of trees around electric lines to prevent power outages. Additionally, tree trimmers and pruners will be needed to help combat infestations caused by new species of insects from other countries. For example, ash trees from Chicago to Washington, DC are under threat by a pest from China, and preventative eradication may be employed to control the pest.

Where the Jobs Are

Landscaping services (53.61%); Local government (8.39%); Self-employed: 24.33%

Resources

American Society of Consulting Arborists (ASCA): asca–consultants.org

California Native Plant Society (CNPS): cnps.org

International Society of Arboriculture (ISA): isa–arbor.com

O*NET OnLine: online.onetcenter.org (see tree trimmers and pruners)

Tree Care Industry Association (TCIA): treecareindustry.org

US Dept. of Labor, Bureau of Labor Statistics: bls.gov/oco/ocos172.htm

 JOHN KIPPING, Certified Arborist,
from an interview with Jim in 2008

How did you get into this career field? What was your education and experience?
I've worked in tree care since 1982. My education and experience prior to that would be a bachelor's degree and master's degree in biology with an emphasis in botany and entomology. Prior to actually getting up and climbing around in trees, my tree-related work experience would have been from more of an educational and public information background, working as an educator and horticulturist at the Strybing Arboretum and Botanical Gardens in Golden Gate Park in San Francisco. I had a job there part-time while I was going to college, which developed into a full-time job as the education director of the Strybing Arboretum Society. We had about 5,000 kinds of plants there. I maintained files on all the plants, helped propagate them and developed educational material for the self-guided nature tours. It was a lot of fun. I also did a lot of teaching at University Extension, that sort of thing — outdoor

education, natural environment programs — and also worked as a river guide in the summer until I started my own business.

What is your current job title and how would you describe the work you do in a typical day? What are your most common tasks?

There's a trade group in the industry called the International Society of Arboriculture. I took their certification program several years ago, so I'm called a certified arborist. I'm also a member of the American Society of Consulting Arborists. So this is sort of the upper echelons of tree work. This involves consulting, diagnosis of tree problems, pests, diseases. Some of my business will be concerned with assessing trees as to their stability and safety — doing sort of forensic arboriculture so we know what happened to the tree, why did it die and is there a chance it might spread to other things? I also do some courtroom work with cases when trees are involved, such as wrongful trespass or logging or somebody mutilating a neighbor's tree to get a view. But I really don't like going to court. I have one suit and one tie that I keep for those dreadful moments of being up on the stand! My typical day might be getting up real early in the morning, getting my paperwork together, meeting my two-person crew and going to a customer's job site. We may be pruning one or more trees and sometimes taking them down. So I'm basically assigning duties, positioning the truck, dealing with the customer and then I usually get up in trees for six or seven hours, off the ground, using hand saws, pole saws and chainsaws. Sometimes we have to install hardware in the tree to help brace it or cable it together when it may be falling apart. Those are my tasks by day, and then in the afternoon, it's run around and do repairs, get supplies, meet new customers, old customers, do bids on future work. And then I go home and answer the phone for two hours.

If you could give advice to a young person who wants to work in this career field someday, what would you tell them? How can they best groom themselves for this field?

There are a few schools that offer a horticulture program that would include maybe a course or two on arboriculture where they might get a little bit of hands-on experience — some of the basics of tree anatomy and tree biology. But that knowledge is very necessary for proper tree pruning. There are a lot of people in my field who are certified arborists who have never climbed a tree. I think that a true arborist really needs to get a hands-on experience and touch the trees to understand them better and to understand exactly what our goals are. I think a lot of people see an arborist doing physical labor, and they think anybody could do that. Whereas we look at it as a very highly skilled job with a lot of inherent risk.

What kind of career advancement opportunities can one expect in this field? What kind of salary range would reflect that career path (from entry-level to the more advanced position)?

I recommend that someone interested in being an arborist take the college classes and then plan to work their way from the ground up. There's not much money being a tree worker. The better money would be in jobs like foreman or salesperson for the big companies or, of course, being an owner of one of those companies. But it's a lot of hard work, it's dirty, it's dangerous, there's a high risk of injury, and it takes a lot of skill. It takes about two years for a person with good abilities and a good attitude to become a fairly competent climber. But a person would have to enjoy hard work and being out of doors in all kinds of weather. I've seen where municipalities start their tree workers/climbers at $40,000 to $50,000 per year — so that's a pretty good salary. A company like mine might pay a journeyman climber $32 per hour, and the ground people anywhere from $18 to $20 per hour.

In your opinion, what are some of the best schools, degrees and certificates for jobs in this career field (as an arborist)?

One good horticulture school I know of is UC Davis. There are also certifications, like that of the International Society of Arboriculture.

How does someone without previous experience in this career field land a job? What are the best strategies for job-hunting in this field?

Probably just making phone calls, knocking on doors and stopping and talking to a tree crew that's out there. The plum jobs would be getting on with the city or county, although a lot of those municipalities are now privatizing their tree crews. Even our local utility company is getting rid of their in-house tree crews. I think part of that is that they don't want to cover the insurance costs.

Are there any professional associations that you would recommend joining?

The best one is the International Society of Arboriculture. And there are many different chapters. It's international, although most chapters are here in the United States and Canada. They have local meetings, and they have student membership rates. They put out excellent journals. There's also the ASCA (the American Society of Consulting Arborists) and the National Arborists Association, which is now called the Tree Care Industry Association.

What emerging or high-growth careers do you see developing now and into the future for this career field? What new technologies will have the greatest impact on this field?

People are always looking for technology to find ways to look inside trees — to look at decay. They've had some very expensive instruments to try to bore into the tree. I've got a $3,000 tool that I use only about twice a year to take corings and get a picture — a graph of what is inside the tree. It makes for a better educated guess as to the tree's stability. And then, of course, there's the whole genetic engineering thing. It's pretty interesting, because it's hard to do breeding programs for trees when they have such long generations compared to something like corn that's an annual. For example, if you do a breeding program for redwood trees, you might have to wait until they're 25–35 years old before they flower and have cones on them. But there's a lot of interest in trying to get disease and insect resistant strains of things. We're getting so many new pests in this country thanks to globalization and rapid transportation. It seems like every year there's a brand new pest that's eating up or devastating some species.

Resources from Q&A

American Society of Consulting Arborists (ASCA): asca–consultants.org
International Society of Arboriculture: isa–arbor.com
Strybing Arboretum & Botanical Gardens: sfbotanicalgarden.org
Tree Care Industry Association (TCIA): tcia.org
University of California, Davis: ucdavis.edu

Water Treatment Plant Operators

Water and liquid waste treatment plant and system operators operate or control an entire process or system of machines, often through the use of control boards, to transfer or treat water or liquid waste.

Qualifications and Advancement

A high-school diploma or equivalent is the typical education/training requirement. However, the completion of an associate's degree or a one-year certificate program in water quality and wastewater treatment technology increases a person's chances for employment and promotion. In some cases, a degree or certificate can be substituted for experience, allowing a worker to become licensed at a higher level more rapidly.

Trainees usually start as attendants or operators-in-training and learn their skills on the job under the direction of an experienced operator. As operators gain experience, they become responsible for more complex treatment processes. Some may be promoted to supervisory positions, while others advance by transferring to a larger facility. With each promotion, the operator must have greater knowledge of federal, state and local regulations. Superintendents of large plants generally need an engineering or science degree.

Salary Survey
Median salary: $36,070 (low/moderate)
Typical range: $28,120 to $45,190

Job Outlook and Employment
Average growth is projected for this occupation in the US, from 110,840 jobs in 2006 to 126,111 in 2016. Opportunities should be good due to the increasing demand for water and wastewater treatment services. As new plants are constructed to meet this demand, new jobs will be created for operators. In addition, many job openings will occur in this occupation as a result of workers with years of experience retiring.

Where the Jobs Are
Local government (78.95%); Water, sewage and other systems (9.17%)

Resources
American Water Works Association: awwa.org
Association of Boards of Certification (ABC): abccert.org
National Environmental Health Association (NEHA): neha.org
National Rural Water Association (NRWA): nrwa.org
O*NET OnLine: online.onetcenter.org (see water and liquid waste treatment
    plant and system operators)
US Dept. of Labor, Bureau of Labor Statistics: bls.gov/oco/ocos229.htm
Water Environment Federation (WEF): wef.org

Q&A **JONATHAN BEALL**
Water Treatment Plant Operator,
El Dorado Irrigation District,
from an interview with Alice in 2008

How did you get into this career field? What was your education and experience, including any green-related training or certification?
I have a love for the rural life and good clean water, having worked on a self-sufficient ranch for many years. I got into the water treatment field at 20 years of age. I started as a seasonal utility worker, cleaning irrigation ditches, when a training position opened. I rated highest on the job's written test because of my abilities in math. At that time, I only had a high-school diploma. So I went to school at night and received my associate of science degree in water quality control and also

continued my advancement through the state certifications for water treatment operator, water distribution operator and wastewater treatment plant operator. I also maintained other certifications from the National Environmental Health Association as environmental health technician and hazardous substance specialist.

What is your current job title and how would you describe the work you do in a typical day? What are your most common tasks?

I'm a water treatment plant operator/distribution operator. I spend many hours on the computer with SCADA (Supervisory Control and Data Acquisition). Through this computer system, I monitor and control the treatment process, pumps and water levels in tanks. Critical work areas are to provide biologically safe water for the consumer and to prevent spills of water — sludge by-products — and treatment chemicals into the environment. A water plant operator must be familiar with basic chemistry and lab procedures to daily test the water and optimize the treatment process. An operator must also respond to customer water quality complaints and water leaks to insure safe delivery of our product to the consumer. Public interaction skills are essential. We may also deal with wasteful water practices and educate homeowners and contractors of water conservation practices.

If you could give advice to a young person who wants to work in this career field someday, what would you tell them? How can they best groom themselves for this field?

This particular field is wide open for young people. The water industry is experiencing a crisis as older workers leave due to attrition, and fewer people are entering the industry. The basic requirements are a high-school diploma and lower-division university credits, which can be achieved through correspondence courses from state universities. To pass the California state tests to become a certified operator, the following areas are helpful: basic knowledge of math to an algebra level, some basic mechanical abilities, a willingness to learn, basic electrical mechanics and very basic chemistry.

What kind of career advancement opportunities can one expect in this field? What kind of salary range would reflect that career path (from entry-level to the more advanced position)?

The career advancement is very good in the water industry. There are many areas of advancement: supervisory, engineering, planning, inspection, hydroelectric, wastewater treatment, warehousing, construction, public outreach.

All these are available at most water districts and are usually hired in-house. For a water treatment plant trainee, the salary is usually $18 to $25 per hour. Once a person is certified at grade 3 or above (after two years experience), the salary ranges are $28 to $35 in this area. These ranges can be much higher, depending on where you work. This field always requires drug testing and basic physical qualifications, such as the ability to lift at least 50 pounds. Advancement in this field usually involves continuing education and testing for higher-grade levels.

In your opinion, what are some of the best schools, degrees and certificates for jobs in this career field, including green-specific training?
Community colleges and state universities provide relevant training. In California, the primary training books are provided by the Office of Water Programs at CSU Sacramento, Attn: Kenneth Kerri, Project Director.

How does someone without previous experience in this career field land a job? What are the best strategies for job-hunting in this field?
The best way is to complete the basic correspondence course from a state university. It is also very helpful if you pass a Grade 2 test from the state. In California, contact the Department of Public Health, Division of Drinking Water and Environmental Management for more information.

Are there any professional associations that you would recommend joining?
The American Water Works Association is one of the largest professional associations in this job field.

What emerging careers do you see developing now and into the future for this career field? What new technologies will have the greatest impact on this field?
Computers are playing a larger and larger role on a daily basis in water treatment. Micro membrane technologies, ultraviolet disinfections and stricter regulations will continue to specialize and move the water treatment plant operator into a more technically advanced career.

Resources from Q&A

American Water Works Association: awwa.org
California Department of Public Health, Division of Drinking Water and
    Environmental Management: cdph.ca.gov/certlic/occupations/Pages/
    DWopcert.aspx
National Environmental Health Association (NEHA): neha.org
Office of Water Programs, CSU Sacramento: owp.csus.edu

Zoologists and Wildlife Biologists, including Marine Biologists

Zoologists and wildlife biologists study the origins, behavior, diseases, genetics and life processes of animals and wildlife. May specialize in wildlife research and management, including the collection and analysis of biological data to determine the environmental effects of present and potential use of land and water areas.

Qualifications and Advancement

A doctorate degree in zoology or wildlife biology is the typical education requirement. The doctorate degree is required for independent research, research administration and for most college and university faculty positions. Those with only a master's degree are limited to jobs in applied research, management, inspection, sales and service or as instructors at community colleges and some four-year colleges. Those with only a bachelor's degree are limited to some non-research jobs, or with the appropriate teaching credential, they may work as high school teachers.

Zoologists and wildlife biologists often gain experience while in college by working as research or laboratory assistants. Entry-level zoologists and wildlife biologists with only a bachelor's degree usually work as laboratory assistants or technicians or in non-research jobs. Those with a master's degree have the additional advantage of qualifying for some jobs in basic research, applied research or product development; they may also qualify to work as a research technician or an educator in a zoo. Those with a doctorate degree often take temporary post-doctoral research positions that provide specialized research experience. These positions often offer the opportunity to publish research findings, which is essential in obtaining a permanent position involving basic research, including for those seeking a permanent college or university faculty position. In private industry, some may become managers or administrators in a zoology or wildlife biology-related field.

Salary Survey

Median salary: $53,300 (high)
Typical range: $41,400 to $67,200

Job Outlook and Employment

Average growth is projected for this occupation in the US, from 20,091 jobs in 2006 to 21,830 in 2016. There will continue to be demand for qualified applicants in this field, but opportunities will be somewhat limited because of the small size of this occupation.

Where the Jobs Are

State government (32.24%); Federal government (24.89%); Research and development (14.2%); Management, scientific and technical consulting services (5.5%); Universities and other educational institutions (4.99%); Zoos (4.41%); Self-employed: 2.12%

Resources

American Association of Zoo Keepers (AAZK): aazk.org

Association of Zoos and Aquariums (AZA): aza.org

O*NET OnLine: online.onetcenter.org (see zoologists and wildlife biologists)

US Dept. of Labor, Bureau of Labor Statistics: bls.gov/oco/ocos047.htm

Physical Geography Group

○ Geographers, including Physical and Geographic Information Systems (GIS) Geographers

○ Physical Geography Professors, including Geographic Information Systems (GIS) Instructors

Geographers, including Physical and Geographic Information Systems (GIS) Geographers

Geographers study nature and use of areas of Earth's surface, relating and interpreting interactions of physical and cultural phenomena. Conduct research on physical aspects of a region, including land forms, climates, soils, plants and animals, and conduct research on the spatial implications of human activities within a given area, including social characteristics, economic activities and political organization.

GIS geographers are experts in the use of geographic information system (GIS) technology, which is a database system designed to work with data referenced by spatial or geographic coordinates.

Qualifications and Advancement

A master's degree in geography is the typical education requirement. However, a doctorate degree is a minimum requirement for most positions with colleges and universities and is also important for advancement to administrative positions. Those with master's degrees usually have better opportunities outside of academia. Bachelor's degree holders have limited opportunities and do not generally qualify for "professional" positions. However, the bachelor's degree does provide a suitable background for many entry-level jobs, including research assistant and GIS specialist or analyst. In fact, some GIS specialist jobs only require an associate's degree in GIS.

There is no typical career path for geographers. Some teach at the college or university level. Some do fieldwork or research in remote locations. Some geographers advise government, real estate developers, utilities and telecommunications firms on where to build new roads, buildings, power plants and cable lines. Some advise on environmental matters, such as where to build a landfill or preserve wetland habitats. With the development of Geographic

Information Systems (GIS), increasing numbers of geographers and GIS specialists can also be found in non-traditional areas, such as emergency assistance, homeland security, defense and planning.

Salary Survey
Median salary: $62,990 (very high)
Typical range: $50,120 to $77,770

Job Outlook and Employment
Slower than average growth is projected for this occupation in the US, from 1,095 jobs in 2006 to 1,162 in 2016. The expected slow growth reflects the relatively few employment opportunities for this occupation outside of the federal government, while overall federal government employment is expected to decline. However, job prospects for GIS-trained geographers and analysts are good — as more and more uses for GIS skills are found in a variety of industries.

Where the Jobs Are
Federal government (60.57%); Local government (5.63%); Self-employed: 5%

Resources
Association of American Geographers (AAG): aag.org
Environmental Sciences Research Institute (ESRI): esri.com
Geography Jobs (article): bls.gov/opub/ooq/2005/spring/art01.pdf
O*NET OnLine: online.onetcenter.org (see geographers)
Occupational Outlook Quarterly: Geography Jobs:
    bls.gov/opub/ooq/2005/spring/art01.pdf
US Dept. of Labor, Bureau of Labor Statistics: bls.gov/oco/ocos054.htm

Physical Geography Professors, including Geographic Information Systems (GIS) Instructors

Geography teachers, postsecondary, teach courses in geography. Includes both teachers primarily engaged in teaching and those who combine teaching and research.

Qualifications and Advancement
A doctorate degree in geography is the typical education requirement, although a master's degree is often adequate for positions with community colleges and some four-year colleges. However, candidates with only a master's degree will find themselves competing against others with a doctorate degree.

Instructors and professors generally begin their careers as graduate teaching assistants. Once they complete their degree, they typically find jobs as lecturers or adjunct (part-time) professors or instructors. Eventually they find a full-time position. The next step for college and university professors is to become tenured — meaning that the professor has received a permanent job contract, granted after a probationary period of several years. Advancement for tenured professors involves moving into administrative positions, such as department chairperson, dean, vice president and president.

Salary Survey
Median salary: $59,000 (very high)
Typical range: $47,300 to $76,630

Job Outlook and Employment
Much faster than average growth is projected for the overall occupation of postsecondary teachers in the US, from 1.7 million jobs in 2006 to 2 million in 2016. (Statistics specific to postsecondary geography teachers is not available.) Projected growth for the summary occupation is primarily due to increases in college and university enrollment over the next decade. This enrollment growth stems from the expected increase in the population of 18- to 24-year-olds, who constitute the majority of students at postsecondary institutions, and from the increasing number of high school graduates who choose to attend these institutions.

Where the Jobs Are
Colleges, universities and professional schools (70.8%); Community colleges (21.54%); Technical and trade schools (3.04%)

Resources
Association of American Geographers (AAG): aag.org
Association of Environmental Engineering and Science Professors (AEESP):
    aeesp.org
Environmental Sciences Research Institute (ESRI): esri.com
Geography Jobs (article): bls.gov/opub/ooq/2005/spring/art01.pdf
Occupational Outlook Quarterly: Geography Jobs:
    bls.gov/opub/ooq/2005/spring/art01.pdf
O*NET OnLine: online.onetcenter.org (see geography teachers,
    postsecondary)
Preparing Future Faculty (PFF) program: preparing–faculty.org
US Dept. of Labor, Bureau of Labor Statistics: bls.gov/oco/ocos066.htm

Q&A SCOTT CROSIER
Professor of Geography/GIS,
Cosumnes River College,
from an interview with Jim in 2008

How did you get into this career field? What was your education and experience, including any green-related training or certification?

I went to school at UC Santa Barbara and got my master's degree in geography. One emphasis in that program was on technology, including GIS and remote sensing. I focused on GIS. When I finished my degree, I went to work at ESRI (Environmental Sciences Research Institute), where I was a technical writer for them. So basically I used the software and then wrote a lot of the user's manuals. From there I went and became the GIS manager at an engineering firm in Santa Barbara. At the same time, I was asked if I would teach night classes in GIS. I realized that I really enjoyed the teaching aspect of it, and so I pursued a full-time teaching position.

What is your current job title and how would you describe the work you do in a typical day? What are your most common tasks?

My official job title is assistant professor of geography. I teach a number of geography classes, as well as the GIS and mapping classes. I research the technologies and see how applicable they are to the level of education that I'm giving to my students and then develop lectures on the material. I also review or write tutorial material so that students can work through exercises in the lab portion of our classes. And then I present the information to the class. That usually is done in lecture form and demonstration form. Besides introducing my students to the technologies, I also want to introduce them to the theories behind GIS in general — what GIS is, how we store data in a GIS, etc. But then there's also the buttons, bells and the whistles of the software. So it's really two different processes.

If you could give advice to a young person who wants to work in this career field someday, what would you tell them? How can they best groom themselves for this field?

If you want to teach a technical skill, you really want to get a good foundation in the knowledge of that skill. The opportunities that I've had to work at ESRI and really digging into the software and figuring out how to do the functions, and how to describe those functions, really prepared me for teaching GIS. So going to work at ESRI or one of the companies that make GIS software offers a great opportunity. ESRI also has a lot of internship opportunities for entry-level positions with them. If someone wanted to become a GIS technician or manager, a lot of the jobs out there require that you have at least a bachelor's degree. Having a bachelor's degree in general just kind of legitimizes you as someone who is educated and can learn things at a professional level. So if that was your goal, you should start off as early in your education as possible with internships. As soon as you can start getting internships and get real-world experience, it does two things for you: first, it gives you on-the-job training, which is really important; and second, it does a great job at letting you see what types of things you like to do and what things you don't like to do. Maybe you prefer to be the field guy collecting data. Or you may prefer to be the office guy processing the data. So getting those internships is valuable, and they can also satisfy a lot of the jobs that may ask for two years of experience.

What kind of career advancement opportunities can one expect in this field? What kind of salary range would reflect that career path (from entry-level to the more advanced position)?
It really depends on where you go with your career: private industry, education or government. A number of my students have been taking GIS classes so that it can help them in a lateral move that may later lead to a promotion. Going to work for a city in their GIS department is usually an entry-level position. And over time you can continue to go up that ladder until you're managing the GIS team. When I worked with the City of Oxnard, their GIS manager was in charge of a crew of about seven people, and those people all had different tasks that they were working on — based on their skills. They managed maps and did various projects for the public works people, the police department, the fire department, community development — all sorts of things. So in government, there's always that ladder to be climbed. In the education sector, you start off usually teaching on a part-time basis and eventually get hired in a full-time position. I'm going through the tenuring process now. I discovered that I loved teaching, and this is what I enjoy doing. So I'm not really looking at where I can go from here. But I think, in any college setting, there are always the administrative positions that a person could eventually move toward.

In your opinion, what are some of the best schools, degrees and certificates for jobs in this career field, including green-specific training?

If a student came to me and said "I want to become a GIS technician," I would probably tell them, "Well, you could take some GIS classes at college A, or you could go to college B where they have a whole GIS program, and you can get an associate's degree or bachelor's degree." College A would be appropriate for the person who wants to be something else, like a biologist, but wants those GIS technical skills. Also, college B is more likely to have internship programs for GIS. If you were going to pursue a bachelor's degree in GIS here in California, many colleges offer GIS programs, usually within their geography program. I am biased towards UC Santa Barbara. They have really been pushing the technology side of GIS for a long time. SUNY (State University of New York) at Buffalo and the University of Maine also have major centers dedicated to spatial technologies. And, yes, there are certainly other colleges throughout the country that have an emphasis in GIS. So I think it would just be a matter of looking them up and talking with the professors and looking at their catalog offerings.

How does someone without previous experience in this career field land a job? What are the best strategies for job-hunting in this field?
To teach at a college, you have to at least have a master's degree in the field you want to teach in, plus have some kind of teaching experience. So some of us got started by having had TA (teacher's assistant) experience while getting our degrees or maybe some other type of teaching or training-related experience. That might get you an opportunity to teach part-time. Then as you gain years of experience, you would hope for an opportunity to teach full-time. Many professional GIS positions require a bachelor's degree, and I would certainly suggest getting as much experience in internships as possible as you go through your schooling.

Are there any professional associations that you would recommend joining?
ESRI, the software company that makes the GIS software, has really been working to build communities. So now many communities will have an ESRI software users group that meets periodically. We go and discuss what we're doing, which is very similar to a professional association. ESRI also has their annual conference down in San Diego every year. It's the type of conference a professional association would put together. They have talks on all sorts of subjects and applications of the software and technologies. And there's the showcasing of the latest and greatest software releases. Going to the conference in San Diego is a mind-boggling experience, because there are thousands of people from all around the world that go. So attending that is a great opportunity. In terms of other associations, GIS is usually tied to geography,

and so there are the associations specific to geographers. That would include, for example, the California Geographical Society and AAG, the Association of American Geographers.

What emerging careers do you see developing now and into the future for this career field? What new technologies will have the greatest impact on this field?
The growth in the use of GIS is just phenomenal. In business it's being used a lot because it's very applicable to figuring out where to put the next store or service. You don't want to be too close to the nearest Starbucks, but you don't want to be too far from the major commuter route. GIS takes that information and combines it together. A lot of environmental applications are also using GIS. As more and more people are taking up space, we need to work on land management. So a lot of city planning is being done with GIS. Also, with population growth, the green space is getting smaller and smaller. So how do we preserve the greatest number of species with the resources that we have? Where do we put our reserve so that the greatest number of endangered species is being preserved? The medical profession is using GIS. How do we track the spread of disease? How is West Nile Virus spreading across the US? We use the computer to do a lot of the analysis, so I see the tool being used everywhere. In fact, it's rare that there is a job field that isn't already using GIS technology.

Resources from Q&A
Association of American Geographers (AAG): aag.org
California Geographical Society: calgeog.org
Environmental Sciences Research Institute (ESRI): esri.com
State University of New York (SUNY) at Buffalo: buffalo.edu
University of California, Santa Barbara: ucsb.edu
University Consortium for Geographic Information Science: ucgis.org

Sustainable
Agriculture Group

○ Agricultural Science Professors, including Organic and Sustainable Agriculture Specialists

○ Agricultural Technicians, including Organic and Sustainable Ag Techs

○ Aquacultural Managers, including Sustainable Aquaculture Farm and Fish Hatchery Managers

○ Farmers and Ranchers, including Organic and Sustainable Farmers and Ranchers

○ Farm workers, including Organic and Sustainable Farm and Ranch Workers

○ Nursery and Greenhouse Managers, including Organic and Native Plant Specialists

Agricultural Science Professors, including Organic and Sustainable Agriculture Specialists

Agricultural science teachers, postsecondary, teach courses in the agricultural sciences. Includes teachers of agronomy, dairy sciences, fisheries management, horticultural sciences, poultry sciences, range management and agricultural soil conservation.

Sustainable agriculture refers to the ability of a farm to produce food indefinitely, without causing irreversible damage to ecosystem health. Organic agriculture excludes the use of synthetic fertilizers and pesticides, plant growth regulators, livestock feed additives and genetically modified organisms.

Qualifications and Advancement
A doctorate degree in agricultural science or a related field is the typical education requirement. However, a master's degree may be adequate for positions with community colleges and some four-year colleges.

Instructors and professors generally begin their careers as graduate teaching assistants. Once they complete their degree, they typically find jobs as lecturers or adjunct (part-time) professors or instructors. Eventually they find a full-time position. The next step for college and university professors is to become tenured — meaning that the professor has received a permanent job contract, granted after a probationary period of several years. Advancement for tenured professors involves moving into administrative positions, such as department chairperson, dean, vice president and president.

Salary Survey
Median salary: $75,140 (very high)
Typical range: $55,630 to $94,150

Job Outlook and Employment
Much faster than average growth is projected for the overall occupation of postsecondary teachers in the US, from 1,671,829 jobs in 2006 to 2,054,077 in 2016. Projected growth in this summary occupation will be primarily due to increases in college and university enrollment over the next decade. This enrollment growth stems mainly from the expected increase in the population of 18- to 24-year-olds, who constitute the majority of students at postsecondary institutions, and from the increasing number of high school graduates who choose to attend these institutions.

Where the Jobs Are
Colleges/universities (70.8%); Junior colleges, public and private (21.54%); Technical and trade schools (3.04%)

Resources
Agroecology Section, Ecological Society of America: esa.org/agroecology/
Association of Environmental Engineering and Science Professors (AEESP): aeesp.org
International Federation of Organic Agriculture Movements (IFOAM): ifoam.org
National Campaign for Sustainable Agriculture: sustainableagriculture.net
O*NET OnLine: online.onetcenter.org (see agricultural science teachers, postsecondary)
Sustainable Agriculture Education Association (SAEA): sustainableaged.org
Sustainable Agriculture Research and Education (SARE): sare.org
UC Santa Cruz, Center for Agroecology and Sustainable Food Systems: casfs.ucsc.edu
US Dept. of Labor, Bureau of Labor Statistics: bls.gov/oco/ocos066.htm

Q&A **Stephen R. Gliessman**
Professor of Agroecology,
University of California, Santa Cruz,
from an interview with Jim in 2008

How did you get into this career field? What was your education and experience, including any green-related training or certification?
After obtaining a PhD in plant ecology and botany at UC Santa Barbara, I left academic work for a nine-year period and worked in tropical agriculture and horticulture as a farmer, researcher, educator and business manager. I developed a way of looking at farming systems as agroecosystems and, from this, founded what is known today as agroecology. Much of my training in agroecology was in the field, alongside farmers.

What is your current job title and how would you describe the work you do in a typical day? What are your most common tasks?
I am the Ruth and Alfred Heller Professor of Agroecology, Department of Environmental Studies, at the University of California, Santa Cruz. A typical day for me involves teaching about agroecology and sustainable food systems, editing manuscripts and thesis projects on sustainable agriculture and directing student activities in a sustainable living center on our campus. I am also co-owner/operator of a small family farm that sustainably grows wine grapes and olives, which we market directly at local farmers' markets to consumers as wine and olive oil.

If you could give advice to a young person who wants to work in this career field someday, what would you tell them? How can they best groom themselves for this field?
I always encourage my students to take advantage of as many opportunities as they can to apply what they learn in the classroom to real-life activities and actions. I also encourage them to live what they believe in and to be an example for others for how to live life sustainably. It is my opinion that unless I have an alternative to propose for something I want to see changed, I can't really criticize the item or system that I don't like. Gain as much actual experience in the green field they want to go into. Internships are a great way to begin.

What kind of career advancement opportunities can one expect in this field? What kind of salary range would reflect that career path (from entry-level to the more advanced position)?

I believe that this field is wide open, from the education side to the technical development side. I especially see lots of opportunities for small-scale local initiatives, especially local food system development. Self-sufficiency, autonomy and sustainability go together well and represent a reversal of the trends towards centralization and concentration we have been seeing. Salary levels range from a living wage at the entry level to six digits for the research and innovation range.

In your opinion, what are some of the best schools, degrees and certificates for jobs in this career field, including green-specific training?

Environmental Studies at UC Santa Cruz, the Sustainable Living Program at Prescott College in Prescott, Arizona, and the Sustainable Food System Program at the Evergreen State College in Evergreen, Washington. There are also numerous training programs in permaculture, agroecology and organic food production, such as the Apprentice Program in Ecological Agriculture at the Center for Agroecology and Sustainable Food Systems at UC Santa Cruz.

How does someone without previous experience in this career field land a job? What are the best strategies for job-hunting in this field?

First do an internship with a green organization, gain experience and in the process develop skills and a reputation as a good worker with a green vision.

Are there any professional associations that you would recommend joining?

The Agroecology Section of the Ecological Society of America, the International Federation of Organic Agriculture Movements (IFOAM) and any local organic farming organization in your region.

What emerging careers do you see developing now and into the future for this career field? What new technologies will have the greatest impact on this field?

As consumers and producers form closer relationships, and local food systems regain the foothold that they had before the corporatization of our food supply, the demand for sustainable food system people will be unlimited, from growing food sustainably, to processing and distribution that promotes green living and natural resource conservation, to networking environmentally and socially aware consumers. People who can manage complex information systems and networks, rather than those who are hunting for the "silver-bullet" answer to problems, will be the ones who will ultimately have the greatest impact and reach the most people with viable alternatives.

Resources from Q&A

Agroecology Section, Ecological Society of America: esa.org/agroecology/
Evergreen State College: evergreen.edu
International Federation of Organic Agriculture Movements (IFOAM):
    ifoam.org
Prescott College: prescott.edu
UC Santa Cruz, Center for Agroecology and Sustainable Food Systems:
    casfs.ucsc.edu
University of California, Santa Barbara: ucsb.edu

Agricultural Technicians, including Organic and Sustainable Ag Technicians

Agricultural technicians set up and maintain laboratory equipment and collect samples from crops or animals. Prepare specimens and record data to assist scientist in biology or related science experiments.

Sustainable agriculture refers to the ability of a farm to produce food indefinitely, without causing irreversible damage to ecosystem health. Organic agriculture excludes the use of synthetic fertilizers and pesticides, plant growth regulators, livestock feed additives and genetically modified organisms.

Qualifications and Advancement

An associate's degree in agriculture or a related field is the typical education/training requirement.

Agricultural technicians are involved in food, fiber and animal research, production and processing. Some conduct tests and experiments to improve the yield and quality of crops or to increase the resistance of plants and animals to disease, insects and other hazards. Some breed animals for the purpose of investigating nutrition. There is not much opportunity for advancement without a graduate degree.

Salary Survey

Median salary: $31,730 (low/moderate)
Typical range: $25,640 to $39,870

Job Outlook and Employment

Slower than average growth is projected for this occupation in the US, from 25,804 jobs in 2006 to 27,516 in 2016. Job prospects should be good, however, as research in biotechnology and other areas of agricultural science will increase as it becomes more important to balance greater agricultural output with protection and preservation of soil, water and the ecosystem. In particular, research will be needed to combat insects and diseases as they adapt to pesticides and as soil fertility and water quality continue to need improvement.

Where the Jobs Are
Colleges and universities (31.22%); Support activities for agriculture (14.64%); State government (6.06%); Meat processing (4.33%); Dairy product manufacturing (4.33%)

Resources from Q&A
O*NET OnLine: online.onetcenter.org (see Agricultural technicians)
US Dept. of Labor, Bureau of Labor Statistics: bls.gov/oco/ocos115.htm

Aquacultural Managers, including Sustainable Aquaculture Farm and Fish Hatchery Managers

Aquacultural managers direct and coordinate, through subordinate supervisory personnel, activities of workers engaged in fish hatchery production for corporations, cooperatives or other owners.

Qualifications and Advancement
A bachelor's degree or higher in wildlife science, fishery biology, fish culture, biological sciences or a related field, plus extensive experience in related occupations, is the typical requirement. For some jobs, an equivalent combination of education and experience is acceptable.

Aquacultural and fish hatchery managers usually begin as seasonal workers or aides. With experience, the next position would likely be a technician. After that, advancement would lead to a supervisor position, followed by advancement to manager. With a master's or doctorate degree, aquacultural and fish hatchery managers could qualify for research or college faculty positions.

Salary Survey
Median salary: $52,070 (high)
Typical range: $39,840 to $71,840

Job Outlook and Employment
Little growth is projected for this occupation in the US, estimated from 258,156 jobs in 2006 to 261,032 in 2016. Nevertheless, aquaculture may continue to provide some new employment opportunities due to concerns about overfishing and the depletion of the stock of some wild fish species. This will likely lead to more restrictions on deep-sea fishing, even as public demand for

the consumption of seafood continues to grow. This has spurred the growth of aquaculture farms that raise selected aquatic species, including shrimp, salmon, trout and catfish. Aquaculture has even increased in landlocked states as farmers attempt to diversify.

Where the Jobs Are

Aquaculture farms and fish hatcheries

Resources

American Fisheries Society: fisheries.org
aquaculturejobs.com: aquaculturejobs.com
Global Aquaculture Alliance: gaalliance.org
National Aquaculture Association (NAA): thenaa.net
O*NET OnLine: online.onetcenter.org (see aquacultural managers)
US Dept. of Labor, Bureau of Labor Statistics: bls.gov/oco/ocos176.htm
US Trout Farmers Association: ustfa.org
World Aquaculture Society (WAS): was.org

Q&A JIM PARSONS
Aquaculturist and Fish Biologist, Troutlodge, Inc., from an interview with Alice in 2008

How did you get into this career field? What was your education and experience, including any green-related training or certification?
I've had a lifelong interest in fish and their habitat, targeting a career in fisheries biology from an early age. My undergraduate training was in fisheries biology at Humboldt State University. After several early jobs in the field, I recognized three things: one, that our fish populations were being overexploited; two, that the demand for fish products continued to climb; and three, that the best way to take pressure off of overexploited fisheries and provide safe, sustainable food for seafood buyers was through aquaculture. This desire led back to grad school for a degree in fish genetics and quantitative genetics in order to better manage brood stock populations and maintain genetic diversity in cultured fish populations.

What is your current job title and how would you describe the work you do in a typical day?

I am senior vice president of our parent company and president of our new marine aquaculture company. My job is extremely diverse, from seeking solutions to questions that require outside collaborative research, usually through grant writing and team building, to direct customer service and fish culture advice, to ensuring our products meet strict international bio-security rules for live product commerce. The most common task is being very flexible!

If you could give advice to a young person who wants to work in this career field someday, what would you tell them? How can they best groom themselves for this field?
I would suggest they study a variety of fields, learn how to communicate with others effectively and define for themselves what environmentalism is and focus their career on what they love. If fish is truly their passion, learn about their needs and how we can impact them and take lessons from how we work with other animals.

What kind of career advancement opportunities can one expect in this field? What kind of salary range would reflect that career?
Opportunities depend upon whether the choice is made to work within an agency, university or private enterprise. As for aquaculture, it's ultimately farming, and farming isn't known for high salaries and large profit margins. It's hard, demanding work that rewards from satisfaction in the work. After 30 years in this career path, I certainly could have made a larger salary focusing on administration or another scientific career path, but I don't believe that my heart would be as happy.

In your opinion, what are some of the best schools, degrees and certificates for jobs in this career field, including green-specific training?
Of course I'm partial to my alma maters, Humboldt State and Washington State University. There are relatively few schools that focus on aquaculture — UC Davis being one of the few on the West Coast — and most fisheries schools will lead towards careers/employment in the conservation/biologist fields. Aquaculture, at this point, is likely best still learned through hands-on experience. Foreign language skills are very advantageous, as this is quickly becoming a global business.

How does someone without previous experience in this career field land a job? What are the best strategies for job-hunting in this field?
Never be afraid to follow your heart. For me that meant several years of volunteer-based internships, low-paying entry-level positions and total im-

mersion and hard work. Networking through attendance at trade shows, such as the World Aquaculture Society annual meetings, is extremely useful.

How much experience is necessary before a person should venture into self-employment in your field? What positions should that experience be in?
I would suggest at least five to seven years of hands-on work with fish culture, trying to get exposed to every aspect one can come up with, including personnel management, financial management and regulatory aspects of the job.

Are there any professional associations that you would recommend joining?
World Aquaculture Society, American Fisheries Society and Global Aquaculture Alliance.

What emerging careers do you see developing now and into the future for this career field?
Animal nutrition will be big for aquaculture, as all animal farming industries attempt to find sustainable alternative sources of protein and lipids. Physiology training, particularly as directly related to fish, will become important as we attempt to better understand the needs of these animals under culture. Veterinary training in fish is a rapidly growing need, as there are few veterinarians with fish training.

Resources from Q&A
American Fisheries Society: fisheries.org
Global Aquaculture Alliance: gaalliance.org
Humboldt State University: humboldt.edu
Troutlodge, Inc.: troutlodge.com
University of California, Davis: ucdavis.edu
Washington State University: wsu.edu
World Aquaculture Society (WAS): was.org

Farmers and Ranchers, including Organic and Sustainable Farmers and Ranchers

Farmers and ranchers, on an ownership or rental basis, operate farms, ranches, greenhouses, nurseries, timber tracts or other agricultural production establishments which produce crops, horticultural specialties, livestock, poultry, finfish, shellfish or animal specialties.

Sustainable agriculture refers to the ability of a farm to produce food indefinitely without causing irreversible damage to ecosystem health. Organic agriculture excludes the use of synthetic fertilizers and pesticides, plant growth regulators, livestock feed additives and genetically modified organisms.

Qualifications and Advancement

Farmers and ranchers do not have education or training requirements. However, while the traditional preparation for this occupation was on-the-job training, the completion of an associate's or bachelor's degree is becoming increasingly important. About 46 percent of new entrants to this occupation have completed some college, and about 16 percent of those have completed a bachelor's degree. The typical degree would be in farm management or business with a concentration in agriculture. Perhaps most important are the managerial skills needed to organize and operate a business.

Advancement usually takes the form of acquiring more acreage or increasing the profitability of one's business. Some successful farmers and ranchers may become consultants or teachers or investors in other business enterprises.

Salary Survey

Median salary: $37,130 (low/moderate)
Typical range: $29,550 to $47,600

Job Outlook and Employment

A slow decline is projected for this occupation in the US, from 1 million jobs in 2006 to 969,000 in 2016. The long-term trend toward the consolidation of farms into fewer and larger ones is expected to continue. Nevertheless, the large number of farmers expected to retire or leave the profession over the next decade will create opportunities. In addition, an increasing number of small-scale farmers (many of them organic farmers) have developed successful market niches that involve personalized, direct contact with their customers. Organic food production is the fastest growing segment in agriculture.

Resources

American Society of Farm Managers and Rural Appraisers: asfmra.org
ATTRA / National Sustainable Agriculture Information Service:
    attra.ncat.org
Ecological Farming Association: eco–farm.org
National Agricultural Library (NAL): nal.usda.gov
National Campaign for Sustainable Agriculture: sustainableagriculture.net
National FFA Organization: ffa.org
O*NET OnLine: online.onetcenter.org (see farmers and ranchers)
Sustainable Agriculture Education Association (SAEA): sustainableaged.org

Sustainable Agriculture Research and Education (SARE): sare.org
Sustainable Farmer: sustainablefarmer.com
US Dept. of Labor, Bureau of Labor Statistics: bls.gov/oco/ocos176.htm

Q&A   NIGEL WALKER
Farmer, Eatwell Farm,
from an interview with Jim in 2008

*How did you get into this career field? What was
your education and experience?*
Before I was 21, I was doing something very
different; I was doing radio engineering. But
I had a grandfather who was a farmer, and so
I decided to pursue my interest in farming. I
was interested in organic farming because one
of my senior projects at school was on solar energy. I built a solar water collector as part of my
final project. And when you get into that, you
read about a lot of other things. So it kind of
snowballed from there. And, for my training, before you could go to an agricultural college in England, you have to work on a farm for a year to see if
you've really got the stuff it takes. So you have to work on a farm and get a
reference from a farmer before you can go to college to do commercial horticulture. And then I did a three-year vocational degree and specialized in
vegetable production. While in college, I worked on an organic farm as part of
my studies, and we were supplying Safeway with all of their organic produce.
When I finished college, Safeway suggested that I go work in Israel for the
Israeli export organization. So I went there and worked on different organic
farms in Israel. It was good experience, and also I could travel around and
work when I wanted. Then I went back to England to manage an organic farm.
I came over here to the States for a conference, and I met Frances, my ex-wife.
We got married and decided to stay here because it would be easiest for us to
start farming on our own here.

*What is your current job title and how would you describe the work you do in a
typical day? What are your most common tasks?*
I'm officially the farmer here at Eatwell Farm. My name is on the promissory
note, so I own the place, along with the bank. But what most people think of
as farming is probably not the reality. I spend quite a bit of time in front of
the computer each week — helping customers and arranging deliveries, doing

the nuts and bolts of supplying those customers and doing what you would call marketing. Then I spend what amounts to half my time actually farming. That means walking the fields, driving the tractor or preparing seeds. Today I spent my whole morning sorting out my seed supply and preparing seeds for the crew who are now starting melons and cucumbers in the field. But I spent the morning sorting out what we needed, soaking the seeds and making sure the crew had everything they needed, so that after lunch they could go straight to planting. I also spend a lot of time writing my blog and my news-letter. As a CSA (Community Supported Agriculture) farm, part of what we do when people get a box of vegetables from us is they're getting information as to what's happening on *their* farm. It's important because people want to be connected to the farm and want to understand what's going on. They're not just buying a box of vegetables. They are also buying that connection.

If you could give advice to a young person who wants to work in this career field someday, what would you tell them? How can they best groom themselves for this field?

They have to have a very good grasp of business skills — what it takes to run a business, because the farm is a business. We don't just grow vegetables here. It's very important how we run the business, how we manage our cash flow, how we get financing, how we have to understand where we are making money and where we are losing money. To be able to read accounts and figure out whether you're making money on a crop is really important. When I look at farmers around me, the ones that are successful are the ones that are good at the business side and not necessarily the ones that are better at farming.

What kind of career advancement opportunities can one expect in this field? What kind of salary range would reflect that career path (from entry-level to the more advanced position)?

Well, it is a vocation without necessarily a set career path. It's very important when you're starting off to be able to look at the skills you need and then find ways to gain those skills. As a young farmer, you need to look at the first ten years of your career as where you work at different farms or even different businesses. I don't think it's necessarily that your work has to be all on a farm to get some of these skills. For example, how to organize people and how to make sure things are done on time. Organizing people with different skill lev-els and different temperaments is very important. So there are a lot of skills you need to be good at. I could be writing in my blog one minute, and the next minute I could be under the tractor trying to fix an oil leak. Problem-solving skills are very important. You have to enjoy multi-tasking and working with people and selling. As far as salary, well, farming is a struggle. It's been a struggle just to get the farm's profit level above ten percent. So I try and take out the least amount I possibly can for myself. And then everything else is reimbursed/reinvested. There are many times when you can't do what you want to do or even what you need to do. You just have to make do. People who are absolute perfectionists can get very frustrated. But on the other hand, the farmers around here are very happy with what they do. After 10–15 years, some of these guys are making a decent living. Not a fabulous living, but I would say they make a good decent living. And we feel good about what we do.

In your opinion, what are some of the best schools, degrees and certificates for jobs in this career field?
I'm not very familiar with agriculture education here in the US, but I've heard good things about the agroecology program at UC Santa Cruz.

How does someone without previous experience in this career field land a job? What are the best strategies for job-hunting in this field?
For jobs on sustainable farms, try Eco-farm.org. They also have an annual conference which is pretty good and they have smart energy courses.

How much experience is necessary before a person should venture into self-employment in your field? What positions should that experience be in?
I think ten years of preparation is about right. You really need to learn from other people for the first ten years. And that's not unreasonable. By the time you're 30, maybe you've got your first piece of land. I don't think that's an unreasonable expectation. You know it's tough. It's a lot of money leasing some land. Or maybe you start earlier, but you start really small. You start part-time. But you need to spend those first ten years working on different farms and working for different farmers.

What emerging or high growth careers do you see developing now and into the future for this career field? What new technologies will have the greatest impact on this field?
There's a huge demand for farmers on the edge of cities to grow food for people who live in the cities. As a business model, the CSA is great because at the beginning of the week you know just how many bunches of this and bags of that and whatever else you're going to pick. There's really no waste. From a planting point of view, you know exactly how much food to plant. As far as technology, we've imported two machines from Switzerland in the last two

years. One of them is a brush weeder, and one is a finger weeder. Both dramatically cut down on how much weeding we do.

Resources from Q&A

Eatwell Farm: eatwell.com

Ecological Farming Association: eco–farm.org

UC Santa Cruz, Center for Agroecology and Sustainable Food Systems: casfs.ucsc.edu

Q&A MOLLY BLOOM
CSA Manager, Eatwell Farm,
from an interview with Jim in 2008

How did you get into this career field? What was your education and experience, including any green-related training or certification?
I worked my first summer as an organic farm intern in 2000. It was during my summer break from Macalester College in St. Paul, Minnesota. I was majoring in international studies, with a focus on non-Western religions, and I wanted to find a way to be outside all summer long, as far from academia as I could be. I'd spent previous summers working at outdoor, overnight camps but needed a change. A friend had signed on as an apprentice at an organic farm in Wisconsin, and I asked her how she found it. She pointed me toward the ATTRA (Appropriate Technology Transfer for Rural Areas) or the National Sustainable Agriculture Information Service website and its internship program. I looked for farms in the Northwest, where I was raised. I found a collective of organic farmers in northwest Washington State and had an incredible experience that summer. It truly changed my life. I was the youngest person I knew, by at least a decade, and I had the opportunity to work with five different organic farmers. I left the summer refreshed, in love with farming, but also uncertain I could make a living doing it — all the farmers I knew had at least one other job. Soon after I finished college, though, I realized I wanted to see whether or not I could do the only job I've truly loved — farming sustainably — and make it financially sustainable for myself. So I worked as an apprentice in an intensive program at Sauvie Island Organics, outside of Portland, Oregon. From that I quickly decided that I'd do whatever I could to make my dream a reality. I'm now working in a farm office, managing the CSA (Community Supported Agriculture)

program at Eatwell Farm and learning how to run a farm as a business before I eventually start my own!

What is your current job title and how would you describe the work you do in a typical day? What are your most common tasks, including those that make yours a green job?

I am currently the CSA Manager for Eatwell Farm. I manage a huge database that keeps track of our 900 or so members and insures that they receive their weekly or bi-weekly deliveries of produce and eggs, either weekly or every other week, depending on whichever schedule they have chosen. I also manage issues via phone or e-mail that arise regarding their subscription and/or pickup of their deliveries. With about 40 drop sites all over the region, problems are sure to arise. In addition, I provide support for my assistant and for our delivery driver and our bookkeeper. My assistant helps with data entry and handles our lavender orders. For the first year I worked here, I also did one day a week of delivery work and one day a week of bookkeeping. After that, I did the CSA management full-time. Most of my job is customer-service oriented. I also edit our weekly newsletter and provide all of the produce care instructions and select the recipes for each week. I educate our members on how to eat seasonally, how to take care of all the produce we send them, make sure they understand our policies and help in selecting what will go into their boxes each week.

If you could give advice to a young person who wants to work in this career field someday, what would you tell them? How can they best groom themselves for this field?

For anyone who would like to get into sustainable farming, I would strongly encourage them to work as a volunteer, intern or apprentice on a variety of sustainable farms. This is a great way to understand first-hand what it means to be a farmer — both the good parts and the more difficult ones. The ATTRA website previously mentioned is a great resource. Another one with an online database of volunteer opportunities is called WWOOF (Worldwide Opportunities on Organic Farms). However, I have no personal experience working with them. When searching for a farm, I would suggest thinking about what it is that you want to learn. There are so many different methods of farming and a plethora of internship set-ups that a great way to narrow down the options is to find what most closely matches what a person wants to learn. I would encourage doing those internships that will work reasonably well for them, both physically and financially. Visiting a farm ahead of time is the best way to know whether or not it will be a good fit.

What kind of career advancement opportunities can one expect in this field? What kind of salary range would reflect that career path (from entry-level to the more advanced position)?

How far any one person can advance in this field depends on what kind of work they choose to pursue. This career path often leads to self-employment and owning one's own farm, though there are also great opportunities to work as the farm manager or greenhouse manager for another farmer. Entry-level jobs in this field would include volunteers, and you can expect produce as compensation for your volunteer work. The next step up would be minimum wage. From there, it's all the way up to $37,000 per year or so — depending on where you live and what kind of farm you work for. Of course, this is based on my own experience and that of my friends, and there may be other opportunities out there.

In your opinion, what are some of the best schools, degrees and certificates for jobs in this career field, including green-specific training?

It's interesting — many folks ask me what kind of education they need to be a farmer. While advanced degrees in sustainable agriculture or a related field would certainly be advantageous, all of my farming experience has been through hands-on learning. Observation, time and talking with other farmers in your region or from similar regions around the world seem to be the best education for farming. Of course, this is my experience and how I've learned, and others may have differing opinions. The only other advanced degree that often shows up among farmers I know is mechanical engineering, as it's great to have a good knowledge of mechanics as a farmer!

How does someone without previous experience in this career field land a job? What are the best strategies for job-hunting in this field?

The volunteering, internship and apprenticeship experience that I have suggested often leads to getting a real job with that farm or with another one in the area. As usual, personal connections are important. That said, however, I must admit that I have found most of my farming opportunities via the Internet.

Are there any professional associations that you would recommend joining?

Many states have their own organic certification organization, and those would be good resources for information — either to join or to find other associations that might be useful. Other than that, specific kinds of farming may have their own associations, such as biodynamic farming, seed farming, animal husbandry, etc.

What emerging careers do you see developing now and into the future for this career field? What new technologies will have the greatest impact on this field?
I see a desire for locally produced and sustainably grown food on the rise across the country, particularly as the economy isn't doing so well and gas prices keep increasing. Folks are turning more and more to local sources of food. Now is a great time to get involved with small-scale farming that markets to local customers. The most difficult hurdle for young farmers, such as myself, is finding land to farm. But there are organizations out there who are trying to help emerging farmers find those special pieces of land. Organizations like California FarmLink and similar organizations in states all over the country are creating ways for older farmers who want their land to continue as a viable farm connect with younger folks in need of a place to grow. I foresee organizations like this becoming more important and widespread in the near future.

Resources from Q&A
ATTRA/National Sustainable Agriculture Information Service: attra.ncat.org
California FarmLink: californiafarmlink.org
Eatwell Farm: eatwell.com
Macalester College: macalester.edu
Sauvie Island Organics: sauvieislandorganics.com
Worldwide Opportunities on Organic Farms (WWOOF): wwoofusa.org

JIM ZEEK
Organic Farmer,
Goodness Orchard,
from an interview with Jim in 2008

How did you get into this career field? What was your education and experience, including any green-related training or certification?
I've always been a gardener — since Victory Garden days in WWII when it was my job to tend the family garden. I had always enjoyed it, and so when I decided to leave the fast lane of New York City professional life in the mid-70s, I thought I would get into subsistence farming. I got property while I was in the construction business for several years, and when it turned out I could get a better water rate doing more than

just subsistence farming, I went a little larger scale. But then my father died of heart disease, and I had a friend who died from cancer related to herbicide use. I would see all these local farmers out in their yellow suits and respirators every ten days, and I thought there had to be a better way. So I got certified as organic back in 1990.

What is your current job title and how would you describe the work you do in a typical day? What are your most common tasks?

I'm an organic farmer. My work depends on the season. I'm typically up at dawn, doing the usual chores of feeding the animals and fixing anything that went wrong in the past 24 hours. During the spring, we work hard to get everything seeded and take care of gophers and other pests. In the summer, we may continue seeding if necessary, or we'll do transplants like the tomatoes from our greenhouse. Obviously we do a lot of harvesting in the fall. And then in the winter we're doing pruning, filling, fence mending, fence building, animal care, planting greenhouse flats and making plans and placing seed orders for the coming year. We've just developed a website this past month. It gets pretty frantic sometimes — in the summertime especially, as it's a crazy matrix of irrigation schedules, irrigation systems and maintenance, harvesting, record keeping, selling, telephoning, delivering, picking up — we have our own market, but we are starting to deliver more. And that all continues right through December.

If you could give advice to a young person who wants to work in this career field someday, what would you tell them? How can they best groom themselves for this field?

The important thing is to find an opportunity either to intern or to work with someone who can be your mentor. There was a young fellow that came to us about three years ago looking for an opportunity. I interviewed him, and he had worked on a couple of organic farms before, but it was already summer and so I had to turn him down. But it eventually worked out, and now he's been co-managing the farm for just over a year. He's knowledgeable, and he's good at what he does.

What kind of career advancement opportunities can one expect in this field? What kind of salary range would reflect that career path (from entry-level to the more advanced position)?

Most of the organic farmers I know didn't actually start out in farming. They were engineers, foresters, physicians, housewives, teachers — and farming was maybe a side activity or maybe just a fantasy. Very few people who grow up on farms go directly into farming themselves, although I think there are a lot who come back to farming after studying and working in other fields. I think most people just do farming because they love it, and they get a sort of spiritual peacefulness and contentment from it all. But the economic turn-out really varies. I know a man who's been farming for 40 years, and he loves farming and watching things grow, but he's never been able to do more than just get by. On the other hand, I know another guy who just started organic farming — it had always been his dream — and he's already very successful and getting ahead.

In your opinion, what are some of the best schools, degrees and certificates for jobs in this career field, including green-specific training?
Of the California schools, I think UC Santa Cruz has the best program. UC Davis is good too, but I think they're more into research, and Santa Cruz is actually developing an organic program. Wherever you go, what's important is finding those specifically organic programs.

How does someone without previous experience in this career field land a job? What are the best strategies for job-hunting in this field?
You need the right skill set. For organic farming, that means having some sense of juggling a lot of balls in the air and having a very strong motivation and work ethic to accomplish your goals.

Are there any professional associations that you would recommend joining?
There are several, including California Certified Organic Farmers. I also belong to our local Apple Hill association, Farm Trails.

Resources from Q&A
California Certified Organic Farmers (CCOF): ccof.org
El Dorado County Farm Trails Association: edc–farmtrails.org
University of California, Davis: ucdavis.edu
University of California, Santa Cruz: ucsc.edu

Farm Workers, including Organic and Sustainable Farm and Ranch Workers

Farm workers and ranch workers attend to farm, ranch or aquacultural animals that may include cattle, sheep, swine, goats, horses and other equines, poultry, finfish, shellfish and bees. Attend to animals produced for animal products, such as meat, fur, skins, feathers, eggs, milk and honey. Duties may include feeding, watering, herding, grazing, castrating, branding, de-beaking, weighing, catching and loading animals. May maintain records on animals; examine animals to detect diseases and injuries; assist in birth deliveries; and administer medications, vaccinations or insecticides as appropriate. May clean and maintain animal housing areas.

Qualifications and Advancement

A minimum level of education is rarely specified for basic farm laborer jobs, which tend to be temporary and seasonal. Workers simply need to have the required physical abilities and the willingness to do hard work and follow directions. But many farm worker jobs, especially those that may provide year-round employment, often require a higher-level skill set and some knowledge of farming or ranching. Ability to operate vehicles, trucks and machinery may be important, as is having some mechanical ability. Sustainable and organic farms will often expect their farm workers to have some knowledge of sustainable and organic farming techniques.

Advancement may lead to tractor driver/machinery operator and to foreman/supervisory positions. Bilingual (English and Spanish) skills may be necessary for promotion to a supervisory position.

Salary Survey

Median salary: $19,060 (very low)

Typical range: $15,770 to $23,830

Job Outlook and Employment

Little growth is projected for this occupation in the US, estimated from 106,843 jobs in 2006 to 109,772 in 2016. Of the two main areas of employment for farm workers, crop farm employment is projected to decline, while animal production (ranching) employment is projected to grow at the average rate.

Where the Jobs Are

Crop production (30.95%); Animal production (24.85%); Farm product raw material merchant wholesalers (7.68%); Employment services (7.66%); Meat processing (4.97%)

Resources

O*NET OnLine: online.onetcenter.org (see farmworkers, farm and ranch animals)

United Farm Workers of America (UFW): ufw.org

US Dept. of Labor, Bureau of Labor Statistics: bls.gov/oco/ocos285.htm

Nursery and Greenhouse Managers, including Organic and Native Plant Specialists

Nursery and greenhouse managers plan, organize, direct, control and coordinate activities of workers engaged in propagating, cultivating and harvesting horticultural specialties, such as trees, shrubs, flowers, mushrooms and other plants.

Qualifications and Advancement

A bachelor's degree or higher in horticulture or plant science, plus extensive experience in related occupations, is the typical requirement. However, smaller nurseries may accept an associate's degree or postsecondary training. Potential nursery and greenhouse managers who plan to supervise large-scale pesticide and herbicide sprayings should check their state regulations to see what training and certification is needed.

Nursery and greenhouse managers often begin in entry-level positions as nursery workers. As they gain experience and knowledge, they may become supervisors, assistant managers and managers. Higher-level advancement may lead to general manager. Some may start their own business.

Salary Survey

Median salary: $52,070 (high)

Typical range: $39,840 to $71,840

Job Outlook and Employment

Little growth is projected for this occupation in the US, estimated from 258,156 jobs in 2006 to 261,032 in 2016. However, job prospects are expected to be good for those who want to go into these fields due to the large number of workers expected to retire over the next decade.

Where the Jobs Are

Nurseries and greenhouses

Resources

American Horticultural Society (AHS): ahs.org

American Nursery and Landscape Association (ANLA): anla.org

California Native Plant Society (CNPS): cnps.org

O*NET OnLine: online.onetcenter.org (see farmworkers, farm and ranch animals)

US Dept. of Labor, Bureau of Labor Statistics: bls.gov/oco/ocos176.htm

Green Jobs with
Electric Utility Companies

Electric utility companies are firms engaged in the generation, transmission and distribution of electric power. Typically, electric power plants utilize highly pressurized steam, flowing water or some other force of nature to spin the blades of a turbine, which generates electricity. Coal is the dominant fuel used to generate steam in electric power plants, followed by nuclear power, natural gas and petroleum. Hydroelectric generators are powered by the release of the tremendous pressure of water, usually at the bottom of a dam. Renewable energy sources such as geothermal, wind and solar are expanding rapidly, but nevertheless comprise only a small percentage of the total current electric power generation.

Most electric utility companies operate as regulated monopolies because electric power distribution tends to require a large investment in facilities and equipment, and it is generally not desirable to have several competing systems of power lines in most areas. Since most of these companies do not face competition, and because the services they provide are so vital to everyday life, they are heavily regulated by public utility commissions. These PUCs set the rates charged to customers and ensure that their utility companies act in the public interest.

Electric utility companies generally operate large plants using expensive and often high-tech equipment. Thus they employ many professional and technical personnel. Most companies have made significant strides in recent years to promote energy efficiency and the use of renewable energy. Jobs that deal directly with these types of programs or initiatives can, of course, be considered green jobs. However, there is some debate as to whether the average electric utility company should be considered green or sustainable — due to their overall heavy carbon footprint. On the other hand, utility companies that operate under state laws that require significant investments in renewable energy and energy efficiency are generally going to have more green career opportunities.

Green Jobs

Green jobs with electric utilities vary from company to company, but typically include manager and staff positions involved in the operation of environmental, conservation, energy efficiency or renewable energy programs. Staff positions may include marketing, sales, engineering, technical, customer service, administrative support and regulatory experts. When an electric utility company makes a significant investment in alternative fuel vehicles, there will also be mechanics and others needed to acquire, maintain and repair that fleet of green vehicles. When the company invests in a renewable-energy power generation facility, probably all jobs associated with building and operating that facility can be considered green jobs.

Job Outlook

The job outlook with electric utility companies depends on whether you focus on job growth or on supply-demand. On one hand, the overall number of jobs in this industry has been in decline due to cutbacks, layoffs, hiring freezes, mergers and consolidations. And while that trend may continue, prospects for qualified job applicants are nevertheless expected to be excellent during the next ten years. That is largely because of the age of the current workforce in this industry and the need to replace the many retiring workers. In addition, if the US government responds aggressively to the need for clean energy on a massive scale, or makes a full commitment to becoming non-dependent on foreign oil, then electric utility companies will be creating additional clean-energy jobs — perhaps numbering in the tens of thousands.

Green Utility Companies

The US Environmental Protection Agency (EPA) has a website where you can evaluate and compare an electric utility company's fuel mix and their average air emissions rates (see link under Resources). This can be helpful in identifying the greener utility companies. However, the EPA's Power Profiler system uses "available data" that is at least two years old and may not be as standardized as it should be for the purposes of drawing conclusions about specific utility companies and their commitment to sustainability. Thus the profiler may be an interesting and even useful tool, but it's probably a good idea not to make hard conclusions based on what the profiler system suggests.

Even though this chapter is about utility companies that are privately owned, it should also be noted that many of the same jobs and career opportunities can also be found with public or municipally owned utilities. See the link to Careers in Public Power under Resources.

Qualifications and Advancement

For electric utility companies, manager and engineering positions generally require a bachelor's degree. Technical positions often require some college or technical training or extensive on-the-job training. Most other positions generally require a high-school level education. Prior experience is more often a preference rather than a requirement. Meter readers often have college degrees, but that's not necessarily because of the position requirements. Rather, this is often an entry-level position for college graduates (and others) that plan to pursue a utility company career path. Customer service is another good point of entry.

Because electric utilities are often large employers, substantial advancement is possible even within a single occupation. For example, there may be several levels for energy efficiency specialist (I, II, II, etc.). However, because utility companies have so many different divisions, products and services, skills developed in one segment of the industry are not always transferable to other segments.

Salary/Compensation

Electric utility companies generally pay well for the same or comparable positions when compared to other industries. For example, electrical engineers generally make about $1 per hour more working for electric utilities than for other industries. Customer service representatives generally make about $3 per hour more. Management positions also pay well, with many managers earning $100,000 per year or more. In addition, most full-time workers in this industry receive substantial benefits in addition to their salaries or hourly wages. About 27 percent of the workers in this industry are union members or are covered by a collective bargaining agreement.

Resources

American Public Power Association (APPA): appanet.org
Build It Green: builditgreen.org
Building Industry Association (BIA): bia.net
Career Guide to Industries: Utilities: bls.gov/oco/cg/cgs018.htm
Careers in Public Power: careersinpublicpower.com
Center for Energy Workforce Development: cewd.org
Green Power Network (GPN): apps3.eere.energy.gov/greenpower/
Occupational Outlook Quarterly: Careers In Energy:
    stats.bls.gov/opub/ooq/2008/fall/art02.pdf
US Environmental Protection Agency Power Profiler:
    epa.gov/cleanenergy/energy-and-you/how-clean.html
US Green Building Council/LEED AP Certification: usgbc.org

WADE HUGHES, SolarSmart Program Manager,
Sacramento Municipal Utility District (SMUD),
from an interview with Jim in 2008

How did you get into this career field? What was your education and experience, including any green-related training or certification?
I had worked in construction for a number of years and went to college for a couple of years, but most of my pertinent experience came from being a roofing contractor. I came to SMUD in 1998 as a meter reader to get my foot in the door. A few years later, a position opened up in the "new construction group" and, with my construction background, it was a good opportunity for me. So then I started working with builders and developers on energy efficiency. I began taking classes internally here at SMUD as well as externally at CSU Sacramento and Pacific Gas and Electric Company's (PG&E) Learning Center. Then I moved to "existing construction programs" at SMUD, and that was my first program management experience — where I started managing eight different efficiency programs, such as the insulation, heating and air conditioning, duct improvement and insulated siding programs. Then I returned to the "new construction program" where I'm now managing the SolarSmart program — which is cost-effective energy efficiency and solar generation related to new housing. I am Build It Green certified and have various other certifications and have taken a multitude of classes.

What is your current job title and how would you describe the work you do in a typical day? What are your most common tasks?
I'm the SolarSmart new homes program manager. On a daily basis, I meet with builders and developers, encouraging energy efficiency and solar electric design in new homes. I lead two inspectors and two support staff in the administration of the program. I work on budgets, forecasts, reports, etc. My most frequent task involves presenting and selling the program to builders and developers. We also spend a lot of time inspecting homes in the program for energy efficiency and solar generation to make sure that everything was installed correctly to meet our design criteria.

If you could give advice to a young person who wants to work in this career field someday, what would you tell them? How can they best groom themselves for this field?
Construction experience in general is good, but any experience with a mechanical or HVAC contractor has additional value. But if you want to be in

a program management capacity at a place like SMUD, education is really important. So you should plan on attending college and completing a bachelor's degree. And then you can get a unique set of experiences by doing internships at utilities.

What kind of career advancement opportunities can one expect in this field? What kind of salary range would reflect that career path (from entry-level to the more advanced position)?
Customer service reps that work with our customers on the phone and meter readers have traditionally been the entry points for those that don't come in with a college degree. Those who do have a degree would usually start at a slightly higher level — perhaps as an energy specialist I or as an energy auditor. You could also start out in engineering services. The income ranges from $40,000 to $45,000 per year up to $100,000 when you work in program management.

In your opinion, what are some of the best schools, degrees and certificates for jobs in this career field, including green-specific training?
Cal Poly, San Luis Obispo, Oregon State and UC Berkeley are good schools for degrees in engineering and architecture. LEED AP certification is important on the commercial building side, while Build It Green certification might be seen as the residential alternative to LEED. PG&E has a great list of classes that they offer.

How does someone without previous experience in this career field land a job? What are the best strategies for job-hunting in this field?
Networking is really important. I still get calls from people who ask "Hey, do you know this guy?" Or "Do you know anyone who has this kind of experience?" And that comes from builders as well as other utility companies. And getting involved in your local BIA (Building Industry Association) and volunteering time there might be advantageous. Also, taking outside classes is going to be really important. Most of the colleges in our area have good classes in energy efficiency, renewable energy and sustainability on an ongoing basis. Even the community colleges have a good set of basic classes to help you get started.

Are there any professional associations that you would recommend joining?
The BIA and Build It Green have been really good associations for me. But there are lots of associations to connect with once you're working in the field. There are also lots of popular trade magazines, such as *Solar Today*.

What emerging careers do you see developing now and into the future for this career field? What new technologies will have the greatest impact on this field?
As a result of the California Solar Initiative, solar is a hot topic right now. The demand for solar is increasing, and most project it to continue to increase. We need a lot of quality people to get the experience necessary to design and install solar systems — both on a residential and commercial level. That's one of the areas we could look at and say, "There's a glaring hole there in our (current) workforce."

Resources from Q&A

Build It Green: builditgreen.org
Building Industry Association (BIA): bia.net
Cal Poly, San Luis Obispo: calpoly.edu
Oregon State University: oregonstate.edu
Pacific Gas and Electric Company (PG&E): pge.com
Sacramento Municipal Utility District (SMUD): smud.org
University of California, Berkeley: berkeley.edu
US Green Building Council/LEED AP Certification: usgbc.org

Q&A BOB KINERT
Manager, Sales Operations
(Energy/Utility Management),
from an interview with Alice in 2008

How did you get into this career field? What was your education and experience, including any green-related training or certification?
I was recruited into the energy field by a utility employee I met in a business class in graduate school. I received my bachelor of arts in business administration with an emphasis in marketing and completed the executive strategic marketing program at Duke University.

What is your current job title and how would you describe the work you do in a typical day? What are your most common tasks, including those that make yours a green job?
Manager of sales operations was a position that I literally was able to create for myself by identifying the critical needs of the organization and proposing solutions to senior leadership. Responsibilities include developing and leading the effort to increase sales-force capability for a business customer sales

and service organization serving over 300,000 customers within a large West Coast gas and electric utility. Typical day-to-day activities involve providing vision and direction to the broader organization, working with senior leadership on a strategic level and making sure sales managers and account executives receive the services they need from sales operations. What makes this a green job is the nature of the products and services provided to customers. The portfolio of products and services include energy management solutions to support increased energy conservation and efficiency, reduction of energy demand, reduction of carbon footprint and acquisition of renewable sources of energy.

If you could give advice to a young person who wants to work in this career field someday, what would you tell them? How can they best groom themselves for this field?
The best advice on preparation is to combine a relevant educational background with internship opportunities. The energy field is broad, and career opportunities are diverse and plentiful right now. Exploring through a variety of internships and informational interviews will help to narrow the focus of interest and provide exposure.

What kind of career advancement opportunities can one expect in this field? What kind of salary range would reflect that career path (from entry-level to the more advanced position)?
Larger companies like gas and electric utilities have nearly unlimited advancement opportunities. The complex nature of utility companies results in many available job functions. Once an individual has established their credibility and reputation through high performance in their job, movement is relatively easy — given understanding the complexity of the company and how it operates carries a significant amount of currency. Pay scales vary by region, but utilities tend to pay well and have excellent total compensation packages. College new hires on the West Coast can expect higher-skilled entry-level management jobs to start in the $50,000 to $60,000 range, with some exceptions both above and below. Leadership positions for middle management often fall in the range of $100,000 to $150,000, plus benefits and performance-based compensation — again, with exceptions on either side of the range.

In your opinion, what are some of the best schools, degrees and certificates for jobs in this career field, including green-specific training?
Top-notch, well-known and respected engineering and business schools are attractive to utilities. Companies tend to develop relationships with schools

on the recruiting side in order to gain access to the best candidates for internships and college new hires.

Within the energy industry, there are numerous entry tracks one can follow. For utilities, there are three that are noteworthy: technical or engineering, business and, more recently, environmental. If one is interested specifically in sales, a background that combines technical and business may create a stronger opportunity. A degree in sales engineering, or a double major of business and engineering are good examples of this.

How does someone without previous experience in this career field land a job? What are the best strategies for job-hunting in this field?
If nearing college graduation, work with the school's career center to see if they have contacts with companies of interest. As with any job seeker, developing and using your networking skills is critical. Joining industry associations is a great way to make contacts in energy.

Are there any professional associations that you would recommend joining?
The Utility Connection (TUC) is a great source for identifying associations on a national and regional level. ACEEE (American Council for an Energy Efficient Economy) and AEE (Association of Energy Engineers) are two great organizations to consider.

What emerging careers do you see developing now and into the future for this career field? What new technologies will have the greatest impact on this field?
There are three areas within energy well worth paying attention to: 1) Energy efficiency is likely to gain increased emphasis nationally, 2) Demand response has been gaining attention and momentum for grid peak load management, and 3) With the advent of global warming, carbon reduction is the hottest area to emerge in recent memory.

Resources from Q&A
American Council for an Energy Efficient Economy (ACEEE): aceee.org
Association of Energy Engineers (AEE): aeecenter.org
Duke University: duke.edu
The Utility Connection (TUC): utilityconnection.com

Additional
Information
and Resources

Career Planning

How do you know which is the best green career for you?

Answering this question is a process of assessment, research and reality testing occupations to determine the best fit for you. Below we've outlined an easy two-step process for career discovery:

Step 1: Career Assessment

Your career assessment is the foundation for discovering your best and most satisfying career. Why is it the best? Because you are the expert on yourself. By understanding all the elements of your best work and personality style, the best career direction for you will become clear.

Elements of your best work include:

- *Values* — what work satisfies you personally?
- *Skills* — what skills give you energy when you use them?
- *Interests* — what content and topics are you most interested in?

Combining the "elements of your best work" assessment results allow you to focus on your best-fit career direction.

Getting Help

There are many career assessment tools and resources to choose from. It is possible to do it on your own without help, but expert help can be invaluable. The National Career Development Association website (ncda.org) is a national resource for finding a certified/registered career counselor in your area who can help with your career assessment and career planning (for a reasonable fee). Sometimes one-stop career centers, community colleges and universities will have a certified/registered career counselor on staff that can help you. But don't assume that anyone who's a counselor or works in a career center is a career development professional. You should ensure that they have the proper credentials before you rely on them for career assessment services.

Local community colleges and universities are easily found in your phone directory or by a Google-type search. Speak with someone in the career or counseling center. Visit in person if possible. Generally, community colleges will provide such services at the lowest possible cost, sometimes for free. In addition to individual services, both community colleges and universities often provide career development classes or workshops.

Finding your local one-stop career center is a bit more difficult because they don't always call themselves "one-stop career centers" and because phone directories don't have consistent categories for these community-based career centers. But virtually every county throughout the US has at least one one-stop career center. These centers usually have a variety of partners and provide free career and job search services to the general public, as well as services to local employers. See America's Service Locator (servicelocator.org) to find your local one-stop career center. They may also provide career development classes or workshops (which would likely be free).

Once you have found your certified/registered career counselor, he/she will administer, score and interpret your assessments and, in some cases, may direct you to the appropriate self-directed career assessment resources.

Self-directed Career Assessment Resources

If you are the self-directed type when it comes to your career planning, you may want to explore some of the following online career assessment resources. Some are fee-based, and some are free or at least partially free. Just make sure that whatever combination of assessment tools you use address your values, skills and interests (i.e., doing only a skills assessment may suggest a career path that is based on your work history more so than on your current interests and future goals).

- Assessment.com: assessment.com
- Bridges Transitions: bridges.com
- Career Cruising: careercruising.com
- Career Decision–making Difficulties Questionnaire (CDDQ): cddq.org
- CareerDNA: careerdna.net
- Career Key: careerkey.org
- CareerMaze: careermaze.com
- CareerStorm Navigator: www.careerstorm.com
- Discover (ACT): act.org/discover/
- Elevations: elevateyourcareer.com
- MCP/Career Dimensions: careerdimension.com
- MyGuidewire: myguidewire.com
- MyMajors.com: mymajors.com
- nextSteps.org (Canadian site): nextsteps.org
- Queendom.com: queendom.com
- SkillScan: skillscan.net

State Career Information Systems

The following list of State Career Information Systems lists only those online systems that offer career assessment resources (as far as we can tell). Note also that many of these systems require a username and password — which needs to be obtained from a participating school, college or other organization, such as a one-stop career center. However, check out the system for your state and see for yourself what it offers in terms of content and access. If we have omitted your state, it simply means we are not aware of an online career information system in your state that provides career assessment resources. In a few cases (e.g., Florida), a state will simply refer its residents to a private resource such as Bridges Transitions (see above under self-directed resources).

- Alaska: AKCIS/Alaska Commission on Postsecondary Education: akcis.org/
- Arizona: AzCIS/Arizona Department of Education: azcis.intocareers.org/
- Arkansas: OSCAR/Occupation and Skill Computer-Assisted Researcher: ioscar.org/ar/
- California: EUREKA/California Career Information System: eurekanet.org; California CareerZone: cacareerzone.com
- Connecticut: Job & Career ConneCTion: www1.ctdol.state.ct.us/jcc/
- Georgia: Georgia Career Information Center: gcic.peachnet.edu/
- Hawaii: Career Kokua (The Hawai'i Career Information Delivery System): careerkokua.org
- Idaho: Idaho Career Information System: cis.idaho.gov
- Illinois: Illinois Career Resource Network: ilworkinfo.com/icrn/
- Indiana: Indiana Career Information System: p16center.educ.indiana.edu/sites/p16/cis/Pages/default.aspx; Learn More Indiana: www.learnmoreindiana.org
- Iowa: Iowa Choices: icansucceed.org/IowaChoices/
- Kentucky: Workforce Kentucky Career Center: workforcekentucky.ky.gov
- Louisiana: OSCAR/Occupation and Skill Computer-Assisted Researcher: ioscar.org/la/; Louisiana Works Career Services: voshost.com/careers.asp
- Massachusetts: MASS CIS/Massachusetts Department of Workforce Development: masscis.intocareers.org
- Michigan: My Dream Explorer: mydreamexplorer.org
- Minnesota: Minnesota Career Information System: mncis.intocareers.org

- Montana: Montana Career Information System: mtcis.intocareers.org
- Nebraska: Nebraska Career Information System: ncis.unl.edu/
- Nevada: Nevada Career Information System: nvcis.intocareers.org/
- New Hampshire: New Hampshire Career Resource Network: nhes.state.nh.us/elmi/nhcrn/index.htm
- New Jersey: New Jersey Career Information Delivery System (NJ CIDS): wnjpin1.dol.state.nj.us/wnjpin_ru/index.htm
- New York: CareerZone: nycareerzone.org
- North Carolina: North Carolina Career Resource Network: ncsoicc.org
- Ohio: Ohio Career Information System: ocis.org
- Oklahoma: OKCIS/Oklahoma Career Information System: okcareertech.org/guidance/
- Oregon: Oregon Career Information System: oregoncis.uoregon.edu/home/
- Pennsylvania: South Central Pennsylvania Career Information System: sccis.org/main/main.htm
- South Carolina: South Carolina Occupational Information System: scois.net
- Tennessee: TCIDS/Tennessee Career Information System: tcids.tbr.edu/
- Texas: OSCAR/Occupation and Skill Computer-Assisted Researcher: ioscar.org/tx/
- Utah: Utah Mentor & Choices: utahmentor.org
- Vermont: Vermont Career Gateway: vtcareergateway.org
- Virginia: Virginia Career VIEW: vacareerview.org
- Washington: WOIS/The Washington Career Information System: wois.org
- Wisconsin: WISCareers: wiscareers.wisc.edu/
- Wyoming: Wyoming Career Information System: uwadmnweb.uwyo.edu/SEO/WCIS/default.asp

Note: Job and employment websites (including the big ones, like Monster.com and Yahoo HotJobs) offer tips and tools for career planning, yet they are limited in depth and scope and generally avoid the subject of basic career assessment and exploration. Even if you are relatively certain of your future career path, you would be wise to conduct an in-depth career assessment before investing thousands of dollars and years of your time on an education program or career path that may not be the right fit for you.

Step 2: Reality Testing

Once you've completed your career assessment, it's time to research your top three career fields of interest to determine which one is the best fit for you. In the career counseling field, this is called "reality-testing." It's a process of reading about the career fields and conducting informational interviews with people already working in that field. Other more active options include internships, volunteer work and job shadowing (if you can find someone who'll let you follow them around for a day on the job).

Note: If you are uncomfortable with the idea of researching only your top three, then expand the number to whatever number feels right to you. But don't go overboard and spend the next ten years reality-testing 100 different occupations! The idea is to *make* a solid career decision, not to avoid making it.

How do you find someone to conduct an informational interview with? There are several options here. One is to talk to a teacher, instructor, professor or counselor and ask if they can help you find someone (appropriate) for the informational interview. Another option is to talk to a prospective employer and ask them the same question. Yet another option is to contact the professional association aligned with that specific career field and ask them for assistance. They may even have a list of association members who have indicated an interest in being mentors. Of course, the ideal situation would be to find someone in your local area so that your informational interview can be done in person.

Prepare a list of questions to use for the informational interview. The following questions may give you some ideas, but you need to create your own customized list based on the types of jobs and employers to which you will apply:

- How did you get into this field?
- What is your training and education?
- What is a typical day/week like?
- What do you like most about your job?
- What do you like least about your job?
- What are the critical skills needed to be successful in this work?
- What are your organization's most pressing, significant and immediate goals?
- What obstacles are getting in the way of achieving these goals?
- What professional association do you recommend joining?

- What would be a high/low income range for this job in this type of industry?
- Is there anyone else I should talk to about this career field?

Try not to ask any question that they may have already answered (within their response to a previous question). Avoid yes/no questions. Don't take up much of their time telling them about you unless they are clearly interested (as evidenced by them asking you direct questions). Spend your time asking them about them, their job and their employer.

Make sure you follow up with a handwritten thank-you note for everyone you meet with during your reality-testing phase. If possible, let them know specifically how they helped you. Try to keep in touch with them if you do proceed on a similar career path. (This is called networking!)

Note: Make sure you conduct at least three informational interviews per career field to maximize the validity of your results. Your first interview may turn out to be someone who is disgruntled, and they may paint a "gloomy" picture of a perfectly good profession. By meeting with at least three people, you'll get a more representative perspective and be better able to determine the best direction for you. You'll also be more likely to have found a mentor.

Online Occupational Information Resources

If you're looking for additional information on any of the career fields in this book, or for information on other types of occupations, these are three excellent online resources to become familiar with — all from the US Department of Labor. Each one has their areas of strength (and weaknesses), but all will provide you with profiles that include descriptions, wages, education/skill requirements, etc. O*NET goes the deepest in terms of occupational knowledge, skills and ability (KSA) information. The Occupational Outlook Handbook is the most readable — since it's based on the content from the book that is the "most read" occupational information resource publication found in career centers and counseling offices across the country. America's Career Info-Net ties the largest number of government-based occupational information sources together in a user-friendly manner and allows you to create customized occupational profiles — or link to other online sources.

- O*NET (America's Occupational Information Network): online.onetcenter.org
- Occupational Outlook Handbook: bls.gov/oco/
- America's Career InfoNet: acinet.org

Top Mainstream Job Boards

- Monster.com: monster.com
- Yahoo! HotJobs.com: hotjobs.yahoo.com
- CareerBuilder: careerbuilder.com

There are hundreds of mainstream job boards. The three listed above are consistently ranked at the top of most "Best Job Board" lists. Each of these sites serves as repositories for huge numbers of job listings posted by employers and recruiters.

Mainstream job boards have much in common as they usually offer the same three features for job seekers:

1. The ability to post resumes (for employers to find)
2. The ability to search for current job openings
3. A resource center giving information and advice to help with job search and career management

The vast majority of mainstream job boards offer these services free to job seekers — usually requiring only that you set up an account. Some sites will charge job seekers for bulk resumé postings and/or for other premium services. Whatever job boards you end up using, remember that job search experts consistently suggest using several of them. Remember also not to overlook traditional offline job-hunting methods. Perhaps the majority of jobs are still filled through the *hidden job market*, i.e., jobs that are not advertised.

Although not a job board in the conventional sense, there is a new generation of job websites based on an Internet search engine rather than a repository for job listings. Think Google-for-jobs, and you begin to get the idea. One of our favorites is called Indeed (indeed.com).

Another mainstream job board that deserves mention here is Craigslist (craigslist.com). Most people don't think of Craigslist as mainstream because it is decentralized into 450 Craigslist websites in 450 different cities around the world. All together, however, Craigslist would probably rank as the top employment site on the Web.

Local Job Boards?
Many excellent job boards are local, so don't overlook their potential value to you as a job seeker. Local job boards are often operated by regional Workforce Investment Boards or One-Stop Career Center Consortiums. To find a local job board website, use one of the top Internet search engines (like Google) and use keywords such as "job" and "Chicago" (insert your geographic area name).

Green/Environmental Career Resources and Job Boards
CoolWorks.com   coolworks.com
This website is about helping you find a seasonal job or career in a great place, like at a national or state park, a ski resort, a theme park or with one of the many state conservation corps or national conservation corps. Note that only some of their jobs would qualify as "protecting the environment." The site includes a privacy policy. CoolWorks.com is based in Gardiner, MT.

Cyber-Sierra's Natural Resources Job Search   cyber-sierra.com/nrjobs/
Very helpful resource for job seekers, created and maintained by Jean Saffell — originally to help her husband find a job in the environmental field!

Earthworks-jobs.com   earthworks-jobs.com
This international job board website is owned by Richard Holt and based in

Cambridge, UK. It includes a wide variety of jobs, including green and environmental jobs, with many different companies throughout the world.

EcoEmploy.com   ecoemploy.com
This environmental job board website is owned by David R. Brierley, an environmental analyst based in Malden, MA. The site includes a privacy policy and job seeker registration is not required. Includes a good list of links.

EnviroNetwork   environetwork.com
EnviroNetwork claims to be the Web's leading environmental job board. However, the troubling thing about this site is that it lacks any disclosure information. It doesn't tell you who owns or operates it, and it provides no privacy policy or terms of use document. A check of the domain name registration indicates that the site is owned by Naturalist.com, Inc., based in New York, NY. This company operates a network of websites featuring news, job postings, product offerings (including weight-loss products), resources and other content related to ecology, wildlife and the environment.

Environmental Career Opportunities   ecojobs.com
ECO is an environmental job board website operated by Betty and Dan Brubach, based in Charlottesville, VA. Without a subscription, you can access 100 current job listings on their website. If you subscribe to their service (for less than $1/day), you get 500 current job listings every two weeks. Registration is not required for non-subscribers.

Environmental Expert   environmental-expert.com
Environmental Expert claims to connect over 500,000 environmental industry professionals (from around the globe) to more than 11,400 companies that hire them. In a test search for environmental engineer job listings (in the US), results showed an impressive total of almost 100 jobs currently posted. However, a closer look at the job listings indicated that most of those were not actually for environmental engineer — which was the search term used. Even though the site's job search tool does not work as efficiently as one might expect, the site is a rich source for industry-related information and resources, including publications, events, articles and news. The site includes privacy policy and terms of use documents. Job seeker registration is not required, but you will need to provide the equivalent information if you try to apply for any of the jobs they have listed. Environmental Expert is based in Madrid, Spain.

EnvironmentalCareer.com   environmentalcareer.com

This environmental job board website marks its 13th year of operation in 2008. The site is owned by the Environmental Career Center, based in Hampton, VA, which has been in operation for 28 years. They also publish the *Green Careers Journal*. The site includes a privacy policy and job seeker registration is not required.

Environmental-Jobs-Online   environmental-jobs-online.com

This website is actually a portal to WorkTree.com, a membership- (fee-) based job search site. WorkTree.com claims to be the largest job search portal in the world, but its fee-based approach makes it somewhat unusual — as job seekers are generally given free access to job listings while employers pay to post their job listings. On the other hand, the fees are actually quite minimal, so if Work Tree.com has found a way to add value that exceeds the competition (such as Monster.com), then they may be offering a fair deal to green career seekers.

GreenBiz.com   greenbiz.com/jobs

GreenBiz is a media company with a mission: To be the leading information resource on how to align environmental responsibility with business success. The site is owned by Greener World Media, Inc., based in Oakland, CA. The site includes a privacy policy and job seeker registration is not required.

Green Career Central   greencareercentral.com

If you're looking for a green career, career counselor and author Carol McClelland created this subscription-based site to provide the guidance and support you need to match your passion for the environment, your skill set and your experience. It includes tools to help you plan your career, find a job and manage and advance in your career. McClelland is the author of *Your Dream Career for Dummies*.

Green Dream Jobs   sustainablebusiness.com/jobs

Environmental job board website owned by SustainableBusiness.com, based in Huntington Station, NY. They also publish a monthly newsletter called the *Progressive Investor*. The site includes a privacy policy and job seeker registration is not required. The site also includes an excellent list of links.

GreenCareers (MonsterTRAK)   monstertrak.com/green_careers/

Monster.com started this new service in late 2007 in collaboration with eco-

America and the Environmental Defense Fund. They promote GreenCareers as the first service exclusively designed to promote the availability of green jobs for college students and recent graduates. It has an advice section with tips for job seekers, a green opportunity section that explains what a green career is and offers news on this emerging area of employment and a links and resources section.

Land Trust Alliance   lta.org

The Land Trust Alliance is the national association that represents more than 1,600 land trusts across America. Their "Alliance Jobs" page may be a bit hard to locate, but this would be a good place to search for administrative positions with land trusts and related organizations.

National Registry of Environmental Professionals   nrep.org

The NREP is a registry that seeks to provide legal and professional recognition of individuals possessing education, training and experience as environmental professionals. Their website does include a "Job Bank," although it has a very small number of job listings. The site does not include privacy policy or terms of use documents for non-registrants; however, job seeker registration is not required and non-registrants are able to access the job listings. The site also offers a "Recruiters" page with a listing of recruitment or headhunting firms that specialize in serving environmental professionals.

National Wildlife Federation   nwf.org

Use this website to learn about jobs, internships and volunteer opportunities with the National Wildlife Federation, whose revenues totaled $115 million in 2006. Most of those resources are spent on programs that include conducting scientific, policy and legislative research; educating the public on issues relating to wildlife conservation policy and legislation; and taking legal action against environmental polluters and violators that threaten wildlife and wildlife habitat.

The Nature Conservancy   nature.org/careers/

The Nature Conservancy has projects in all 50 states and in more than 30 different countries around the world. It employs people in a variety of jobs that protect the lands and waters that our plants, animals and natural communities need to survive. This is their career website for browsing or searching the Nature Conservancy job listings.

New Scientist   newscientist.com

Environmental science news, blogs and special reports from the website of *New Scientist* magazine. This site also has a job board called "New Scientist Jobs." The site includes privacy policy and terms of use documents, and job-seeker registration is not required.

North American Association for Environmental Education   naaee.org

Based in Washington, DC, NAAEE is a professional association for people involved in environmental education. Their website includes a job board called "EE Jobs," which is a good place to search for jobs in the environmental education field. In addition, the NAAEE site is an excellent resource for identifying environmental-related education programs. The site does not include privacy policy or terms of use documents for non-members; however, job seeker registration is not required and non-members are able to access the job listings.

The Orion Society   orionsociety.org

The Orion Society is a non-profit organization based in Great Barrington, MA. Its mission is to inform, inspire and engage individuals and grassroots organizations in becoming a significant cultural force for healing nature and community. They publish *Orion* magazine, which the *Boston Globe* calls "America's finest environmental magazine." The Orion Grassroots Network connects and empowers groups working for positive social and environmental change across North America and beyond. Orion's Internship and Career Service has hundreds of job listings, internships and AmeriCorps positions with members of the Orion Grassroots Network. The Orion Society also undertakes educational initiatives, including the Nature Literacy Series. Their job board does not include privacy policy or terms of use documents for non-members; however, job seeker registration is not required and non-members are able to access the job listings.

The School for Field Studies   fieldstudies.org

SFS is an international non-profit educational organization that provides environmental education and conducts research through its field-based programs. A very small job board includes both academic and nonacademic job openings in the US and abroad, as well as some internships.

TreeHugger   treehugger.com

TreeHugger describes itself as the leading media outlet dedicated to driving sustainability mainstream. With an impressive team of international writers,

TreeHugger has become one of the most respected and visited environmental sites on the Web in just three short years. In addition to the articles and the job board, TreeHugger offers green-themed blogs, weekly and daily newsletters, weekly video segments and a weekly radio show. The site includes a privacy policy and job seeker registration is not required.

USAJOBS   **usajobs.opm.gov**
This is a website of the US Office of Personnel Management and is the Federal Government's official one-stop source for federal jobs and employment information.

Industry- and Occupation-specific Resources and Associations
Advertising and Public Relations Services Industry (Green)
- American Advertising Federation (AAF): aaf.org
- American Association of Advertising Agencies (AAAA): aaaa.org
- American Marketing Association (AMA): marketingpower.com
- Career Guide to Industries: Advertising and Public Relations Services: bls.gov/oco/cg/cgs030.htm
- Council of Public Relations Firms: prfirms.org
- Institute for Public Relations (IPR): instituteforpr.org
- International Association of Business Communicators (IABC): iabc.com
- National Association for Interpretation (NAI): interpnet.com
- Public Relations Society of America (PRSA): prsa.org
- Sales & Marketing Executives International (SMEI): smei.org
- True Spin Conference: truespinconference.com

Agriculture and Food Industry
- Agroecology Section, Ecological Society of America: esa.org/agroecology/
- American Fisheries Society: fisheries.org
- American Horticultural Society (AHS): ahs.org
- American Nursery and Landscape Association (ANLA): anla.org
- American Society for Horticulture Science (ASHS): ashs.org
- American Society of Agricultural and Biological Engineers: asabe.org
- American Society of Farm Managers and Rural Appraisers: asfmra.org
- aquaculturejobs.com: aquaculturejobs.com
- Association of Environmental Engineering and Science Professors (AEESP): aeesp.org
- ATTRA, National Sustainable Agriculture Information Service: attra.ncat.org

- California Native Plant Society (CNPS): cnps.org
- Career Guide to Industries: Agriculture, Forestry and Fishing: bls.gov/oco/cg/cgs001.htm
- Career Guide to Industries: Food Manufacturing: bls.gov/oco/cg/cgs011.htm
- Career Guide to Industries: Food Services and Drinking Places: bls.gov/oco/cg/cgs023.htm
- Career Guide to Industries: Grocery Stores: bls.gov/oco/cg/cgs024.htm
- Ecological Farming Association: eco-farm.org
- Global Aquaculture Alliance: gaalliance.org
- International Federation of Organic Agriculture Movements (IFOAM): ifoam.org
- National Agricultural Library (NAL): nal.usda.gov
- National Aquaculture Association (NAA): thenaa.net
- National Campaign for Sustainable Agriculture: sustainableagriculture.net
- National FFA Organization: ffa.org
- National Sustainable Agriculture Information Service (ATTRA): attra.ncat.org
- North American Fruit Explorers (NAFEX): nafex.org
- Sustainable Agriculture Education Association (SAEA): sustainableaged.org
- Sustainable Agriculture Research and Education (SARE): sare.org
- UC Santa Cruz, Center for Agroecology and Sustainable Food Systems: casfs.ucsc.edu
- United Farm Workers of America (UFW): ufw.org
- US Department of Agriculture (USDA): usda.gov
- US Trout Farmers Association: ustfa.org
- World Aquaculture Society (WAS): was.org

Alternative Fuel Vehicles Industry

- biodiesel-jobs.com: biodiesel-jobs.com
- Career Guide to Industries: Motor Vehicle and Parts Manufacturing: bls.gov/oco/cg/cgs012.htm
- Electric Auto Association: eaaev.org
- Electric Vehicle Association of the Americas (EVAA): evaa.org
- ethanol-jobs.com: ethanol-jobs.com
- Fuel Cells 2000 from the Breakthrough Technologies Institute (BTI): fuelcells.org

- Hybrid Cars & Alternative Fuels by Christine and Scott Gable: alternativefuels.about.com
- Hydrogen and Fuel Cell Job Board: hydrogenassociation.org/jobs/
- National Alternative Fuels Association: altfuels.us
- National Alternative Fuels Training Consortium (NAFTC): naftc.wvu.edu
- National Hydrogen Association: hydrogenassociation.org
- Tesla Motors, Inc.: teslamotors.com

Bicycle Industry
- Bicycle Manufacturers Association of America: no website
- Bicycle Retailer & Industry News: bicycleretailer.com
- National Bicycle Dealers Association (NBDA): nbda.com

Biotech/Life Sciences Industry
- BayBio: baybio.org
- BIO Career Guide: accessexcellence.org/RC/CC/bio_intro.php
- Biotechnology Industry Organization (BIO): bio.org
- Career Guide to Industries: Pharmaceutical and Medicine Manufacturing: stats.bls.gov/oco/cg/cgs009.htm
- Career Guide to Industries: Scientific Research and Development Services: bls.gov/oco/cg/cgs053.htm
- GeneRef.com: science.bio.org
- Jobs in Biotechnology: bls.gov/opub/ooq/2002/fall/art03.pdf

Building Industry (Green/Sustainable)
- American Institute of Architects (AIA): aia.org
- American Solar Energy Society: ases.org
- Americas Glass Association: americasglassassn.org
- Architects/Designers/Planners for Social Responsibility (ADPSR): adpsr.org
- Associated Builders and Contractors (ABC): trytools.org
- Associated General Contractors of America (AGC): agc.org
- Association of the Wall and Ceiling Industry (AWCI): awci.org
- BigGreen Discussion Group (sustainable design and construction): biggreen.org
- BuildingGreen.com: buildinggreen.com
- Building Industry Association (BIA): bia.net
- California Solar Energy Industries Association (CALSEIA): calseia.org
- Career Guide to Industries: Construction: bls.gov/oco/cg/cgs003.htm

- Certified Floorcovering Installers Association (CFI): cfiinstallers.com
- Certified Sustainable Development Professional (CSDP) Program: aeecenter.org/certification/csdppage.htm
- Engineering Central: engcen.com
- Flooring Contractors Association (FCICA): fcica.com
- Green Building Initiative (GBI): thegbi.org
- Green Energy Jobs: greenenergyjobs.com
- Habitat for Humanity: habitat.org
- Home Builders Institute: hbi.org
- Independent Electrical Contractors (IEC): ieci.org
- Insulation Contractors Association of America (ICAA): insulate.org
- Intern Development Program (IDP): aia.org/ep_home_getlicensed
- International Brotherhood of Electrical Workers (IBEW): ibew.org
- International Society of Sustainability Professionals (ISSP): sustainabilityprofessionals.org
- International Union of Bricklayers and Allied Craftworkers (BAC): bacweb.org
- International Union of Painters and Allied Trades (IUPAT): iupat.org
- Mason Contractors Association of America (MCAA): masoncontractors.org
- Masonry Institute of America (MIA): masonryinstitute.org
- Master Painters and Decorators Association (MPDA): paintinfo.com/assoc/mpda/
- National Association of Home Builders (NAHB): nahb.org
- National Center for Construction Education and Research (NCCER): nccer.org
- National Concrete Masonry Association (NCMA): ncma.org
- National Council of Architectural Registration Boards (NCARB): ncarb.org
- National Electrical Contractors Association (NECA): necanet.org
- National Insulation Association (NIA): insulation.org
- National Joint Apprenticeship Training Committee (NJATC): njatc.org
- National Roofing Contractors Association (NRCA): nrca.net
- National Society of Professional Engineers: nspe.org
- National Sustainable Building Advisor Program (NaSBAP): nasbap.org
- National Terrazzo and Mosaic Association (NTMA): ntma.com
- National Tile Contractors Association (NTCA): tile-assn.com
- Natural Building Network: naturalbuildingnetwork.org

- North American Board of Certified Energy Practitioners (NABCEP): nabcep.org
- Operative Plasterers and Cement Masons International Association (OPCMIA): opcmia.org
- Painting & Decorating Contractors of America (PDCA): pdca.org
- Plumbing–Heating–Cooling Contractors Association (PHCC): phccweb.org
- Solar Energy Industries Association: seia.org
- Solar Energy International (SEI): solarenergy.org
- Solar Living Institute: solarliving.org
- Solar Rating and Certification Corporation (SRCC): solar-rating.org
- United Association of Journeymen and Apprentices of the Plumbing and Pipefitting Industry: ua.org
- United Brotherhood of Carpenters and Joiners of America (UBC): carpenters.org
- United Union of Roofers, Waterproofers and Allied Workers: unionroofers.org
- US Green Building Council/LEED AP Certification: usgbc.org

Cleaning and Janitorial Services Industry (Green Cleaning)
- Association of Residential Cleaning Professionals (ARCSI): arcp.us
- DestinationGreen: destinationgreen.com
- Global Cleaning Association, Cleaning and Janitorial Business Owner Forum: globalcleaningassociation.com/forums/
- Green Clean Schools: healthyschoolscampaign.org/campaign/green_clean_schools/
- Green Cleaning for Dummies: greencleaningfordummies.com
- Green Cleaning Network: greencleaningnetwork.org
- Institute of Inspection Cleaning and Restoration (IICRC): iicrc.org
- International Janitorial Cleaning Services Association (IJCSA): ijcsa.org
- International Window Cleaner Certification Institute: iwcci.org
- International Window Cleaning Association (IWCA): iwca.org
- ISSA (Worldwide Cleaning Industry Association): issa.com
- Power Washers of North America (PWNA): pwna.org
- Zero Waste Alliance: zerowaste.org

Clothing and Accessories Industry (Organic/Natural/Recycled Material)
- Career Guide to Industries: Clothing, Accessory and General Merchandise Stores: bls.gov/oco/cg/cgs022.htm

- Career Guide to Industries: Textile, Textile Product and Apparel Manufacturing: bls.gov/oco/cg/cgs015.htm
- Career Guide to Industries: Wholesale Trade: bls.gov/oco/cg/cgs026.htm
- Organic Clothing News and Views from LotusOrganics.com: lotusorganics.com/NewsViews.aspx
- Organic Consumers Association: organicconsumers.org/clothes/
- Organic Directory from the Soil Association: whyorganic.org/involved_organicDirectory.asp
- Organic.org: organic.org
- Organic Trade Association (OTA): ota.com

Ecotourism Industry

- EcoBusinessLinks: ecobusinesslinks.com
- International Ecotourism Society (TIES): ecotourism.org
- Leave No Trace: lnt.org
- Planeta.com: planeta.com
- Tourism Concern: tourismconcern.org.uk
- Tread Lightly!: treadlightly.org

Engineering Services Industry (Green)

- Air and Waste Management Association (A&WMA): awma.org
- American Academy of Environmental Engineers (AAEE): aaee.net
- American Association for Aerosol Research (AAAR): aaar.org
- American Chemical Society (ACS): acs.org
- American Geophysical Union (AGU): agu.org
- American Institute of Chemical Engineers (AIChE): aiche.org
- American Society of Agricultural and Biological Engineers: asabe.org
- American Society of Certified Engineering Technicians (ASCET): ascet.org
- American Society of Civil Engineers (ASCE): asce.org
- American Society of Mechanical Engineers (ASME): asme.org
- American Solar Energy Society (ASES): ases.org
- Association of Conservation Engineers (ACE): conservationengineers.org
- Association of Environmental Engineering and Science Professors (AEESP): aeesp.org
- Association for Environmental Health and Sciences (AEHS): aehs.com
- Association of Environmental Professionals (AEP): califaep.org
- Career Guide to Industries: Chemical Manufacturing: bls.gov/oco/cg/cgs008.htm

- Career Guide to Industries: Management, Scientific and Technical Consulting Services: bls.gov/oco/cg/cgs037.htm
- Engineering Central: engcen.com
- EnvironmentalEngineer.com: environmentalengineer.com
- Green Chemistry Institute: chemistry.org
- Green Energy Jobs: greenenergyjobs.com
- greenengineeringjobs.com: greenengineeringjobs.com
- Green Mechanical Council (GreenMech): greenmech.org
- Institute of Electrical and Electronics Engineers: ieeeusa.org
- National Institute for Certification in Engineering Technologies (NICET): nicet.org
- National Society of Professional Engineers: nspe.org
- Natural Resources Conservation Service (NRCS): nrcs.usda.gov
- Solar Energy Industries Association (SEIA): seia.org
- US Green Building Council/LEED AP Certification: usgbc.org

Environmental Health and Safety Services Industry (Consulting)
- American Board of Industrial Hygiene (ABIH): abih.org
- American Industrial Hygiene Association (AIHA): aiha.org
- American Society of Safety Engineers: asse.org
- Association for Environmental Health and Sciences (AEHS): aehs.com
- Board of Certified Safety Professionals (BCSP): bcsp.org
- Career Guide to Industries: Management, Scientific and Technical Consulting Services: bls.gov/oco/cg/cgs037.htm
- Council on Certification of Health, Environmental and Safety Technologists (CCHEST): cchest.org
- EHSCareers.com: ehscareers.com
- Environmental Protection Agency (EPA): epa.gov
- Indoor Air Quality Association (IAQA): iaqa.org
- Indoor Environmental Institute (IEI): ieinstitute.org
- Institute of Inspection, Cleaning and Restoration Certification (IICRC): iicrc.org
- National Association for EHS Management (NAEM): naem.org
- National Environmental Health Association (NEHA): neha.org
- National Safety Council (NSC): nsc.org

Environmental and Hazardous Materials (HazMat) Services Industry
- Academy of Certified Hazardous Materials Managers (ACHMM): achmm.org
- American Academy of Forensic Sciences (AAFS): aafs.org

- American Association for the Advancement of Science (AAAS): aaas.org
- American Association of Pharmaceutical Scientists (AAPS): aapspharmaceutica.com
- American Association of State Climatologists (AASC): stateclimate.org
- American Association of Zoo Keepers (AAZK): aazk.org
- American Chemical Society (ACS): acs.org
- American Geological Institute (AGI): agiweb.org
- American Geophysical Union (AGU): agu.org
- American Institute of Biological Sciences (AIBS): aibs.org
- American Institute of Hydrology (AIH): aihydro.org
- American Institute of Physics (AIP): aip.org
- American Meteorological Society (AMS): ametsoc.org
- American Physical Society (APS): aps.org
- American Society of Agronomy (ASA): agronomy.org
- American Society for Biochemistry and Molecular Biology (ASBMB): asbmb.org
- American Society of Consulting Arborists (ASCA): asca-consultants.org
- American Society for Microbiology (ASM): asm.org
- American Society of Plant Biologists (ASPB): aspb.org
- American Water Works Association: awwa.org
- Association of American Geographers (AAG): aag.org
- Association of Boards of Certification (ABC): abccert.org
- Association of Consulting Foresters of America (ACF): www.acf-foresters.org
- Association of Environmental & Engineering Geologists (AEG): aegweb.org
- Association of Environmental Engineering and Science Professors (AEESP): aeesp.org
- Association for Environmental Health and Sciences (AEHS): aehs.com
- Association of Environmental Professionals (AEP): califaep.org
- Association of Zoos and Aquariums (AZA): aza.org
- Biophysical Society: biophysics.org
- Career Guide to Industries: Management, Scientific and Technical Consulting Services: bls.gov/oco/cg/cgs037.htm
- Continuing Challenge Hazmat Workshop: hazmat.org
- Ecological Society of America (ESA): esa.org
- EHSCareers.com: ehscareers.com
- EnvironmentalEngineer.com: environmentalengineer.com
- Environmental Sciences Research Institute (ESRI): esri.com

- Forest Guild: forestguild.org
- Geography Jobs (article): bls.gov/opub/ooq/2005/spring/art01.pdf
- Global Association of Online Foresters (GAOF): foresters.org
- Health Physics Society (HPS): hps.org
- International Association for Ecology (INTECOL): intecol.net
- International Association for Environmental Hydrology: hydroweb.com
- International Association of Hazardous Materials Technicians (IAHMT): iahmt.com
- International Association of Hydrogeologists (IAH): iah.org
- International Association of Meteorology and Atmospheric Sciences (IAMAS): iamas.org
- International Society of Arboriculture (ISA): isa-arbor.com
- International Society for Environmental Epidemiology (ISEE): iseepi.org
- International Society of Sustainability Professionals (ISSP): sustainabilityprofessionals.org
- Journal of Exposure Science and Environmental Epidemiology: nature.com/jes/
- Marine Geology and Geophysics at MIT: web.mit.edu/mit-whoi/www/research/mgg/
- National Association of Conservation Districts (NACD): nacdnet.org
- National Association of Environmental Professionals (NAEP): naep.org
- National Environmental Health Association (NEHA): neha.org
- National Oceanic and Atmospheric Administration (NOAA): noaa.gov
- National Rural Water Association (NRWA): nrwa.org
- National Weather Service: nws.noaa.gov
- Natural Resources Conservation Service (NRCS): nrcs.usda.gov
- Occupational Safety and Health Administration (OSHA): osha.gov
- Pharmaceutical Research and Manufacturers of America (PhRMA): phrma.org
- Restoration Industry Association (RIA): ascr.org
- Society of American Foresters (SAF): safnet.org
- Society of Environmental Toxicology and Chemistry (SETAC): setac.org
- Society of Toxicology (ST): toxicology.org
- Soil and Water Conservation Society (SWCS): swcs.org
- Soil Science Society of America (SSSA): soils.org
- Tree Care Industry Association (TCIA): treecareindustry.org
- USAJOBS: usajobs.gov
- US Dept. of Agriculture, Forest Service: fs.fed.us

- US Dept. of Agriculture, National Resources Conservation Service: nrcs.usda.gov
- US Environmental Protection Agency (EPA): epa.gov
- US Geological Survey ,Water Resources of the United States: water.usgs.gov
- Water Environment Federation (WEF): wef.org

Geography and GIS Services Industry
- Association of American Geographers (AAG): aag.org
- Association of Environmental Engineering and Science Professors (AEESP): aeesp.org
- Environmental Sciences Research Institute (ESRI): esri.com
- Occupational Outlook Quarterly, Geography Jobs: bls.gov/opub/ooq/2005/spring/art01.pdf
- University Consortium for Geographic Information Science: ucgis.org

Government
- American Academy of Forensic Sciences (AAFS): aafs.org
- American Association for Health Education (AAHE): aahperd.org/aahe/
- American Association of Pharmaceutical Scientists (AAPS): aapspharmaceutica.com
- American Association of State Climatologists (AASC): stateclimate.org
- American Chemical Society (ACS): acs.org
- American Fisheries Society: fisheries.org
- American Geological Institute (AGI): agiweb.org
- American Geophysical Union (AGU): agu.org
- American Horticultural Society (AHS): ahs.org
- American Institute of Biological Sciences (AIBS): aibs.org
- American Institute of Hydrology (AIH): aihydro.org
- American Institute of Physics (AIP): aip.org
- American Meteorological Society (AMS): ametsoc.org
- American Physical Society (APS): aps.org
- American Planning Association (APA): planning.org
- American Society of Agronomy (ASA): agronomy.org
- American Society for Biochemistry and Molecular Biology (ASBMB): asbmb.org
- American Society for Microbiology (ASM): asm.org
- American Water Works Association: awwa.org
- AmeriCorps: americorps.org
- Association of American Geographers (AAG): aag.org

- Association of Boards of Certification (ABC): abccert.org
- Association of Collegiate Schools of Planning (ACSP): acsp.org
- Association of Environmental and Engineering Geologists (AEG): aegweb.org
- Association of Environmental Engineering and Science Professors (AEESP): aeesp.org
- Association of Environmental Health Academic Programs (AEHAP): aehap.org
- Association for Environmental Health and Sciences (AEHS): aehs.com
- Association of Environmental Professionals (AEP): califaep.org
- Association of National Park Rangers (ANPR): anpr.org
- ATTRA / National Sustainable Agriculture Information Service: attra.ncat.org
- Biophysical Society: biophysics.org
- Career Guide to Industries: Federal Government: bls.gov/oco/cg/cgs041.htm
- Career Guide to Industries: State and Local Government: bls.gov/oco/cg/cgs042.htm
- Centers for Disease Control and Prevention (CDC): cdc.gov
- DOE Jobs ONLINE from the US Department of Energy: chris.doe.gov/jobs/
- Ecological Farming Association: eco-farm.org
- Ecological Society of America (ESA): esa.org
- Engineering Central: engcen.com
- Environmental Lawyers.com: environmentallawyers.com
- Environmental Sciences Research Institute (ESRI): esri.com
- Forest Guild: forestguild.org
- Occupational Outlook Quarterly: Geography Jobs: bls.gov/opub/ooq/2005/spring/art01.pdf
- Global Aquaculture Alliance: gaalliance.org
- Global Association of Online Foresters (GAOF): foresters.org
- Health Physics Society (HPS): hps.org
- Institute for Public Relations (IPR): instituteforpr.org
- International Association for Environmental Hydrology: hydroweb.com
- International Association of Hydrogeologists (IAH): iah.org
- International Association of Meteorology and Atmospheric Sciences (IAMAS): iamas.org
- International Code Council (ICC): iccsafe.org/training/contract/insp-c.html

- International Network for Environmental Compliance and Enforcement (INECE): inece.org
- International Society for Environmental Epidemiology (ISEE): iseepi.org
- International Society of Sustainability Professionals (ISSP): sustainabilityprofessionals.org
- Journal of Exposure Science and Environmental Epidemiology: nature.com/jes/
- National Agricultural Library (NAL): nal.usda.gov
- National Aquaculture Association (NAA): thenaa.net
- National Association of Conservation Districts (NACD): nacdnet.org
- National Association of Environmental Professionals (NAEP): naep.org
- National Association for Interpretation (NAI): interpnet.com
- National Campaign for Sustainable Agriculture: sustainableagriculture.net
- National Commission for Health Education Credentialing (NCHEC): nchec.org
- National Environmental Health Association (NEHA): neha.org
- National Oceanic and Atmospheric Administration (NOAA): noaa.gov
- National Parks Conservation Association (NPCA): eparks.org
- National Recycling Coalition (NRC): nrc-recycle.org
- National Registry of Environmental Professionals (NREP): nrep.org
- National Rural Water Association (NRWA): nrwa.org
- National Society of Professional Engineers: nspe.org
- National Weather Service: nws.noaa.gov
- Natural Resources Conservation Service (NRCS): nrcs.usda.gov
- North American Association of Environmental Education (NAAEE): naaee.org
- North American Wildlife Enforcement Officers Association (NAWEOA): naweoa.org
- Occupational Safety and Health Administration (OSHA): osha.gov
- Planetizen: The Planning & Development Network: planetizen.com
- Public Relations Society of America (PRSA): prsa.org
- Recycler's World: recycle.net
- Society of American Foresters (SAF): safnet.org
- Society of Environmental Toxicology and Chemistry (SETAC): setac.org
- Society for Public Health Education (SOPHE): sophe.org
- Society for Range Management (SRM): rangelands.org/srm.shtml
- Society of Toxicology (ST): toxicology.org
- Soil Science Society of America (SSSA): soils.org

- Soil and Water Conservation Society (SWCS): swcs.org
- Solid Waste Association of North America (SWANA): swana.org
- Sustainable Agriculture Education Association (SAEA): sustainableaged.org
- Sustainable Agriculture Research and Education (SARE): sare.org
- UC Santa Cruz, Center for Agroecology and Sustainable Food Systems: casfs.ucsc.edu
- USAJOBS: usajobs.gov
- US Army Corps of Engineers: usace.army.mil
- US Department of Agriculture, Forest Service: fs.fed.us
- US Department of Agriculture, National Resources Conservation Service: nrcs.usda.gov
- US Department of Energy (DOE): doe.gov
- US Department of the Interior, Bureau of Land Management (BLM): blm.gov
- US Department of the Interior, National Park Service: nps.gov
- US Department of Justice, Environment and Natural Resources Division (ENRD): usdoj.gov/enrd/
- US Environmental Protection Agency (EPA) Environmental Accounting Resources: epa.gov/oppt/library/pubs/archive/acct-archive/resources.htm
- US Fish and Wildlife Service: fws.gov
- US Forest Service: fs.fed.us
- US Geological Survey: usgs.gov
- US Geological Survey, Water Resources of the United States: water.usgs.gov
- US Green Building Council/LEED AP Certification: usgbc.org
- Water Environment Federation (WEF): wef.org
- World Aquaculture Society (WAS): was.org

Investment Services Industry (Sustainable/Socially Responsible Investing/SRI)

- Career Guide to Industries: Securities, Commodities and Other Investments: bls.gov/oco/cg/cgs029.htm
- Ceres (Coalition for Environmentally Responsible Economies): ceres.org
- Green Energy Jobs: greenenergyjobs.com
- Green VC (news and resources on green venture capital, funding and start-ups): www.greenvc.org
- Social Investment Forum: socialinvest.org

- Sustainable Investments Directory: ecobusinesslinks.com/sustainable-investments.htm

Journalism and Publishing Industry (Green/Sustainable)

- American Society of Newspaper Editors: asne.org
- Association of American Publishers: publishers.org
- Career Guide to Industries: Publishing: bls.gov/oco/cg/cgs013.htm
- Committee of Concerned Journalists (CCJ): concernedjournalists.org
- Green Press Initiative: greenpressinitiative.org
- Magazine Publishers of America: magazine.org
- Newspaper Association of America: naa.org
- Project for Excellence in Journalism (PEJ): journalism.org
- Society of Environmental Journalists (SEJ): sej.org

Landscaping and Habitat Restoration Services Industry (Green)

- American Society of Consulting Arborists (ASCA): asca-consultants.org
- American Society for Horticulture Science (ASHS): ashs.org
- American Society of Landscape Architects (ASLA): asla.org
- Association for Environmental Health and Sciences (AEHS): aehs.com
- Association of Professional Landscape Designers (APLD): apld.com
- California Native Plant Society (CNPS): cnps.org
- California Society for Ecological Restoration (SERCAL): sercal.org
- Council of Landscape Architectural Registration Boards: clarb.org
- International Society of Arboriculture (ISA): isa-arbor.com
- North American Fruit Explorers (NAFEX): nafex.org
- Occupational Outlook Quarterly: Careers in the Green Industry (for people with green thumbs): bls.gov/opub/ooq/2005/spring/art03.pdf
- Professional Landcare Network (PLANET): landcarenetwork.org
- Primer on Ecological Restoration from SER International: ser.org/pdf/primer3.pdf
- Professional Grounds Management Society (PGMS): pgms.org
- Society for Ecological Restoration (SER): ser.org
- Tree Care Industry Association (TCIA): treecareindustry.org
- US Department of Agriculture (USDA): usda.gov

Legal Services Industry (Environmental and Land Use Law)

- American Bar Association (ABA): abanet.org
- Earthjustice: earthjustice.org
- Environmental Law Alliance Worldwide (ELAW): elaw.org
- Environmental Law and Policy Center (ELPC): elpc.org

- Environmental Lawyers.com: environmentallawyers.com
- lawjobs.com Career Center: law.com/jsp/law/careercenter/index.jsp
- Law School Admission Council (LSAC): lsac.org
- Lawyers Weekly Jobs: lawyersweeklyjobs.com
- National Association for Law Placement (NALP): nalp.org
- US Department of Justice, Environment and Natural Resources Division (ENRD): usdoj.gov/enrd/

Natural Sciences Consulting Services
- American Academy of Forensic Sciences (AAFS): aafs.org
- American Association for the Advancement of Science (AAAS): aaas.org
- American Association of Pharmaceutical Scientists (AAPS): aapspharmaceutica.com
- American Association of State Climatologists (AASC): stateclimate.org
- American Association of Zoo Keepers (AAZK): aazk.org
- American Chemical Society (ACS): acs.org
- American Geological Institute (AGI): agiweb.org
- American Geophysical Union (AGU): agu.org
- American Institute of Biological Sciences (AIBS): aibs.org
- American Institute of Hydrology (AIH): aihydro.org
- American Institute of Physics (AIP): aip.org
- American Meteorological Society (AMS): ametsoc.org
- American Physical Society (APS): aps.org
- American Society of Agronomy (ASA): agronomy.org
- American Society for Biochemistry and Molecular Biology (ASBMB): asbmb.org
- American Society for Microbiology (ASM): asm.org
- American Society of Plant Biologists (ASPB): aspb.org
- Association of Consulting Foresters of America (ACF): acf-foresters.org
- Association of Environmental and Engineering Geologists (AEG): aegweb.org
- Association of Environmental Engineering and Science Professors (AEESP): aeesp.org
- Association for Environmental Health and Sciences (AEHS): aehs.com
- Association of Environmental Professionals (AEP): califaep.org
- Association of Zoos and Aquariums (AZA): aza.org
- Biophysical Society: biophysics.org
- California Native Plant Society (CNPS): cnps.org

- Career Guide to Industries: Management, Scientific and Technical Consulting Services: bls.gov/oco/cg/cgs037.htm
- Ecological Society of America (ESA): esa.org
- Forest Guild: forestguild.org
- Global Association of Online Foresters (GAOF): foresters.org
- Health Physics Society (HPS): hps.org
- International Association for Ecology (INTECOL): intecol.net
- International Society for Environmental Epidemiology (ISEE): iseepi.org
- International Association for Environmental Hydrology: hydroweb.com
- International Association of Hydrogeologists (IAH): iah.org
- International Association of Meteorology and Atmospheric Sciences (IAMAS): iamas.org
- International Society of Sustainability Professionals (ISSP): sustainabilityprofessionals.org
- Journal of Exposure Science and Environmental Epidemiology: nature.com/jes/
- Marine Geology and Geophysics at MIT: web.mit.edu/mit-whoi/www/research/mgg/
- National Association of Conservation Districts (NACD): nacdnet.org
- National Association of Environmental Professionals (NAEP): naep.org
- National Oceanic and Atmospheric Administration (NOAA): noaa.gov
- National Weather Service: nws.noaa.gov
- Natural Resources Conservation Service (NRCS): nrcs.usda.gov
- Pharmaceutical Research and Manufacturers of America (PhRMA): phrma.org
- Society of American Foresters (SAF): safnet.org
- Society of Environmental Toxicology and Chemistry (SETAC): setac.org
- Society of Toxicology (ST): toxicology.org
- Soil and Water Conservation Society (SWCS): swcs.org
- Soil Science Society of America (SSSA): soils.org

Non-profit Organizations (Green/Environmental)

- Acterra: Action for a Sustainable Earth: acterra.org
- Adirondack Mountain Club: adk.org
- Allegheny Land Trust: alleghenylandtrust.org
- American Bird Conservancy (ABC): abcbirds.org
- American Bison Society (ABS): americanbisonsocietyonline.org
- American Clean Skies Foundation (ACSF): cleanskies.org
- American Farmland Trust (AFT): farmland.org

- American Forests: americanforests.org
- American Public Gardens Association (APGA): publicgardens.org
- American Society for the Prevention of Cruelty to Animals: aspca.org
- Appalachian Mountain Club (AMC): outdoors.org
- Appalachian Trail Conservancy (ATC): appalachiantrail.org
- Appalachian Voices: appvoices.org
- Arbor Day Foundation: arborday.org
- As You Sow: asyousow.org
- Association of Environmental Professionals (AEP): califaep.org
- Association of Northwest Steelheaders (ANWS): nwsteelheaders.org
- Bark: bark-out.org
- Blacksmith Institute: blacksmithinstitute.org
- Blue Ridge Parkway Foundation: brpfoundation.org
- Bonneville Environmental Foundation (BEF): b-e-f.org
- Boone and Crockett Club: boone-crockett.org
- Branford Land Trust: branfordlandtrust.org/blt.html
- Bullitt Foundation: bullitt.org
- California League of Conservation Voters (CLCV): ecovote.org
- California Native Plant Society (CNPS): cnps.org
- Californians Against Waste: cawrecycles.org
- Calumet Stewardship Initiative: calumetstewardshipinitiative.org
- Capitol Land Trust (CLT): capitollandtrust.org
- Career Guide to Industries: Advocacy, Grantmaking and Civic Organizations: bls.gov/oco/cg/cgs054.htm
- Center for Biological Diversity: biologicaldiversity.org
- Center for Northern Studies (CNS): sterlingcollege.edu/CNS/about.htm
- Ceres (Coalition for Environmentally Responsible Economies): ceres.org
- Chesapeake Bay Program: chesapeakebay.net
- Chewonki Foundation: chewonki.org
- Citizens for Alternatives to Chemical Contamination (CACC): caccmi.org
- Citizens for Pennsylvania's Future (PennFuture): pennfuture.org
- Clean Air Campaign: cleanaircampaign.com
- Clean Air Conservancy: cleanairconservancy.org
- CleanCOALition: cleancoalition.org
- Clean Edge: cleanedge.com
- Clean Water Action: cleanwateraction.org

- Climate Counts: climatecounts.org
- Coalition on the Environment and Jewish Life (COEJL): coejl.org
- Colorado Conservation Voters (CCV): coloradoconservationvoters.org
- Committee for Green Foothills: greenfoothills.org
- Conservation International (CI): conservation.org
- Conservation Law Foundation (CLF): clf.org
- Defenders of Wildlife: defenders.org
- Ducks Unlimited: ducks.org
- Earth Force: earthforce.org
- Earthjustice: earthjustice.org
- Earth Policy Institute: earth-policy.org
- Earth Share: earthshare.org
- Earthwatch Institute: earthwatch.org
- ecoAmerica: ecoamerica.net
- Ecosystem Marketplace: ecosystemmarketplace.com
- Ecotrust: ecotrust.org
- Elephant Sanctuary (Tennessee): elephants.com
- Environment California: environmentcalifornia.org
- Environmental and Energy Study Institute (EESI): eesi.org
- Environmental Defense Fund (EDF): edf.org
- Environmental Law Alliance Worldwide (ELAW): elaw.org
- Environmental Law and Policy Center (ELPC): elpc.org
- Environmental Working Group (EWG): ewg.org
- Food & Water Watch: foodandwaterwatch.org
- Friends of the Earth (US): foe.org
- Georgia Wildlife Federation: www.gwf.org
- Global Water Policy Project (GWPP): globalwaterpolicy.org
- GLOBIO: globio.org
- Great Smoky Mountains Association (GSMA): smokiesinformation.org
- Great Swamp Watershed Association: greatswamp.org
- Green Corps: greencorps.org
- Green Energy Jobs: greenenergyjobs.com
- Green Light New Orleans: greenlightneworleans.org
- Green Project: thegreenproject.org
- Hazon: hazon.org
- High Rock Lake Association (HRLA): hrla.com
- High Uintas Preservation Council (HUPC): hupc.org
- Honor The Earth: honorearth.org
- Hudson River Sloop Clearwater: clearwater.org

- Humane Society of the United States: humanesociety.org
- Hummingbird Society: hummingbirdsociety.org
- Huron Mountain Wildlife Foundation: hmwf.org
- INFORM: informinc.org
- Institute for Energy and Environmental Research (IEER): ieer.org
- Institute for Marine Mammal Studies (IMMS): imms.org
- Institute for Social Ecology: social-ecology.org
- Integration and Application Network (IAN): ian.umces.edu
- International Rivers: internationalrivers.org
- Izaak Walton League: iwla.org
- Land Institute: landinstitute.org
- Land Trust Alliance: landtrustalliance.org
- Marine Mammal Center: marinemammalcenter.org
- Mercury Policy Project (MPP): mercurypolicy.org
- Montana Wilderness Association: wildmontana.org
- Monterey Bay Aquarium Foundation: montereybayaquarium.org
- Murie Science and Learning Center: murieslc.org
- National Audubon Society: audubon.org
- National Coalition for Marine Conservation (NCMC): savethefish.org
- National Council for Science and the Environment (NCSE): ncseonline.org
- National Fish Habitat Action Plan: fishhabitat.org
- National Parks Conservation Association (NPCA): npca.org
- National Wildlife Federation (NWF): nwf.org
- Native Forest Council: www.forestcouncil.org
- Natural Lands Trust: natlands.org
- Natural Resources Defense Council (NRDC): nrdc.org
- Nature Centers in the United States: en.wikipedia.org/wiki/List_of_nature_centers_in_the_United_States
- The Nature Conservancy: nature.org
- Nature's Classroom: naturesclassroom.org
- New American Dream: newdream.org
- New England Grassroots Environment Fund (NEGEF): grassrootsfund.org
- New York–New Jersey Trail Conference (NYNJTC): nynjtc.org
- Northeast Wilderness Trust: newildernesstrust.org
- Northwest Service Academy (NWSA): northwestserviceacademy.org
- Ocean Arks International: oceanarks.org
- Ocean Conservancy: oceanconservancy.org

- Oceana: oceana.org
- Office of Response and Restoration (OR&R): response.restoration.noaa.gov
- Ohio Citizen Action: ohiocitizen.org
- Open Space Institute (OSI): osiny.org
- Oregon Water Trust (OWT): owt.org
- Pacific Islands Conservation Research Association (PICRA): picra.net
- Pheasants Forever: pheasantsforever.org
- Planetfesto: planetfesto.org
- Plenty International: plenty.org
- Property and Environment Research Center: perc.org
- Public Employees for Environmental Responsibility (PEER): peer.org
- Rainforest Action Network: ran.org
- Rainforest Alliance: rainforest-alliance.org
- RE3.org: re3.org
- Reef Ball Foundation: reefball.org
- Republicans for Environmental Protection (REP): repamerica.org
- The Resource Foundation (TRF): resourcefnd.org
- Resources for the Future (RFF): rff.org
- Reverb: reverbrock.org
- Rewilding Institute: rewilding.org
- Riverkeeper: riverkeeper.org
- Rocky Mountain Institute (RMI): rmi.org
- Round River Conservation Studies: roundriver.org
- Rural Action: ruralaction.org
- Save-the-Redwoods League: savetheredwoods.org
- Seafood Watch: montereybayaquarium.org/cr/seafoodwatch.asp
- SeaWorld & Busch Gardens Conservation Fund: swbg–conservationfund.org
- Sempervirens Fund: sempervirens.org
- Sierra Club: sierraclub.org
- Sierra Club Foundation: tscf.org
- Sierra Nevada Alliance: sierranevadaalliance.org
- Sierra Student Coalition (SSC): ssc.org
- Social Venture Network (SVN): svn.org
- Sound Adirondack Growth Alliance (SAGA): soundgrowth.info
- Soundkeeper: soundkeeper.org
- Southeastern Cave Conservancy, Inc. (SCCi): scci.org
- Southern Alleghenies Conservancy: sac-sarcd.org

- Southern Utah Wilderness Alliance (SUWA): suwa.org
- Student Conservation Association (SCA): thesca.org
- Student Environmental Action Coalition (SEAC): seac.org
- Sudbury Valley Trustees (SVT): sudburyvalleytrustees.org
- Superfund Basic Research Program (SBRP): niehs.nih.gov/research/supported/sbrp
- Tellus Institute: tellus.org
- Tennessee Native Plant Society: tnps.org
- Time's Up!: times-up.org
- TreePeople: treepeople.org
- Tri-State Bird Rescue and Research, Inc.: tristatebird.org
- Trust for Public Land (TPL): tpl.org
- Trustees of Reservations (TTOR): thetrustees.org
- Ucross Foundation: ucrossfoundation.org
- Union of Concerned Scientists (UCS): ucsusa.org
- Upper Chattahoochee Riverkeeper (UCR): ucriverkeeper.org
- US Institute for Environmental Conflict Resolution: ecr.gov
- Vermont Institute of Natural Science (VINS): vinsweb.org
- Vermont Land Trust: vlt.org
- Vermont Natural Resource Council: vnrc.org
- Voyageurs National Park Association: voyageurs.org
- WILD Foundation: wild.org
- Wildlife Society (TWS): wildlife.org

Printing Industry (Green/Sustainable)
- Career Guide to Industries: Printing: bls.gov/oco/cg/cgs050.htm
- Conservatree: conservatree.org
- Environmental Paper Network: environmentalpaper.org
- Green Printing News from Barefoot Press: barefootpress.com/blog/
- International Imaging Technology Council (Int'l ITC): i-itc.org
- Press Relations: How green printing can make a good impression: grist.org/biz/tp/2006/01/03/printing/
- Printing Industries of America: gain.net

Recycling Industry (Green)
- Engineering Central: engcen.com
- International Solid Waste Association (ISWA): iswa.org
- National Recycling Coalition: nrc-recycle.org
- National Society of Professional Engineers: nspe.org
- Recycler's World: recycle.net

- Recycling Today: Association Central: recyclingtoday.com/associations/
- Solid Waste Association of North America (SWANA): swana.org

Renewable Energy Industry

- American Solar Energy Society (ASES): ases.org
- American Wind Energy Association: awea.org
- California Biomass Energy Alliance (CBEA): calbiomass.org
- California Solar Energy Industries Association (CALSEIA): calseia.org
- Engineering Central: engcen.com
- Green Energy Jobs: greenenergyjobs.com
- Independent Energy Producers Association: iepa.com
- International Solar Energy Society (ISES): ises.org
- National Association of Energy Service Companies (NAESCO): naesco.org
- National Renewable Energy Laboratory (NREL): nrel.gov
- National Society of Professional Engineers: nspe.org
- North American Board of Certified Energy Practitioners (NABCEP): nabcep.org
- Solar Electric Power Association: solarelectricpower.org
- Solar Energy Industries Association (SEIA): seia.org
- Solar Energy International (SEI): solarenergy.org
- Solar Living Institute: solarliving.org
- Solar Rating and Certification Corporation (SRCC): solar-rating.org
- Sustainable Buildings Industry Council: sbicouncil.org
- USA Biomass: usabiomass.org
- US Department of Energy, Biomass Program: eere.energy.gov/biomass/
- US Department of Energy, National Energy Technology Laboratory (NETL): netl.doe.gov

Utilities Industry

- Alliance to Save Energy: ase.org
- American Gas Association (AGA): aga.org
- American Public Energy Agency (APEA): apea.org
- American Public Gas Association: apga.org
- American Public Power Association: appanet.org
- American Public Works Association (APWA): apwa.net
- Association of Energy Engineers: aeecenter.org
- Association of Energy Services Professionals AESP: aesp.org
- Career Guide to Industries: Utilities: bls.gov/oco/cg/cgs018.htm
- Edison Electric Institute (EEI): eei.org

- Electric Power Research Institute (EPRI): my.epri.com
- Electric Power Supply Association: epsa.org
- Engineering Central: engcen.com
- Green Energy Jobs: greenenergyjobs.com
- Institute of Public Utilities: ipu.msu.edu
- National Hydropower Association (NHA): hydro.org
- National Society of Professional Engineers: nspe.org
- Propane Gas Association: National: npga.org
- US Department of Energy, National Energy Technology Laboratory (NETL): netl.doe.gov
- Utility Wind Integration Group (UWIG): www.uwig.org

Hidden Job Market

The "hidden job market" refers to the vast world of job openings that get filled but are never advertised. Why? Because employers often don't need or want to advertise a job opening. They find that they can staff their business in whole or in part through word of mouth, referrals and unsolicited job applicants. Small employers in particular often rely on personal referrals because it's easier, cheaper and, they contend, better. Another factor is the belief that people tend to work harder when they are not only representing themselves, but also the person who helped them get the job.

Three ways to take advantage of the hidden job market:

1. **Network.** Make it known that you're looking for work. This means network, network, network. And if that didn't make an impression, repeat that last sentence ten times! Talk with your family members, friends, former supervisors and co-workers and even new acquaintances to let them know that you're looking for work. Mention the kind of job you're looking for, the reasons why and the skills you have and enjoy using. Be enthusiastic. Network in person, by phone and online. Utilize social networking websites. Any social networking site! If something seems promising, follow up a few days later. Always be sure to thank people for any help they may try to provide.

2. **Temp or Volunteer.** Part-time, temporary, freelance and volunteer positions are excellent ways to network and maybe even bring in a little income in the meantime. A temporary staffing/placement firm can put you in several different worksite locations (temporarily) in just a few short weeks. Think of that as several opportunities to show someone you have what it takes. In a way, it's like getting paid for an interview. Temp jobs commonly lead to full-time employment if you can show that you have what they're looking for.

3. **Apply.** Develop your own list of employers that you would like to work for and then apply with each. If an employer is not accepting applications, ask when you can/should check back. There are various ways to create your list, and you can always ask a librarian or a career center staff person for help. Sometimes the biggest challenge here is being (and staying) focused. It may seem like sending out 10,000 resumés will increase your chances of getting a job, but it tends to work in just the opposite manner. The more

effective method is to pick a reasonable number of employers (start with a dozen or so) that are a good fit for you and then give them your full attention. This would include informational interviewing, job shadowing (if possible), offering to volunteer or starting out as a part-time or temp worker. Make sure you understand how to apply for a job properly, including how to correctly complete an employment application. And make sure you practice the job interview with someone who will be honest, but not overly critical. The worst interviewees can be divided into two groups: those who have no confidence and those who have false confidence.

Glossary of Green Terminology

Alternative energy: Energy produced from renewable sources, such as sunlight or wind. It has the added benefit of not generating heat-trapping greenhouse gases.

Alternative fuel vehicles: Vehicles that run on a fuel other than traditional gasoline or diesel. Includes fuel-cell-powered vehicles.

Alternative fuels:
- biodiesel: can be used safely in any diesel engine vehicle
- compressed natural gas (CNG): vehicle conversions cost about $3,000
- electric/hybrid: requires OEM vehicle
- ethanol: 85% alcohol blend (ethanol) requires a flexible-fuel vehicle
- hydrogen: new technologies being developed show great promise
- liquefied natural gas (LNG): requires OEM vehicle designed for this fuel
- liquefied petroleum gas (LPG): vehicle conversions cost about $3,000

Biodegradable: Organic substances that are broken down by the enzymes produced by living organisms.

Biofuels: Solid, liquid or gas fuel derived from recently dead biological material, most commonly plants. This distinguishes it from fossil fuel, which is derived from long-dead biological material.

Carbon footprint: Details how much carbon dioxide an individual, family or organization adds to the atmosphere.

Carbon-neutral: Refers to neutral (zero) total carbon release that is achieved by balancing the amount of carbon released with the amount offset. Being carbon-neutral is increasingly seen as good corporate and state social responsibility. A growing list of corporations announcing dates for when they intend to become fully carbon-neutral include: Dell, Google, PepsiCo and Tesco. When an individual or an organization sets out to become carbon neutral, it is usually achieved by combining the following three steps: a) Limiting energy usage and emissions from transportation (walking, using bicycles or public transport, avoiding flying, using low-energy vehicles), as well as from buildings, equipment and processes; b) Obtaining electricity from a renewable energy source either directly by generating it (installing solar panels on the roof for example) or by selecting an approved green energy provider and by using low-carbon alternative fuels such as biofuels; and c) Offsetting the remaining emissions that can't, for the moment, be avoided or generated from renewables in a responsible carbon project, or by buying carbon credits.

CFCs: Chlorofluorocarbons. Used in refrigerants, cleaners and aerosols and in the making of plastic foams. CFCs are greenhouse gases. They also cause ozone depletion in the stratosphere.

Compact fluorescent bulb: A smaller version of a fluorescent lamp that fits into a standard light bulb socket. Fluorescent bulbs create light in a more energy-efficient way.

Energy audit: The process of determining the energy consumption of a building or facility.

Environmental footprint: The impact of an organization in categories such as resource use and waste generation. See also Carbon footprint.

Ethanol: An automotive fuel derived from grass, sugar cane or corn. Burning ethanol adds carbon dioxide to the atmosphere, but it is seen as a renewable fuel, like solar power, that does not deplete natural resources.

Greenhouse effect: The warming of the Earth's atmosphere attributed to a buildup of carbon dioxide and other gases that retain heat and warm the planet's surface, a.k.a. global warming.

Green careers: Careers involving jobs that are focused on sustainability or on environmental protection and preservation — determined either by the nature and purpose of the job or by the nature and purpose of the employer.

Greens: Supporters of the Green movement or political ideology that places a high importance on ecological and environmental goals and on achieving those goals through broad-based, grassroots participatory democracy.

Hybrid vehicles: Autos with a small, fuel-efficient gas engine, combined with a battery-powered electric motor that assists the engine when accelerating, and an energy-recovery system from braking that fuels the battery.

Methanol: An alcohol that can be used as an alternative fuel or as a gasoline additive.

Sustainable: A method of harvesting or using a resource so that the resource is not depleted or permanently damaged.

Sustainable agriculture: Refers to the ability of a farm to produce food indefinitely, without causing irreversible damage to ecosystem health.

Sustainable business: Involves an organizational commitment to conserve energy, use renewable energy sources, prevent pollution, reduce waste and conserve water. A higher standard would also include a commitment to the greening of buildings and facilities, including the extensive use of renewable energy.

Alphabetical Listing
of Real People Q&A

Nelson, Les: Western Renewables Group, page 117.

Ortiz, Tony: Solar Installer Foreman, Aztec Solar, Inc., page 83.

Overhaug, Debora (Debe): President/CEO, PRC Technologies (soy-based print cartridges), page 120.

Parsons, Bobette: Conservation Specialist, US Dept. of Agriculture, National Resources Conservation Service, page 249.

Parsons, Jim: Aquaculturist and Fish Biologist, Troutlodge, Inc., page 277.

Pushnik, Jim: Earth Sciences Professor, California State University, Chico, page 221.

Reich, Lee: Horticultural Consultant and Writer, page 122.

Riley, Jr., George A.: Civil Engineering Technician, Natural Resources Conservation Service, page 18.

Rivard, Tom: Senior Environmental Health Specialist, City/County of San Francisco, page 52.

Rockhold, John: Managing Editor, *Mother Earth News*, page 184.

Ryan, John P.: Recycling Facility Manager, Waste Connections, Inc., page 134.

Samarya-Timm, Michéle: Health Educator, Franklin Township Health Department, page 170.

Scott, Lilia: Senior Transportation Planner, Santa Clara Valley Transportation Authority/URS Corporation, page 65.

Sewell, Linda: Senior Health Physicist, Pacific Gas and Electric, page 245.

Steinmetz, Camas J.: Land Use Attorney, Manatt, Phelps & Phillips, LLP, page 176.

Steinmetz, Jim: Reusable Lumber Company, page 124.

Thomson, Neil: Carpenter/Project Manager, GreenBuilt Construction, page 80.

Walker, Nigel: Farmer, Eatwell Farm, page 281.

Weisbrod, Annie: Toxicologist, The Procter & Gamble Company, page 209.

Wood, Fred: Greenlight Magazine/Pattiwood Productions, page 127.

Zeek, Jim: Organic Farmer, Goodness Orchard, page 287.

Zierden, David F.: State Climatologist, Florida State University, page 203.

Alphabetical Listing
of Career Profiles (Occupations)

About the Authors

ALICE RUSH, MA, RPCC, MCC, is a certified and registered career counselor and founder of CareerU® — a counseling practice in the Sacramento, California, foothills. She has over 15 years experience in career development counseling and education, providing counseling to the general public and consulting to Fortune 500 companies. Projects she has worked on have been documented in *Harvard Business Review, Fortune, Personnel Journal, Training Magazine* and televised on PBS. She is author of

Paid to Play (Random House/Prima Games) and is devoted to helping people pursue values-driven work. Alice's passion for protecting the environment began 30 years ago as the daughter of innovative environmentalist/land conservationist and elected official Nonette Hanko, while growing up in Palo Alto, California, in the 1960s.

JIM CASSIO is a career information and workforce development professional who has been commissioned to conduct hundreds of labor market studies and has published many occupational resource books, including the *Career Pathways Handbook* (Trafford). Jim specializes in green workforce issues, as well as industry, occupation and skills research, analysis and resource product development. In addition to hundreds of research projects performed over two decades for local and regional clients,

Jim has coordinated research and development projects for state and federal agencies, including O*NET pilot projects sponsored by the US Department of Labor. Jim lives with his wife and two daughters in Folsom, California, and is also a former park ranger and an avid kayaker and hiker.

If you have enjoyed *Green Careers*, you might also enjoy other

Books to Build a New Society

Our books provide positive solutions for people who
want to make a difference. We specialize in:

Sustainable Living • Ecological Design and Planning

Natural Building & Appropriate Technology • New Forestry

Environment and Justice • Conscientious Commerce

Progressive Leadership • Resistance and Community • Nonviolence

Educational and Parenting Resources

New Society Publishers

ENVIRONMENTAL BENEFITS STATEMENT

New Society Publishers has chosen to produce this book on recycled
paper made with 100% post consumer waste, processed chlorine
free, and old growth free.

For every 5,000 books printed, New Society saves the following
resources:[1]

36	Trees
3,297	Pounds of Solid Waste
3,628	Gallons of Water
4,732	Kilowatt Hours of Electricity
5,994	Pounds of Greenhouse Gases
26	Pounds of HAPs, VOCs, and AOX Combined
9	Cubic Yards of Landfill Space

[1]Environmental benefits are calculated based on research done by the Environmental
Defense Fund and other members of the Paper Task Force who study the environmental impacts of the paper industry.

For a full list of NSP's titles, please call 1-800-567-6772 *or check out our web*

site at: **www.newsociety.com**

NEW SOCIETY PUBLISHERS